Undoing Work,
Rethinking Community

Undoing Work, Rethinking Community

A Critique of the Social Function of Work

James A. Chamberlain

ILR Press
AN IMPRINT OF
CORNELL UNIVERSITY PRESS
ITHACA AND LONDON

First published 2018 by Cornell University Press

Printed in the United States of America

Library of Congress Cataloging-in-Publication Data

Names: Chamberlain, James A., 1980– author.
Title: Undoing work, rethinking community : a critique of the social function of work / James A. Chamberlain.
Description: Ithaca : Cornell University Press, 2018. | Includes bibliographical references and index.
Identifiers: LCCN 2017011822 (print) | LCCN 2017014074 (ebook) | ISBN 9781501714870 (epub/mobi) | ISBN 9781501714887 (pdf) | ISBN 9781501714863 (cloth : alk. paper)
Subjects: LCSH: Work—Social aspects. | Work—Philosophy. | Work ethic.
Classification: LCC HD4904 (ebook) | LCC HD4904. C45 2018 (print) | DDC 306.3/6—dc23
LC record available at https://lccn.loc.gov/2017011822

Cornell University Press strives to use environmentally responsible suppliers and materials to the fullest extent possible in the publishing of its books. Such materials include vegetable-based, low-VOC inks and acid-free papers that are recycled, totally chlorine-free, or partly composed of nonwood fibers. For further information, visit our website at cornellpress.cornell.edu.

CONTENTS

Acknowledgments

Chapter 3 is an extended version of the essay, "Bending over Backwards: Flexibility, Freedom, and Domination in Contemporary Work," which appeared in *Constellations: An International Journal of Critical and Democratic Theory* 22, no. 1 (March 2015): 91–104.

I would like to thank the following friends and colleagues for their support, advice, feedback, and suggestions at various stages of this project: Christine Di Stefano, Jamie Mayerfeld, Jack Turner, Michael McCann, Nancy Hartsock, Michael Forman, Matthew Walton, Larry Cushnie, Carolina Johnson, Glenn Mackin, Amy Allen, Robyn Marasco, Hauke Brunkhorst, Chris Watkin, and Frances Benson. Various anonymous reviewers, conference panel chairs, discussants, and audience members at the conferences I have attended as this project has unfolded have also helped improved the book, but of course, any errors are my own. Without the unstinting support and encouragement of Stasha McBride, this book would not have been possible. Her parents, Michael and Pamela, also helped with childcare at key stages of the process, which in turn meant that I could focus more on writing. I dedicate the book to our beautiful children, who help me keep it all in perspective.

Undoing Work, Rethinking Community

1

The Ends of Work

Despite the polarized and rancorous nature of the US presidential election in 2016, candidates from across the political spectrum found common ground on the need to get more Americans working. At his first press conference after winning the election, President Donald Trump repeated earlier boasts that he would be "the greatest jobs producer that God ever created."[1] Trump's campaign rhetoric also included the empirically false claim that immigrants reduce job opportunities for native-born Americans, thus calling for more restrictive immigration policies, while he struck another nationalist chord by promising to return offshored jobs to the United States. Meanwhile, Senator Bernie Sanders ran on a platform committed to establishing full employment in the United States. Sanders explained that "work is part of what being human is about," while he also acknowledged "the horrors of unemployment" and the effects of "not having a job, not being part of the community, being isolated, feeling worthless."[2]

These examples express a commitment to the value of work that goes beyond the United States and its recent presidential election. For example, in August 2011, riots involving up to fifteen thousand people convulsed British society. As the media broadcast scintillating images of looted shops and burning vehicles, the public's attention inevitably turned to the causes of the unrest and how to prevent future inflammations. The fact that the rioters failed to articulate a coherent set of demands arguably exacerbated the sense of collective anxiety and left politicians and commentators grasping at familiar themes of criminality, moral degradation, and social exclusion to account for their disturbing behavior. Despite predictable disagreement over the relative weight of structural factors and individual agency, though, a consensus emerged across the political spectrum that employment—or more accurately, the lack thereof—had played a key role in the outbreak of social unrest. The then prime minister David Cameron summed up these views when he claimed in the aftermath of the riots that "work is at the heart of a responsible society. So getting more of our young people into jobs- or up and running in their own businesses is a critical part of how we strengthen responsibility in our society."[3]

As all three examples show, the value of employment in contemporary society far exceeds its function of distributing material rewards and enabling us to satisfy various needs and wants. In addition, they suggest that full inclusion in the political community requires earning an income and that employment lays the foundation of a just, stable, and harmonious community. This book argues that, in the contemporary work society, good citizenship does indeed entail gainful employment but that this requirement substantially undermines freedom, equality, and justice. Given this, I examine the openings and limitations for freedom offered by the regime of flexibility as well as by the possible introduction of an unconditional basic income. While these measures offer some prospects for greater freedom and equality, I argue that they do not suffice to break fully with the work society. Rather, it is also necessary to reconfigure the value and place of paid work in our lives. We need to rethink the meaning of community at a deeper level and, in particular, abandon the view that community is constructed by work, whether paid or not. As will become clear, this task raises significant political and theoretical challenges, as work is deeply embedded in the way we tend to think about society, community, and even civilization. Moreover, capitalism stands in fundamental tension

with the view of community that I propose, such that undoing the perni-
cious effects of work requires both a rethinking of community and the
struggle against capitalism.

In developing these arguments it will become clear that two thinkers
in particular—André Gorz and Kathi Weeks—have served as important
sources of inspiration and intellectual support for this project. They and
I are concerned with understanding, criticizing, and ultimately moving
beyond the work society. All three of us share a broadly Marxist orientation that informs our critiques as well as our visions and hopes for
the future. And all three of us recognize the emancipatory potential of
the unconditional basic income (although this is true of Gorz only in his
later works) alongside the need to reduce the hold of paid work on our
lives to make room for activities that better match our needs, desires, and
values. Yet despite my debt to and agreement with these pioneering thinkers, this book diverges from their analyses most markedly in its focus on
community.

Weeks provides a comprehensive account of the work ethic but offers
relatively little to help us understand the construction of the work society
as a social order. Similarly, she shies away from offering a vision of the
postwork society, preferring to present two "utopian demands"—for the
reduction of work without loss of income and for an unconditional basic
income. Meanwhile, although Gorz helpfully explains how paid work integrates individuals into society, his post-wage-based society carries forward important features of the existing work society, thus undermining its
ability to address all the injustices that flow from the present connection
between work and citizenship. In sum, while my project is broadly complementary to theirs, it moves beyond them by foregrounding the question
of community and showing how we need a new conception of community
to put the work society behind us.

To clear the way for the analysis of the next chapter, this chapter dis-
entangles three prominent threads that run through popular and scholarly
discourses on the meaning and value of work: the work ethic, independence, and citizenship. As will become apparent, these familiar themes
intertwine and support one another in lending a positive valence to paid
work. Yet existing analyses of these narratives do not supply an exhaus-
tive account of the political dimensions and normative force of paid work
in contemporary society. In particular, in chapter 2, I will show how work

not only constructs individual subjects; it also structures the social order as a whole, making up the work society.

The Work Ethic, Independence, Citizenship

No discussion of the work ethic would be complete without reference to the seminal work of Max Weber. In *The Protestant Ethic and the Spirit of Capitalism*, Weber famously analyzed the reversal in attitudes to work that occurred when the Protestant Reformation helped unseat the "traditional" culture of work and replace it with the "modern" work ethic. Whereas the traditional culture saw work as a necessary evil and something to avoid whenever possible, Weber shows how the Protestant ethic sanctified work, framed it as a religious duty, and encouraged people to see successes derived from it as a sign of God's grace. In Weber's account, the orientation to work promoted by the Protestant ethic long outlived strict religious observance and was in fact bound up with a set of processes that undermined the appeal and hold of religion itself. This in turn brought alarming consequences for human freedom because, whereas the "Puritan wanted to work in a calling; we are forced to do so."[4] In many ways this book shares the critical thrust of Weber's conclusion, but I will take a more overtly political approach by identifying work as a mechanism that helps fabricate a social order from and by individuals who are presumed to exist prior to it.

The impact of the Reformation on the American work ethic appears both in the nineteenth-century doctrine of usefulness and in the belief that regular work would consume sexual passions, dispel violence, doubts, and despair, distract from radicalism, and reform convicts. But in addition to the utilitarian and disciplining functions of work, employment became seen as a pathway to success and as a creative act.[5] Furthermore, unlike in Europe, where work was viewed as an end in itself, in the United States labor promised an eventual release from the "repulsive necessity to work for others" and thus provided a pathway to greater independence.[6] Abraham Lincoln, for example, publicly proclaimed that through hard work, a white wage laborer could one day become an independent citizen who owned his own land.[7]

It is important to note that the valorization of work does not appeal only to religion for its ethical support. As Weeks puts it, "Once the world is made hostile to the religious basis of the Protestant ethic, new rationales emerge for what remains a fundamentally similar prescription." Thus, in the industrial era the work ethic framed work as a conduit to social mobility and "achievement in this life," while the postindustrial ethic that developed in the last decades of the twentieth century treats work "as a path to individual self-expression, self-development and creativity."[8] As Weeks understands it, the postindustrial work ethic arose in part out of the movements of the 1960s and early 1970s that opposed the "disciplinary subjectivity of the Fordist period and the problem of worker alienation that they helped to publicize."[9] In this regard, as I will show in chapter 3, the postindustrial work ethic has close ties with the discourse and practices of flexibility, which emerged around the same time and, at least in part, respond to similar dissatisfaction with the Fordist organization of work. Like flexibility, all three versions of the work ethic also amount to "an individualizing discourse" in that each presents achievement and success as a reflection of the individual's character. As Weeks points out, this means that every individual, rather than the community as a whole, bears the moral obligation to work.[10] These observations will also provide support for my argument that the work society is based on an individualist social ontology, meaning that society appears as an association of individuals who are integrated into it by means of work.

The sanctification of paid work as a means to personal advancement within the work ethic overlaps with the idea that paid work can ensure independence. In the first half of the nineteenth century, the American preoccupation with independence as a core republican value called into question the status of the increasing numbers of those who were dependent on wage labor for their livelihoods. If the American citizen was neither a slave nor an aristocrat, it was necessary to distinguish between wage and slave labor for the nonslave workforce to credibly claim citizenship.[11] Thus, although in the 1840s white workers invoked white slavery and wage slavery to protest their loss of freedom and independence at the hands of increasingly overbearing and profit-driven masters, it was ultimately free labor that won out as a description of wage labor by the 1860s.[12]

Whereas slaves, paupers, colonial natives, and housewives, with all their connotations of dependency, were antithetical to a notion of citizenship premised on independence, the white male breadwinner who supported his family through hard work eventually embodied the ideal citizen of the Fordist-Keynesian regime.[13] Despite being excluded from full citizenship, the figure of the housewife represented a "good" form of dependency during the industrial era; but as Nancy Fraser and Linda Gordon point out, in contemporary postindustrial society all forms of dependency have now become "suspect." From the pervasive but usually subtle liberal denunciation of middle-class women who refuse a career in favor of full-time parenting to the more explicit demonization of the so-called "underclass" (including single mothers who receive welfare and the often racialized long-term unemployed), it is clear that the "independence" that paid work affords has helped make the figure of the worker the norm to which all must conform on pain of social marginalization.

By the modern industrial period in the United States and Britain, employment had thus become a core attribute of citizenship.[14] Indeed, in 1945 the British sociologist T. H. Marshall pronounced that "today all workers are citizens" and that "we have come to expect that all citizens should be workers."[15] As the state subjected workplaces to greater legal regulation, as workers gained rights to collective bargaining, and as welfare rights were largely addressed to workers, participation in the labor market came to undergird much of the substance of modern legal citizenship. Despite the neoliberal remaking of state and society—a process that could not leave untouched the organization and experience of work, as I will show in chapter 3—the tie between work and citizenship remains alive and well. In fact, the crumbling of the welfare state and the transformation of the social citizen have only intensified the economic imperative of paid work, while at the level of ideology, employment still constitutes a paramount civic duty.

Children, seniors, and people with disabilities are to some extent exempt from the civic duty of paid work, but members of these groups rarely enjoy comparable social status to most full-time workers. In addition, their exemption is temporary and often conditional on an assessed incapacity to work. Thus, although it is no longer considered acceptable in the United States or Britain for children to work full time, it is expected that they participate in some form of full-time education, in no small part designed and increasingly justified on economic grounds as preparation for a subsequent life of paid work.[16] Even though retirees are "free from" paid work, they are only legitimately so if they have "paid their dues" by participating in a lifetime of paid work. The very wealthy often are at pains either to point out that they earned their income through hard work or that their wealth helps create jobs for others. People who cannot work due to mental or physical incapacity are exempted from the civic duty of paid work, but only after government agencies have made every effort to ensure that they are not faking it, and not without experiencing loss of privacy and social esteem. Ultimately, these exceptions from the civic duty of paid work prove its rule.

The connection between employment and citizenship is especially apparent when the latter is thought of not as a legal category but in terms of social recognition. As Judith Shklar points out, when one says that people must engage in paid work to become "full-blown citizens," this means that employment earns them not only wages but "social standing." That paid work confers social standing on those who engage in it is most obvious when one looks to those who do not work, for their fellow citizens scorn them, and they "feel dishonored, not just . . . poor."[17] According to Shklar, this is because earning is not simply a means of making money but, alongside voting, one of two key attributes of American citizenship. While this argument helps one understand the psychological burden of unemployment in a nation that so highly values paid work, it remains unclear why work is considered to be an attribute of citizenship.

In her discussion of the work ethic, Weeks considers the relationship between work and citizenship, observing that the obligation to work "is fundamental to the basic social contract; indeed, working is part of what is supposed to transform subjects into the independent individuals of the liberal imaginary, and for that reason, is treated as a basic obligation of citizenship." She also asserts that "work is the primary means by which individuals are integrated not only into the economic system, but also into social, political and familial modes of cooperation."[18] Finally, in her analysis, this "glorification of work as . . . the key both to social belonging and individual achievement, constitutes the fundamental ideological foundation of contemporary capitalism."[19]

Although I agree with all three of these claims—that work counts as a fundamental social obligation in contemporary society, that it integrates individuals into broader structures of cooperation, and that this makes it functional to the needs of capital for docile and productive workers[20]—they are insufficiently elaborated and thus cannot tell the whole story of the work society or how to move beyond it. While it is clear that capitalism benefits from the belief that social belonging depends on paid work, how and why does this ideology succeed in "gripping" workers? The work ethic cannot supply an answer here because it focuses on the individual rather than social benefits of work. Instead, we need to consider what sort of view of human coexistence makes it possible and even necessary to think of "individuals" being integrated into "society" in the first place and why it is believed that this process ought to occur via work (whether paid or not). As I will show in chapter 5, these considerations also help lay the groundwork for theorizing a postwork community that can improve on the visions offered by André Gorz, as well as by Michael Hardt and Antonio Negri.

Denaturalization and Critique

This book seeks to denaturalize the position of work in society and underline its political significance. When one succumbs to thinking of processes and social arrangements as "natural" they acquire an aura of inevitability and an effective shield against critical assessment. Why consider the impact on freedom and justice of something that cannot be otherwise? Why expend precious time and energy trying to oppose it? To *de*naturalize practices or a set of arrangements means to open them up to precisely the scrutiny from which they ordinarily enjoy protection because of the misperception that they constitute immutable facts of life.

The core contention of this book—that full membership of contemporary capitalist society depends on the performance of paid work—works against the depoliticization and naturalization of work by capturing the dual political character of the requirement to work for pay. First, it shows that whether a person works shapes not simply his or her ability to consume commodities but the extent to which he or she enjoys social respect and inclusion as a full member of the political community. Second, as a contingent social fact, the need to sell one's labor power to receive material, social, and psychological benefits rests on a set of beliefs and practices that are seldom contested and come to appear as part of our common sense.

At a deeper level, this book also denaturalizes the connection commonly made between work (whether paid or not), society, and community. This process begins in chapter 2, where I analyze the contemporary work society, and continues in chapter 5, where I consider two prominent leftist visions of postcapitalism. In this sense, the postwork community that I propose is not synonymous with the post-wage-based society (a phrase used by Gorz as the subtitle to his book *Reclaiming Work*), in which wage labor has been radically reduced or even eliminated in favor of various cooperative and autonomous activities. More radically, the postwork community refers to a form of community that is no longer premised on work—even unpaid work—as the basis of membership. The choice of the term "community" is both an attempt to visibly distinguish my vision from that of thinkers like Gorz and Weeks and an expression of my debt to thinkers like Jean-Luc Nancy and Roberto Esposito, who have encouraged me to reclaim the term from its connotation of an organic and often totalitarian whole. As such, the book seeks to challenge common assumptions about the meaning and requirements of community in the hope that we might one day live in a manner that better reflects our interdependence and relationality, at the same time overcoming the significant incursions on freedom engendered by the contemporary work society.

To be clear, denaturalization does not necessarily entail rejecting or modifying norms or practices, and its value does not lie exclusively in its ability to spur social change. Indeed, after careful consideration, we may judge that the status quo realizes our goals better than other possible alternatives. But even in that case, denaturalization would have helped in the cultivation of what I would like to call an "ethic of authenticity." This ethic rests on the conviction that being aware of and taking responsibility for the consequences of our actions, whether individual or collective, is ethically preferable to a life of willful ignorance and the denial of responsibility for how we live.[21] Moreover, grasping the contingency of that which appears necessary and natural constitutes what one might call, in Foucauldian language, "an ethical work upon ourselves," because it lets us see that how we relate to ourselves need not, and has not, remained fixed and frozen for all time, but rather can always be modified.[22] In heightening awareness of the contingency of our fundamental beliefs about work and how we organize work, I thus hope to spur reflection and informed judgment or, as Hannah Arendt put it, "to think what we are doing."[23]

Having dissolved the protective membrane around largely unquestioned practices and values, we of course find ourselves confronted with the possibility, even the duty, to assess them normatively. To do so, I appeal here to the intersecting values of freedom, equality, and justice. Western philosophy includes innumerable attempts to define freedom, but rather than reviewing this rich literature and becoming embroiled in its more technical debates, I propose a fairly straightforward definition of freedom as the capacity of agents to act according to their own values, needs, and desires, or ends, for short.[24] Clearly, this view of freedom demands more than noninterference or noncoercion: to discern, formulate, and then act on one's ends also entails the satisfaction of basic biological needs and a social context that facilitates individual and collective expression, deliberation, and experimentation.

Not everyone will agree with such an expansive understanding of freedom. For example, Friedrich Hayek claims that "the range of physical possibilities from which a person can choose at any given moment has no relevance to freedom."[25] Yet even classical liberals like John Stuart Mill understand freedom not just as negative liberty but also as self-expression, or, to put it in terms that resonate more clearly with my definition, the deployment and development of capacities in ways that best suit the agent's character and fundamental values.[26] To treat freedom as more than simply the absence of coercion thus hardly constitutes a radical position within Western political thought and practice.

Based on the understanding of freedom as the capacity of agents to act according to their own ends, the ideology and practices of work constrain freedom in four primary ways. The first centers on the structural coercion we face to enter the labor market. In a word, very few people have a meaningful choice about whether to work for money. The ideology of work helps make this requirement to work appear inevitable, natural, and legitimate, yet it remains a contingent and thus contestable and potentially alterable social fact. In particular, because in capitalism the bulk of humanity's needs and wants takes the form of commodities, people need to obtain money, which for most means earning a wage. This process forms a vicious circle: as paid work engulfs our lives, we have less time to develop noncommoditized means of meeting our needs, which only reinforces the material pressure to earn a living through paid work. For this reason, the provision of an unconditional basic income is a necessary (albeit insufficient) condition for moving beyond the work society.

At a second, more widely recognized level, numerous incursions on freedom can and do take place both inside and outside the workplace: in the first case, restrictions on freedom of assembly and the unlawful firing of workers who try to unionize; in the second, invasions of privacy by employers who then punish workers for private acts of which they disapprove.[27] Moreover, under the guise of deregulation, the neoliberal push for greater flexibility in both the labor market as a whole and in individual worksites has reduced the power of workers relative to employers and has thus diminished the capacity of the former to shape the terms and conditions of their work. I will pay particular attention to the perverse effects of flexibility on freedom in chapter 3, since proponents of flexibility boast of its ability to liberate and empower workers. Of course, a common defense of these abridgments of freedom rests on the claim that one can leave an unsatisfying, unsafe, or morally objectionable workplace; thus by staying, one tacitly consents to whatever working conditions prevail. Yet such arguments rarely take account of the enormous monetary and social costs of leaving a job, factors that call into question the authenticity of one's presumed consent.[28]

To be clear, workers do enjoy a degree of choice as to where and how they labor, and individuals often try to exercise this freedom in ways that reflect their values, needs, and desires, whether this means devoting themselves to a particular vocation, like teaching and research, or minimizing the amount of time spent doing paid work to free up time for unpaid pursuits, like bicycling. Yet notwithstanding this freedom, and aside from the fact that accidents of birth leave some people with more choices than others, almost no one is immune from the intense material and social pressures to place gainful employment in some shape or form at the center of life. As a result, we must squeeze our values, needs, and desires either into, or as is more often the case, around paid work. The third way that the ideology and practices of work constrain freedom, then, is by reducing the time, energy, and institutional spaces needed to act in ways that genuinely reflect one's values, needs, and desires, whether these take the form of service, care, play, love, or rest.

Precisely this shortage of time for nonmarket pursuits makes personal or political reflection on fundamental values, including the place of work in one's life, more difficult. Yet the opportunity to engage in individual and collective reflections about the meaning, priority, and realization of one's values, needs, and desires constitutes a prerequisite for freedom: only this reflexivity can shield the subject against the ever-present threat of unthinkingly conforming to tradition or the ends of others. To be clear, I do not privilege acts of dissent or attempts to transform social reality within this account of freedom but assign equal significance to the signs of autonomy within more modest attempts to modify social structures and practices, and even within acts that deliberately affirm the status quo.

Not only does the requirement to work keep many people too busy to engage in deep reflections on fundamental questions of collective existence, but the ideology of work erodes freedom by constructing paid work as an unassailable good and by placing it outside the realm of "reasonable" or "realistic" debate. By encouraging people to see the requirement to work for pay as an inevitable or even natural feature of collective existence, the ideology of work therefore chips away at their freedom to even imagine alternative futures in which paid work might play a different role (or none at all) and thus reduces people's capacities to act according to their own ends. When a great number of individuals do not even question whether society can or should organize production and distribution differently, this ought to register as a loss of freedom.

Taking inspiration from Jean-Jacques Rousseau, Karl Marx, and most recently, Étienne Balibar, I see freedom and equality not as mutually exclusive but as mutually reliant. In that case, we cannot critique the work society from the perspective of freedom without also considering its negative effects on equality. As Balibar points out, "Equality and freedom are contradicted in exactly the same conditions, in the same situation, because there is no example of conditions that suppress or repress freedom that do not suppress or limit—that is, do not abolish—equality, and vice versa."[29] Bringing these two terms together, one can understand justice as equality of freedom or, more specifically, the equal ability of all members of society to act in ways that reflect their own ends.[30]

The hypervalorization of work in contemporary society undervalues those who perform many socially necessary activities—often on account of their being associated with women, people of color, and immigrants—and marginalizes those who do not or cannot work for pay at all, such as elderly or disabled persons, residents of economically disadvantaged areas, and full-time parents and caregivers.[31] As a result, these persons cannot participate on an equal footing with members of more privileged groups in the major institutions of social life, thus constraining their freedom. The low value placed on their contributions also limits the financial remuneration they receive, once again limiting the extent to which they can act according to their own ends. Given this manifold incursion on freedom and equality, we need to move beyond the work society. As I will argue in chapter 6, while some progress on this front could be made within the confines of capitalism, not only does capitalism limit the degree of control ordinary people can have over work, but it also presents an insuperable obstacle to the achievement of the form of community that I propose.

Work and Political Theory

Before offering a more detailed overview of the chapters that follow, I want to briefly touch on the way that I understand work and how this relates to a certain reading of Karl Marx and to the thought of Hannah Arendt. Although these two thinkers differ dramatically in their criticisms of modernity, both can be seen as basing their critiques, at least in part, on assumptions about the true meaning of work. For example, the broad substance of Marx's critique of alienated labor is that paid work robs us of a putatively more authentic experience of work as creative self-actualization or as the externalization of ourselves through the transformation of matter.[32] When joined to a philosophical anthropology that identifies work as the defining feature of humans, this in turn treats the debasement of work in capitalism as an instance of severe dehumanization.

My critique of the work society does share the concern that the imposition of paid work reduces the scope of human freedom. But this is not to say that paid work robs us of access to the experience of "true" work, nor do I assume that this work is the sine qua non of humanity. While I certainly do not doubt the necessity and pleasures of work as productive and reproductive activity, one risk with treating work as of the essence of humanity is that society makes work—however it is defined—an instrument of exclusion and oppression. Moreover, my own philosophical leanings direct me away from the ascription of any particular essence to humans, whether politics, as Aristotle thought, or work, as Marx appears to have thought in his humanist writings. I am rather more inclined to the thought that people are, as Giorgio Agamben puts it, "devoid of any specific vocation."[33]

While Hannah Arendt famously avoids the notion of human nature, preferring instead "the human condition" (the title of one her best-known works), she goes to great lengths distinguishing among three sets of activities that constitute that condition—namely, labor, work, and action. While labor comprises the cyclical performance of activities concerned with the assurance of life and the maintenance of the body, work involves the fabrication of what she calls the "human artifact," and action refers to the necessarily collective and public practice of politics as the exercise of our freedom to make new and unpredictable beginnings in the world.[34] For Arendt, this typology generates a critical perspective on the tendencies that have coalesced in modern society under the banner of the "rise of the social"—the ascension of what should be private matters to the realm of the public and the handling of collective issues on the model of the household, both of which result in the eclipse of action. Another modern trend, which involves the impetus to accumulate wealth, leads us to treat "all use objects as though they were consumer goods, so that a chair or a table is now consumed as rapidly as a dress and a dress used up almost as quickly as food."[35] As a result, the laborer (who produces mere consumer items) has steadily replaced the workman (who produces use goods), and we thus find ourselves in a society of laborers at the cost of permanence, stability, and durability.[36]

While Arendt no doubt uses these distinctions to powerful critical effect, they are less helpful for understanding how and why paid work acts as a precondition for full membership of the political community. Indeed, in the contemporary work society what matters more than whether you are engaged in reproductive or directly productive activities is that you are paid for them. In other words, work today colloquially means paid employment, not a particular kind of activity defined by its product or goal. As I will argue in chapter 5, however, we should also be wary of basing membership of the community on *unpaid* work. In both cases, what matters more than how an individual philosopher might choose to define work is how what counts as work at a given time and place operates politically as a mechanism of inclusion and exclusion. To make these arguments, I therefore do not need a context-transcendent definition of true work, nor do I need to make any philosophical claims about the importance of work to self-realization or to the human condition. Nevertheless, I define work very broadly as the manipulation of matter, symbols, and affect through the application of physical, intellectual, or emotional energy. As such, I do not expect that a life without work is either possible or desirable, but I believe we can adjust the way we organize and experience work and how it relates to community.

As I will show in chapter 2, Gorz offers a compelling account of how paid work integrates individuals into society. And yet, despite criticizing what he calls the "ideology of work," in his early work he also affirms the social obligation to perform paid work on the grounds that removing it—such as by introducing an unconditional basic income—would deny individuals of their social existence. From this internal tension in Gorz's thought, I then derive the hypothesis that the work society operates on the basis of an individualist social ontology that needs a mechanism like that of paid work to bring individuals together in social order and harmony. Moreover, I argue that what makes work a particularly appealing mechanism for this purpose is the common tendency to view society or civilization as a whole as the product of work. To put the argument bluntly, the good citizen is a worker because society itself is commonly understood, as John Rawls famously put it, as "a cooperative venture for mutual advantage."[37]

Chapter 3 explores the regime of flexibility as a neoliberal instantiation of freedom in relation to work, thus providing an empirically grounded account of the contemporary organization of work that can help us understand the general lack of resistance to the work society. In addition, it disrupts the hegemony of flexibility by drawing out the perverse effects of a regime that touts its ability to maximize individual freedom. I will show that flexibility constructs and naturalizes an individualistic social formation by dismantling collective institutions, particularly unions, and empowering individual employees through a menu of rights and norms. Moreover, the decollectivizing and individualizing modes of flexibility that I identify compel and reward a spirit of self-entrepreneurialism and adaptability. By developing a portrait of the flexible worker, I argue that flexibility comes at the price of the increasing encroachment by work into the once-more-bounded sphere of private life. Rather than the flexible worker taking control of work, work has enveloped the life of the flexible worker and created a subject more committed than ever to devoting his or her energies to its demands, which in turn imperils nonmonetary activities such as leisure, care, and community service. To capitalize on the emancipatory potential of flexibility to reduce the domination of work, I suggest that we need to overcome our dependence on paid work as the primary source of income and to displace work from the center of personal identity.

The Unconditional Basic Income (UBI) appears to be a simple way to achieve these goals. As I argue in chapter 4, however, while proposals for a UBI seem to make a strong challenge to the work society, many arguments for it in fact extol its capacity to boost employment. Drawing on post-structural political theory, I argue that proposals for the UBI on the basis of its employment-boosting potential remain attached to what I call the "fantasy" of the work society. To be sure, a UBI motivated by the goal of expanding employment and introduced within a society still committed to the central value of paid work would offer benefits in terms of distributive justice. But I argue that such a scheme would fail to tackle three core problems with contemporary work: the pervasive mismatch between the social recognition that an occupation confers on a person and the contribution it makes to society; the marginalization of those who cannot or will not perform paid work, despite the fact that many nonetheless contribute to society through various unpaid activities; and the pressure that paid work puts on the panoply of nonpaid activities that make up a rich and rewarding life. To counter these risks, it is essential therefore to argue for the UBI in conjunction with a critique of the work society and its hypervaloriza-tion of work and thus as a measure that can take us beyond it.

In chapter 5 I begin to consider the outlines of the postwork society in more detail by examining the work of André Gorz, and Michael Hardt and Antonio Negri. All three thinkers share a commitment to the UBI and see in contemporary capitalism openings for radical transformation. As persuasive as these arguments are, however, I will show that the specter of the work society haunts them, specifically in their view of community as constructed by work. Given the harms that the current work society inflicts and the risk that these alternative societies incur of perpetuat-ing them, thinking of community as distinct from work or cooperation (which, of course, literally means working together) is a task of both great philosophical difficulty and political urgency. In this chapter I turn to the work of Jean-Luc Nancy, and specifically his concept of the inoperative community (better translated in my view as the "unworked community"), for guidance. In place of a community based on work, Nancy proposes the "communionless communism of singular beings," which takes place "in the unworking and as the unworking of all its works."[38] In chapter 6, I draw out some more concrete implications of this analysis, specifically concerning the relationship between capitalism and the postwork community, and the possibility of maintaining ethical duties within it. Against a left-liberal view that we can transcend the work society without challenging capitalism, I argue that capitalism would thwart the postwork community and that anticapitalism therefore constitutes an essential component of the struggle against the work society.

2

THE WORK SOCIETY

Judging by the crescendo of applause and cheering from the audience, Vice President Joe Biden tapped into deep-seated moral feelings when, at the US Democratic National Convention in 2012, he relayed his father's observation that "a job is about a lot more than a paycheck. It's about—it's about your dignity. It's about respect. It's about your place in the community."[1] In the context of the global economic crisis and its aftermath, in which millions found themselves jobless or underemployed, Mr. Biden's statement, as well as its reception by the audience, poignantly demonstrates the leading role of employment in twenty-first-century life. His succinct statement of the enduring significance of work encapsulates three key points: the material necessity of earning a wage in a capitalist economy; the dignity and respect that doing so confers upon workers; and the social inclusion that gainful employment facilitates.

In this chapter I want to focus on the last of these observations and to consider how and why a job is "about your place in the community." I argue that the connection between work and social belonging captured by Biden in this speech reflects two key features of the work society: an individualist social ontology, which treats society as an association of preexisting individuals who are integrated into it by means of their paid work, and the ability of paid work to perform this role, not only because it involves social interaction and cooperation but because we see society itself as the product of work (though not necessarily paid) and justify its existence with the claim that working together enables people to do better than they could alone.

To help develop these arguments, in this chapter I turn first to the work of André Gorz, who observes that "the values of work, time, and money" have acted as the "bases of the social order established over the last 150 years."[2] As an astute analyst and critic of contemporary capitalism over the course of several decades—Herbert Marcuse wrote a blurb for Gorz's *Strategy for Labor* describing it as "one of the most important contributions to the analysis of contemporary industrial society"—Gorz offers valuable insights into the political significance of work. One modest goal of this chapter, then, is to reconstruct Gorz's analysis of both the work society and the supporting ideology of work as it appears across several of his texts. In the course of doing so, however, I will reveal a tension in his thought that will serve as a provocation for further reflections on the question of social ontology and the very meaning and purpose of society and its relation to work.

To understand this tension, it is essential to first consider Gorz's summation of the ideology of work, in which he suggests that:

> It is a feature of "work-based societies" that they consider work as at one and the same time a moral duty, a social obligation and *the* route to personal success. The ideology of work assumes that, the more each individual works, the better off everyone will be; those who work little or not at all are acting against the interests of the community as a whole and do not deserve to be members of it; those who work hard achieve social success and those who do not succeed have only themselves to blame.[3]

Related to these features of the ideology of work are the ideas of work as a vocation as well as the norm of full-time work, which clearly overlaps the first element's assertion that "more is better." In keeping with his Marxist leanings, Gorz highlights the functionality of the ideology of work to the maintenance of capitalism, particularly as it serves the interests of employers in maintaining domination. Gorz thus presents the ideology of work, especially under conditions of scarce employment opportunities, as an instrument wielded by the ruling class to secure adherence to a regime of production that fails to serve the interests of ordinary people.

Alongside his analysis of the ideology of work, however, Gorz also offers an account of the way paid work integrates private individuals into society and gives them an identity as citizens, a process that he calls "functional integration." Although this mechanism might also help explain popular support for the ideology of work in a manner that avoids the implication of false consciousness—Gorz is committed to the view that, under the right conditions, work really can integrate individuals into society—he does not directly address the relationship between this mechanism and what he calls the "ideology of work." More curiously still, even as Gorz defines work precisely as "an imposition, a heterodetermined, heteronomous activity" and calls for its abolition "as a central activity" of our lives and society, he maintains that its complete elimination is neither possible nor desirable.[4] In particular, despite criticizing aspects of the organization and social value of paid work in contemporary society, throughout many of his writings he maintains that work in the modern sense—that is, an "activity in the public sphere, demanded, defined and recognized as useful by other people and, consequently, as an activity they will pay for"[5]—is valuable because it "gives us an identity as citizens."[6]

As is shown in chapter 5, Gorz's later texts place less emphasis on this macrosocial work, with Gorz even advocating the eventual elimination of wage labor. In this chapter I am not offering a complete account of Gorz's oeuvre. Rather, I consider why he affirms the social role that work plays in terms of integration even though this brings him close to the second element of the ideology of work, according to which "those who work little or not at all are acting against the interests of the community as a whole and do not deserve to be members of it." The particular value of this exercise lies in a deeper understanding of Gorz's thought and, more importantly, in the way it illustrates the hold of certain beliefs about the value of work even on those who sharply criticize it. To make sense of the tension between Gorz's criticism of the ideology of work and his affirmation of the functional integration that work facilities, I argue that it is his ethical and ontological commitment to the individual subject—whereby he positively values the individual subject of autonomy and takes it for granted as a presocial reality—that commits him to a view of society as an association of individuals who are and need to be bound together by economic and social ties.[7]

The implications of this argument extend beyond the interpretation of Gorz's work. In particular, to the extent that Gorz accurately reflects the dynamics of work-based integration in contemporary society—that is, explains how a job is "about your place in the community"—he helps us see that an individualist ontology also lies at the heart of the work society and that the social value of work derives in part from the resultant need for a mechanism that would bring individuals together and allow them to live harmoniously with one another. Indeed, it is evident from the previous discussion that the work ethic acts as an individualizing discourse; moreover, in chapter 3 I will discuss how the discourses and practices of flexibility help construct an individualistic social formation. Under these conditions, work both individualizes and brings subjects together into society understood along the lines of an association.

As Gorz demonstrates, one does not have to be especially committed to the intrinsic value of work as expressed by any or all versions of the work ethic to support treating work as a social obligation. In his case, this is due to the insight that the performance of paid work brings a private individual into the public realm, transforming her or him into a social individual and a citizen with rights and duties. While Gorz explains this mechanism persuasively, the final section of this chapter considers the meaning and purpose of society or civilization at a more basic level. There we find that Sigmund Freud's *Civilization and Its Discontents* links work and society at a deeper level than even Gorz's analysis of functional integration by casting civilization itself as the product of work. While there is some evidence in Gorz's texts that he takes a similar approach, the broader implication of this finding is that such a view of coexistence helps provide the justification for society needed by an individualist social ontology. That is, Freud's approach to civilization helps show how work can become a properly social obligation.

Gorz's Ideology of Work

As Gorz explains in *Critique of Economic Reason*, the ideology of work is highly rational from the perspective of capitalism because it helps motivate and control the workforce. To do so, the ideology of work "must preserve the workforce's adherence to the work ethic, destroy the relations of solidarity that could bind it to the less fortunate, and persuade it that *by doing as much work as possible* it will serve the collective interest as well as its own private interests."[8] In fact, however, under the conditions of "an increasing structural glut of workers and an increasing structural shortage of secure, full-time jobs,"[9] the ideology of work encourages workers to "enter into increasingly fierce competition with each other," which in turn drives down wages and promises the "rebirth of a dynamic form of capitalism."[10] In sum, the "ultra-competitive egoism and careerism" that the Thatcherite ideology of work promotes[11] and that dovetails with the individualizing effects of the discourses and practices of flexibility that are considered in the next chapter goes against "the common interest of waged workers," who should instead organize collectively in trade unions to negotiate better conditions with employers and abandon the work ethic.[12]

As Gorz writes in *Paths to Paradise*, the "fundamental aim of keeping full-time work as the norm" is to "*maintain the relations of domination based on the work ethic.*" Although the elaboration of the three parts of the ideology of work previously quoted does not appear in this earlier text, Gorz treats the norm of full-time work as part of "the ideological bases of domination."[13] Indeed, as I have suggested, this norm clearly conforms to the "more is better" claim of the first component of the ideology of work that Gorz theorizes in *Critique of Economic Reason*. Similarly, in *Farewell to the Working Class*, Gorz asks, "Why does the right always prefer to reduce the number of workers in employment by 10 percent rather than cut working hours by 10 percent?" He attributes this stance to ideology: if people had options about how to spread this work out over the months, years, or even a lifetime, then they "would—or could—define themselves with reference to their free time activities rather than their paid work."[14] But this reduction of working time would make it hard to maintain the "relation of existential submission to employers."[15] Moreover, employers recognize the "disciplinary force" of unemployment, in that the scarcity of jobs makes it easier to exclude "trouble-makers, militants and layabouts."[16] Finally, especially in the Fordist model, the norm of full-time employment represents the attempt to "shape individual ways of life and the model of individual consumption as functions of economic rationality,

that is, of the need to obtain a return on growing quantities of capital."
Thus *"people must be prevented from choosing to limit their working
hours so as to prevent them choosing to limit their desire to consume."*[17]

Not only does the ideology of work reflect the interests of capitalists
in maintaining domination, but, according to Gorz, ideology is a matter
of concealment, and support for it on the part of workers is evidence of
impaired or deficient consciousness of reality. For example, Gorz analyzes
the so-called new-style workers as part of the "ideology of 'human resources.'" As he puts it, these workers "must be capable of reacting rapidly, must co-operate with their fellow workers sharing out tasks between
them as they themselves see fit in response to different situations, and
must show both independent initiative and a sense of responsibility."[18]
This picture of work as providing the conditions for personal fulfilment
clearly resonates with Weeks's account of the postindustrial work ethic,
while the human resources movement has an important place within the
post-Fordist discourses and practices of flexibility. What bears emphasis,
though, is that Gorz sees it as "an essentially ideological invention" in that
it "conceals the real transformations that have taken place"—in particular, automation and the resulting marginalization of a mass of workers
who then compose a "reserve army of labour."[19]

Similarly, to preserve the work ethic, Gorz notes that it is "necessary
to conceal" the structural surplus of workers and structural shortage of
jobs and that therefore "work can no longer serve as the basis of social
integration." Nonstructural accounts of unemployment—that is, claims
that "casual labourers and the unemployed are not serious about looking for work, do not possess adequate skills, are encouraged to be idle by
overgenerous dole payments and so on"—help conceal these structural
problems in the labor market.[20] Although he does not make the connection here, these "alternative explanations" resemble the third component
of Gorz's version of the ideology of work—namely, that "those who work
hard achieve social success and those who do not succeed have only themselves to blame."

In a later text, Gorz also refers to the ideology of work as a "bad
joke" for those with limited employment opportunities. In particular, he
suggests that "the *reality disguised* by extolling 'human resources' or the
work of the new skilled industrial personnel" is that only a privileged minority has access to "stable, full-time, year-round employment throughout

an entire lifetime."[21] Gorz mentions that "an appreciable section of the traditional Left and the unions" adheres to the ideology of work "without perceiving (or without wishing to acknowledge)" that maintaining their privileges comes at the cost of the "growing mass of unemployed people, temporary and casual workers."[22] Thus, as he writes in *Capitalism, Socialism, Ecology*, "The ideology of work, which argues that 'work is life' and demands that it be taken seriously and treated as a vocation, and the attendant utopia of a society ruled by the associated producers, play right into the hands of the employers, consolidate capitalist relations of production and domination, and legitimate the privileges of a work elite."[23]

Gorz's comments on the stability of capitalism also partake of this play of appearance and reality. For example, he claims that the bourgeoisie has destroyed "what consciousness the proletariat might have of its sovereign creativeness," thus preventing workers from perceiving the contradiction between their subjugation "to the realm of necessity and the fact that this sphere has already been transcended by the *gratuitousness* (the non-necessity, the non-utility) of the wealth produced."[24] Finally, Gorz suggests that "the possibility of building an *apparently* growing sphere of individual autonomy outside of work" helps placate workers who might be aggrieved by the "dispossession and growing constraints experienced at work," thus helping ensure the stability of capitalism.[25]

As these examples show, Gorz consistently opposes appearance and reality, suggesting that from an empirical perspective the claims of ideology are simply false. Indeed, this chapter later shows that Gorz opposes the first proposition of the ideology of work that "the more each individual works, the better off everyone will be" with the claim that we ought to reduce working time so that everyone can work and thus be better off (if not monetarily). Similarly, the third part of the ideology of work—"those who work hard achieve social success and those who do not succeed have only themselves to blame"—provides an individualizing account of unemployment (like Weeks's work ethic) that covers over the structural surplus of workers and lack of jobs. But what about the second element of the ideology of work, that "those who work little or not at all are acting against the interests of the community as a whole and do not deserve to be members of it"?

On one hand, the ideology of work as a social obligation also seems disjointed from reality from Gorz's perspective, since he implies that those who maintain full-time employment are in fact selfishly clinging onto an indefensible privilege. Indeed, he writes that the ideology of work "legitimate[s] the privileges of a work elite which, despite the existence of millions of unemployed, views a reduction in working hours which could create extra jobs as incompatible with its professional pride and ethic of productivity."[26] In other words, given the current availability of jobs, the principle that membership of the community should depend on the performance of full-time work simply serves to exclude a mass of less fortunate and less successful persons from society.

On the other hand, Gorz not only explains how paid work integrates individuals into society, he also defends this process, fearing that without the social obligation to perform paid work individuals would remain trapped in a narrowly private existence and lack the public identity of a citizen. To be sure, this does not amount to an endorsement of the ideology of work as he theorizes it, because Gorz does not make a normative argument about which individuals deserve to be full members of the community; rather, his is a sociological explanation of the way paid work bestows a public existence upon individuals. Yet in offering these reflections, Gorz suggests another set of reasons that we support the work society beyond those that fall under the heading of the "work ethic." Indeed, while his official account of the ideology of work tends to imply that its supporters are being duped by a set of claims that only benefits the ruling class, Gorz's unofficial account of the ideology of work—his theorization of functional integration—offers additional insight into the stabilization of a contingent social order.[27]

Work, Citizenship, and the Market

Similar to Marx's claim that "the exchange of exchange values is the productive, real basis of all *equality* and *freedom*,"[28] Gorz observes that when I enter into an employment contract, the general character of labor that I sell "designates me as being a *generally* social, generally useful individual, as capable as anyone else and entitled to the same rights as they are. In other words, it designates me as a *citizen*."[29] This claim suggests an important link between citizenship and paid work, but it is necessary to note the context in which it appears to appreciate its nuance. In the chapter bearing the title "The Limits of Economic Rationality," Gorz explores which of a variety of activities constitute "economically rational work."[30] In particular, he suggests that "economic rationality seems properly applicable to activities which: (a) create use value; (b) for exchange as commodities; (c) in the public sphere; (d) in a measurable amount of time, at as high a level of productivity as possible."[31]

While not all activities that one might conceive of as work meet these criteria for "economically rational work," when he refers to the way that the sale of labor designates a person as a "*generally* social, generally useful individual . . . as a *citizen*," it is in the context of his analysis of "work in the economic sense as emancipation."[32] This suggests that Gorz's claim about the connection between work and citizenship is not intended to merely describe the ideology of work and the work society, but that his purpose is to discern which paid activities can successfully ground citizenship and which, regardless of official ideology, cannot. Although, as will become apparent shortly, his support for functional integration to some extent resembles the ideology of work as a social obligation against the "current ideologues" who advance a "view of work as an undifferentiated entity" and the "ideology of jobs for jobs' sake,"[33] Gorz consistently stresses the need to insulate certain activities performed for their own sake from commodification.[34]

Gorz emphasizes in particular the fact that economically rational work is exchanged as a commodity in the public sphere, which "immediately denotes it as being a socially useful activity."[35] Later, in *Critique of Economic Reason*, he expands on the publicity criterion by explaining that "work in an economic sense . . . is governed by universal rules and relations which liberate the individual from particular bonds of dependence and define her or him as a universal individual, that is, as a citizen."[36] The public dimension of this work sets it apart from the labor performed in private in premodern societies, which he notes "was never a factor of social integration" but in fact a "criterion of exclusion."[37] In his examples of the "farmer's daughter who goes to work in a canning factory" and "the 'housewife' who gets a job in a school canteen," Gorz argues that both women are "finally being able to break free of their confinement within the private sphere and *gain access to the public sphere*." Overcoming the duties of the private sphere, which are "dictated by the intangible obligations of love and family membership," not only grants the women in these examples "a legal existence as *citizens*," it is also part of a broader set of processes by which the public and private spheres are demarcated.[38]

"Work in the economic sense as emancipation" is necessarily exchanged in the public sphere as a commodity; in addition, the capacity of paid work to designate a person as a citizen derives from the abstraction and generality of labor in capitalism. Gorz explains that as capitalists needed to "calculate and forecast labour costs accurately," they began to conceive of workers and their work as "interchangeable and comparable to that of any other workers"—that is, they made sure workers entered "the process of production stripped of their personality and their individuality, their personal goals and desires."[39] As alienating as this process was and is, it also helped construct the social individual, whose very economic activity now incorporated him or her into society's broader network of production and exchange.

This notion of abstract labor thus relates to Gorz's fourth criterion of activities to which economic rationality applies—namely, that activities should be done "in a measurable amount of time, at as high a level of productivity as possible." One reason that economic rationality does not apply to helping and caring activities, in Gorz's view, is that their efficiency is "impossible to quantify." Gorz thus suggests that these activities would be better performed "on a voluntary basis within the framework of mutual aid networks," rather than as paid work.[40] But it is also worth noting that, in more recent work, Gorz points to the destruction of abstract labor by "the individualization of pay rates, together with the transformation of employees into sessional or self-employed workers." As a result, "wage-labour is losing the emancipatory function of freeing workers from the relations of subjection which prevailed in traditional society."[41]

Finally, it is worth noting that although Gorz would eventually support the UBI in *Reclaiming Work*, his arguments against it prior to that demonstrate his commitment to work not on the basis of the work ethic, but instead because of its role in producing social individuals. Thus he worries that "when society expects nothing of me," as would be the case with the payment of a genuinely unconditional basic income, one loses one's "reality as a social individual in general."[42] That is, the problem with the UBI is not only that it would allow individuals to opt out of the very activity that would otherwise confer on them the identity of a citizen. In addition, he stresses, the provision of the UBI would relieve people of social obligations and, in particular, the "obligation to 'earn my living' by working," and that this in turn means that "I cease to exist as an 'interchangeable social individual as capable as any other'; my only remaining existence is private and micro-social."[43]

For Gorz, both the performance of socially useful work in the public sphere and the understanding of this as a duty establish a person's claim to citizenship. As he explains, he does "not propose this in order to save 'work-based society,' the work ethic or biblical morality, but to maintain the indispensable dialectical unity between rights and duties."[44] While Gorz does not exactly reiterate the second part of the ideology of work that he describes—namely, that only those who work deserve to be members of the community—he does take for granted the role of work in effecting functional integration. Thus, for Gorz, the solution to social marginalization and the dual economy (of secure and contingent employment) is to spread the available work out more evenly across the population rather than trying to challenge the link between work and social membership.

While Gorz's account of the relationship between work and citizenship is generally compelling, his argument that activities must meet all four criteria to ground citizenship does not perfectly reflect the ideology of the work society, which, by contrast, lays all the emphasis on the fact of a given activity being paid. Indeed, as has been shown, it is precisely in opposition to the "ideologues" who wish to make jobs out of tasks that people previously did for themselves that Gorz proposes to demarcate the proper sphere of economic rationality. For example, what Gorz calls "servants' work" does not create a use value and is only partially performed in public, since "it consists not just in supplying a certain amount of labour at a certain price as stated in their contract, but also in giving pleasure, in giving of themselves." In this case, Gorz clearly states that service workers are deprived of "chances of economic and social integration."[45]

Similarly, although helping and caring activities create use value and are exchanged in the public sphere for commodities and thus presumably qualify as being socially useful, Gorz judges that they lack the fourth criterion, since it is impossible to quantify their efficiency. In both cases, however, when Gorz claims that these activities are incapable of grounding citizenship, he parts ways with official ideology. While the child minder enjoys considerably less social esteem than a lawyer, for example, it seems odd to say that a physician—whose work on Gorz's account also falls outside the proper sphere of economic rationality—does not enjoy considerable recognition as a citizen on the basis of her or his employment. It is thus evident that Gorz is in fact less interested in explaining the connections between work and citizenship in contemporary society than he is in providing an account of which activities should continue to be economicized.

While Gorz disapproves of the marketization of any and all activities, he does not challenge the link between (some forms of) paid work and citizenship. One problem with this approach is that it suggests that the work he thinks should not be paid also should not serve as the basis of citizenship. It would be unfair to Gorz to suggest that he does not recognize the value of care work. For example, he argues that childcare should not be considered "socially necessary" because "we do not bring children into the world out of social necessity, nor do we raise them for that reason."[46] In seeking to defend household-based activities from economic rationality, moreover, Gorz also anticipates Kathi Weeks's concern that, by arguing that care work is "real work and should be recognized and valued as such," this risks "tapping into and expanding the scope of the traditional work ethic."[47]

And yet there is another option here, one not explored by Gorz—namely, to uncouple citizenship from paid work altogether. Indeed, theorists committed to raising the social value of care work suggest that this requires treating it as a social contribution equal to more highly valued activities like paid work.[48] Yet Gorz cannot take this route because he has not only explained how paid work integrates individuals into society, he has endorsed the process. Unless care work is paid—a possibility that Gorz rejects on the grounds that it operates according to a noneconomic rationality—he cannot conceive of how it might form the basis of full citizenship. As I will argue later in this chapter and in chapter 5, to see those who do not perform paid work, as well as those who do not perform even unpaid work, as full members of society will require a different, more social social ontology.[49]

Even though Gorz does not accept the ideology of work wholesale, his account of functional integration nevertheless provides additional insight into why we support the work society: work in the public sphere performed for wages confers on a person a public identity that enables him or her to transcend the merely private one to which he or she would otherwise remain confined. I now want to consider in more detail what Gorz means by integration and how he sees work performing it, since the claims that he makes about the relation between individual and society that underpin these arguments can also help us understand the presuppositions of the work society.

Shortages of Work and the Limits of Social Integration

In 1980, Gorz observed that the "abolition of work is a process already underway and likely to accelerate" due to automation and the "technological revolution."[50] Eight years later, in *Critique of Economic Reason*, Gorz claimed that the " 'society of work' is obsolete" because insufficient demand for work means that it "can no longer serve as the basis of social integration."[51] By 1991, Gorz would write that "we are no longer living in a society of producers, in a work-based civilization. Work is no longer the main social cement, the principal source of socialization, nor each person's main occupation, their chief source of wealth and well-being, the meaning and focus of our lives."[52] In this regard, Gorz seems to be in broad agreement with Zygmunt Bauman, who argues in *Work, Consumerism, and the New Poor* that we no longer inhabit a society of producers.[53]

Whereas Bauman speaks of a society of consumers replacing the work society, however, Gorz describes "a society of phantom work, spectrally surviving the extinction of that work by virtue of the obsessive, reactive invocations of those who continue to see work-based society as the only possible society and who can imagine no other future than the return of the past."[54] Gorz thus implies that to deserve the description "work society," a society must not only prize paid work in its values, it must also ensure the social integration of all or at least most of its members through the availability of sufficient jobs. In my view, this "positivistic" approach risks occluding the very real harms produced by society's continuing commitment to the values of work. In other words, even if "work is no longer the main social cement" as Gorz claims, this does not justify jettisoning the term "work society," since the ideology of work continues to significantly structure social relations. Indeed, Gorz himself seems to recognize this when he notes that, instead of accepting the need to envision a new society in which full-time work is no longer the norm, the prevailing tendency is to try to replace the jobs lost through automation with new ones that perform activities that people previously did for themselves.[55]

The shortage of work is not the only factor that Gorz identifies as undermining its function of social integration. In *Critique of Economic Reason*, he argues that the social division and specialization of work mean that "work is *no longer* a source of *social* integration," only of functional integration.[56] Gorz points out that the growing complexity of society results in functionality as a form of rationality that programs the agent's activities according to the needs of the organization, which are beyond his or her individual comprehension.[57] While the socialist regimes and workers' movements claimed to be able to avoid the alienating effects of this functionalism by encouraging an approach to work as a fulfillment of both the personal goals of individuals and the needs of society,[58] Gorz suggests that this failed because the coincidence of functional work and personal activity "is ontologically unrealizeable *on the scale of large systems*."[59]

In other words, we do not achieve social integration through work (which Gorz defines as heteronomous) because the system into which it integrates us "remains external to us," instead of being "a web of co-operative relations established for the purpose of attaining common goals." As the source of functional integration, work still gives "us an identity as citizens, as defined in a series of codified rights and duties," but this is clearly distinct from giving us an identity "as 'members' each assuming the goals sought by all as our own."[60] Note that Gorz here points to a distinction between society and community. In *Reclaiming Work*, he also writes that society is "the substitution of juridical relations between emancipated individuals for communal bonds based on a traditional *order* which assigns each person his/her place and governs all aspects of daily life, including relations between man and wife or parents and children." This means that "there is no concrete community and immediate lived solidarity" between citizens who make up a society, although "economic and social citizenship establishes" what he calls "abstract solidarity."[61]

In *Capitalism, Socialism, Ecology*, first published in 1991, Gorz makes a similar claim about the impossibility of individual being coinciding with social being. In Gorz's view, guild-based society and the industrial working class, "with its culture, solidarities, associations and counter-society," had enabled the individual to belong "in his or her entirety to society and community—in work, lifestyle, ethics, milieu and position within the social totality." In what he calls "complex modern society," by contrast, existence is differentiated into various "spheres of activity" with the individual performing a "multiplicity" of distinct roles such that the subject cannot seek "his or her unity in any of them."[62] By the time of *Reclaiming Work*, first published in 1997, however, Gorz claims that work "was *never* a source of 'social cohesion' or integration, whatever we might have come to believe from its retrospective idealization."[63] In other words, we (including Gorz himself) have imagined a community based on work that never existed.

The distinction that Gorz draws between functional integration, on one hand, and social integration, on the other, thus corresponds to the difference in his thought between society and community. If Gorz believes that "social existence inevitably carries a degree of alienation because we do not and cannot recognize society as something we have freely created through voluntary co-operation with everyone else,"[64] this raises the question of why we should not abandon it in favor of smaller-scale communities, in which we can experience a "lived, existential bond" with others.[65] As I will show in chapter 5, one direct answer that Gorz gives is that we have become accustomed to the benefits of modern society, which flow from the efficiency of production, specialization, and the division of labor. Another reason he offers, which I will also consider at greater length in that chapter, is that the tight integration of communal life threatens individual liberty.

Despite these advantages of society, however, Gorz does not dismiss the value of community as the level of interaction at which we most directly experience the existential bond and as the precise site at which social bonds are produced.[66] In other words, Gorz does not think we have to choose between community and society; rather, we need to make sure each is kept within its proper bounds. While Gorz is therefore certainly not advocating radical individualism—not just for the reasons already noted, but also because autonomous behavior "always occurs within a socially determined field, with socially pre-given instruments"[67]—it becomes clear from these reflections that underlying his account of both functional and social integration is an individualist social ontology.

Social Ontology

Gorz's intellectual and political positions have been the subject of some debate among his readers. As Finn Bowring puts it, Gorz "has been accused of both 'bourgeois individualism' and 'backward-looking romanticism.' Depending on the critic, Gorz is an erstwhile 'quasi-Stalinist' or a reformed 'anti-Stalinist,' an advocate of 'postmodern politics' or simply an 'intellectual charlatan.' "[68] While I do not wish to affirm any of these accusations, Gorz's individualist social ontology is clear and worthy of further discussion for the light that it can shed not only on his attachment to functional integration, but also on the contemporary work society. Insofar as Gorz's account of functional integration accurately reflects the social effects of paid work in contemporary society, it makes sense to attribute individualist ontological presuppositions to the latter. Moreover, both the work ethic and the discourse and practices of flexibility foster an individualist social ontology in the work society.

How does Gorz's account of integration betray an individualist social ontology? To put it simply, by theorizing the processes of integration, Gorz implies the possibility of nonintegration. In other words, for Gorz integration is akin to a property that individuals either have or don't have, thus making (private) individuals ontologically prior to the society into which they are integrated. Another way to put this is that society is the outcome of the functional integration of individuals—and in parallel fashion, community in his sense of the term is the outcome of the social integration of individuals—with those unsuccessfully integrated falling at its margins or completely outside of it.

Here I want to focus on how this ontology influences common understandings of society, including Gorz's. When one starts out from an individualist social ontology, it becomes necessary to offer a justification for society—that is, an account of what the presumptively ontologically prior individuals who make it up gain by taking part in the association and what the terms and conditions of membership are.[69] As I will argue in the next section with the help of Freud's *Civilization and its Discontents*, common understandings of society couch such an account in terms of the advantages of cooperation—that is, of working together. Gorz's thought captures (although uncritically) the fact that, in contemporary society, paid work is at once a form of cooperation on a macrosocial scale that promises material benefits that would be unavailable to individuals working alone and a disciplinary mechanism that integrates individuals into society, thus helping bring about social order and harmony.

Other evidence of Gorz's individualist social ontology abounds. For example, Gorz suggests that the so-called humanism of work needs to be replaced with the "humanism of free activity and of self-management at all levels." Whereas the former treats individuals as "means of society and of production," the latter "presupposes that individuals . . . be seen and see themselves as ends."[70] Finally, although Gorz does not develop a detailed critique of poststructuralism, it is worth noting that he does clearly distance himself from what he calls "structuralism," for fear that its account of the subject is complicit with the separation that techniciza-tion and economic rationality perform between thought, on the one hand, and "examination and criticism," on the other.

In a passage directly referring to Michel Foucault and obliquely to Gilles Deleuze, Gorz identifies as a core principle of structuralism the no-tion that "the subject is spoken by the language, there are only speaking, desiring machines, and so on."[71] Although it is well known that "post-structuralism" is a term that originated outside of France to describe vari-ous thinkers, including Foucault and Deleuze, by the end of the 1980s the term was in common usage, so it seems reasonable to take Gorz's use of "structuralism" as further evidence of his unfavorable view of this broad intellectual movement.[72] Indeed, he claims that (post)structuralism's de-nial of the individual subject amounts to "the ideology of triumphant technicism"—that is, that it reflects the fact that "technicization allows subjects to be absent from the operations they themselves carry out," but that this experience of work is now "elevated to the level of a universal truth" about man.[73]

For Gorz, this "technique of thinking" makes "living individuals strang-ers to the reified world which is nonetheless their product."[74] In his view we must therefore maintain a commitment to the individual as the funda-mental unit of social analysis, because forsaking it risks complicity with the very social formation that he wants to criticize. As will become clear in chapter 5, I take a different approach, appealing in particular to Jean-Luc Nancy's singular-plural ontology, according to which "*being-one . . . can only be understood by starting from being-with-one-another*,"[75] and to his theory of the inoperative community to ground an alternative postwork community to those projected both by Gorz and by Hardt and Negri. The point I want to emphasize here, however, is that although he criticizes both the content of work and its scarcity and maldistribution, Gorz does not challenge the underlying individualist social ontology of the work society. Indeed, Gorz accepts the complex operation that he observes employment performing on the subject in the contemporary work society: on one hand, it emancipates the individual from relations of personal dependence, and on the other, it brings the individual into an association with others, thus forming society.

When Gorz identifies a structural surplus of workers and a structural lack of jobs, these factors disturb a reassuring and appealing image of society as fully integrated and harmonious. In response to this crisis, one solution is to attempt to create new jobs, but Gorz dismisses this approach on the grounds that noneconomically rational work does not offer genuine social and economic integration. Another response, or rather a set of different responses that I will examine in chapter 4, is to propose the unconditional basic income (UBI). As already noted, only in his later work does Gorz accept this response, insisting on the necessity of a social obligation to work on the grounds that removing it would result in the disintegration of society. It is now evident that viewing society as an association of individuals is precisely what makes the specter of disintegration so alarming. In calling for the reduction and redistribution of work, Gorz does not want to save the work society, but to prevent the widespread dissolution of social bonds. While I doubt that Gorz would have approved of David Cameron's appraisal of the 2011 riots mentioned in chapter 1, the connections made between the disorder and joblessness (whatever the plausibility of these claims) and the claim that "work is at the heart of a responsible society" represent a particularly dramatized version of this concern.

Work, Repression, Civilization

In the preceding sections of this chapter I have shown that Gorz does not merely describe work's role of securing functional integration; he also affirms it and even emphasizes the importance of treating work as a social obligation. I suggested that we can understand these prescriptions in terms of Gorz's individualist social ontology, which in turn leads to a view of society as an association that stands in need of justification to its members. In this section I want to continue to dwell on how and why the justification for society, and hence the social obligations of its members, might be linked with work. Freud's theorization of civilization as a social contract for the mutual repression of instinctual satisfactions provides rich material with which to explore this question, since it directly connects civilization with work.[76]

Here I will emphasize two of Freud's claims: first, the unavoidable necessity of work (Freud's reality principle); and second, the notion that society exists, at least in part, to help us meet our needs more effectively. In Herbert Marcuse's interpretation of Freud, we put up with the subordination of work because the idea of rejecting this order fills us with guilt, as it "appears as the crime against the whole of human society."[77] The similarity between this proposition and Gorz's formulation of the ideology of work as a social obligation is striking. What Freud and Marcuse add to Gorz's analysis, however, is an explanation of *why* work plays such an important social role.

I do not mean to suggest, of course, that either Gorz or supporters of the work society have all read and accepted Freud's speculations on the origins of civilization. Rather, Freud illustrates how certain assumptions about civilization and collective life not only lend support to the work society, but also make it difficult to envision a social order that is not significantly structured by and around work. As I will show in chapter 5, even in Gorz's postindustrial socialism or multiactivity society, "co-operation on the basis of solidarity within voluntary communities and associations is the basis *par excellence* for social integration and the production of social bonds."[78] Although Gorz distinguishes this cooperation from work defined in his narrow sense, "cooperation" still connotes work, albeit not of a commoditized nature. As such, I will argue that Gorz continues to view society as inextricably linked with work.

While Freud regards the purpose of life as a religious question, this does not prevent him from observing that what people strive for is happiness, where this means both "the absence of pain and unpleasure, and . . . the experiencing of strong feelings of pleasure." Although the "most enticing" way of life might involve the "unrestricted satisfaction of every need," Freud notices that this "soon brings its own punishment" because it means privileging enjoyment over all else, including caution. Freud therefore identifies an aporia at the heart of human existence: on one hand, the purpose of life is set by what he calls the "pleasure principle," and yet on the other, "all the regulations of the universe run counter to it." Freud identifies three principal sources of human suffering—that is, barriers to the gratification of pleasure: other people, the external world, and "our own body."[79]

Given the unsustainability of gratifying one's every need, Freud suggests that people eventually learn to accommodate themselves to the more modest goal of avoiding unhappiness and to surviving their suffering. Corresponding to the three sources of suffering, Freud discusses three types of responses: turning away from the world in "voluntary isolation," "becoming a member of the human community," and trying to "influence our own organism," for example, by intoxication.[80] Even if voluntary isolation can bring the "happiness of quietness," Freud notes that by working alone one can only turn away from the external world. More relevant for this volume's purposes are the second and third responses. Let me examine each in its turn.

Rather than withdrawing from the external world, Freud suggests that by working with others, and with the help of science, humanity can attack nature and bring it under its will. By joining the human community "one is working with all for the good of all."[81] I will show later that Marcuse sees what precisely it means to join the human community and work for the good of all as historically variable, a notion that he tries to capture with his performance principle. For now, though, the important point is Freud's more general claim that "we recognize as cultural all activities and resources which are useful to men for making the earth serviceable to them, for protecting them against the violence of the forces of nature, and so on." So, for example, "the first acts of civilization were the use of tools, the gaining of control over fire and the construction of dwellings." More broadly, Freud treats civilization as the sum of man's "achievements" and "regulations" that serve to "protect men against nature and to adjust their mutual relations."[82]

As a third means by which to keep suffering at bay, Freud points to forms of work that make use of one's instincts and that yield the type of satisfactions enjoyed by artists and scientists. Specifically, these shift "the instinctual aims in such a way that they cannot come up against frustration from the external world."[83] As he points out, however, most people do not pursue work as a "path of happiness" as assiduously as they do other activities, although the postindustrial work ethic that Weeks discusses, as well as the ideology of human resources briefly mentioned earlier in this chapter, do cast work as a site of self-realization.

Freud concludes this reflection with the allusive claim that "the great majority of people only work under the stress of necessity, and this natural human aversion to work raises most difficult social problems."[84] Unfortunately, he does not expand on this point, but one might surmise that he has in mind problems that stem from not displacing "narcissistic, aggressive or even erotic" libidinal components onto socially useful activities, as well as perhaps the difficulties of trying to impose work on recalcitrant subjects. Indeed, while Freud argues that love and the "compulsion to work" were the two foundations of humans' earliest communal life in the so-called band of brothers of totemic culture,[85] he sees the connective power of work as weaker than that of Eros,[86] which, for reasons that Freud does not attempt to explain, combines "single human individuals, and after that families, then races, peoples and nations, into one great unity, the unity of mankind."[87]

Although Freud does not make this point explicitly, it seems reasonable to infer that at least part of the weakness of work as a social glue stems from his assumption of our natural aversion to it. Yet, at the same time, our lack of a natural instinct for work and the need to sacrifice our libido to it is precisely what makes it central to culture and civilization. As Marcuse explains, "If there is no original 'work instinct,' then the energy required for (unpleasurable) work must be 'withdrawn' from the primary instincts—from the sexual and from the destructive instincts." Quoting Freud, Marcuse then notes that culture "obtains a great part of the mental energy it needs by subtracting it from sexuality."[88] The association Freud makes between civilization and the withdrawal of "psychical energy" from sexuality and its displacement onto work is closely related to the yielding of the pleasure principle to the reality principle.

Marcuse explains the "transformation of the *pleasure principle* into the *reality principle*" in terms of the development of the "animal man" into a "human being." As he puts it, while the pleasure principle involves "immediate satisfaction, pleasure, joy (play), receptiveness, and absence of repression," the reality principle encompasses "delayed satisfaction, restraint of pleasure, toil (work), productiveness, security."[89] It is worth noting how much this schema corresponds with the conservative columnist Max Hastings's depiction of those who took part in the UK riots in 2011: "They respond only to instinctive animal impulses—to eat and drink, have sex, seize or destroy the accessible property of others."[90] Quoting Freud, Marcuse explains that "society's motive in enforcing the decisive modification of the instinctual structure is thus 'economic; since it has not means enough to support life for its members without work on their part, it must see to it that the number of these members is restricted and their energies directed away from sexual activities on to their work.'"[91] But Hastings suggests another motive for enforcing this modification: the assumption that only disciplined human beings operating under the reality principle can live together in a peaceful and orderly fashion.

In light of this recapitulation, it is evident why Marcuse writes that, for Freud, "civilization is first of all progress in *work*—that is, work for the procurement and augmentation of the necessities of life." Indeed, at the very outset of *Eros and Civilization*, Marcuse writes that "Freud's proposition that civilization is based on the permanent subjugation of the human instincts has been taken for granted." Conventional readings of Freud, according to Marcuse, thus see civilization as entailing the subordination of happiness to "the discipline of work as full-time occupation" and culture as "the methodical sacrifice of libido, its rigidly enforced deflection to socially useful activities and expressions."[92] One difficulty with these claims, of course, is that modern society is exceptional in that it does not exclude people who work. In other words, surely Freud is simply wrong in claiming that civilization in general requires full-time work.

One possible response would be to say, following Carole Pateman, that when Freud speaks of civilization he is actually referring to a historically specific, modern social formation. As she points out, "Conjectural histories of the development of the patriarchal family or civil society . . . are presented as stories of the origin of human society or civilization." In reality, however, "'Civilization' refers to an historically and culturally specific form of social life," only coming into usage in the late eighteenth century, "preceded by 'civility,'" "closely bound up with the emergence of the idea of 'civil society,'" and assuming the pinnacle of social progress.[93] Following this line of argument, one could then conclude that premodern societies in which work was not a factor of inclusion, rather of exclusion, simply fall outside the scope of Freud's reflections on civilization. Yet when Freud writes that "the first acts of civilization were the use of tools, the gaining of control over fire and the construction of dwellings,"[94] he clearly does not mean to limit civilization to modernity.

Marcuse himself suggests another approach, which allows one to recognize the importance of work to premodern societies without losing sight of the historical specificity of what I have been calling "the work society" and the principle that membership of it rests on the performance of paid work. It is important to note that Marcuse's project in *Eros and Civilization* is to question the assumption that civilization requires repression. As Marcuse puts it, "Freud's theoretical conception itself seems to refute his consistent denial of the historical possibility of a non-repressive civilization," while "the very achievements of repressive civilization seem to create the preconditions for the gradual abolition of repression."[95] In this regard, one of Marcuse's main contributions to Freudian thought is the historicization of the reality principle.

As Marcuse argues, "The various modes of domination (of man and nature) result in various historical forms of the reality principle. For example, a society in which all members normally work for a living requires other modes of repression than a society in which labor is the exclusive province of one specific group." The performance principle is thus a historically specific form of the reality principle, characteristic of "an acquisitive and antagonistic society in the process of constant expansion." Specifically, the performance principle justifies the hierarchical ordering of society based on its members' economic contribution.[96] Whereas at earlier periods the reality principle made work the "exclusive province of one specific group," and work did not even constitute a factor of social inclusion, the performance principle generalizes the expectation of work and accords social respect on the basis of a person's fulfillment of it.

As this section has shown, Freud approaches civilization as the product of work. In this sense, he adopts what Jean-Luc Nancy calls an "operative view of community," while the challenge Nancy sets himself, as will be considered at greater length in chapter 5, is to think an *in*operative community—that is, one that is "neither a work to be produced, nor a lost communion."[97] On the collective level, civilization and culture (the same German word, *Kultur*, is translated with both of these English terms) refer to people's joint attempts to subdue and use nature for their own purposes, thus reducing if not eliminating the external barriers to the satisfaction of their pleasures. That is, Freud suggests a justification for society based on work and the satisfactions it promises.

Of course, I am not suggesting that Freud has or deserves to have the final say on the justification of society. Rather, I have examined his speculative history of civilization as an example of the type of assumptions and reasoning that might support the view of work as a social obligation. In case Freud's view of society seems somehow unconventional, I want to close this section with a quotation from John Rawls's *A Theory of Justice*:

> Let us assume, to fix ideas, that a society is a more or less self-sufficient association of persons who in their relations to one another recognize certain rules of conduct as binding and who for the most part act in accordance with them. Suppose further that these rules specify a system of cooperation designed to advance the good of those taking part in it. Then, although a society is a cooperative venture for mutual advantage, it is typically marked by a conflict as well as by an identity of interests. There is an identity of interests since social cooperation makes possible a better life for all than any would have if each were to live solely by his own efforts. There is a conflict of interests since persons are not indifferent as to how the greater benefits produced by their collaboration are distributed, for in order to pursue their ends they each prefer a larger to a lesser share.[98]

While I hope that this chapter helps shed new light on Gorz's thought, my purpose is broader. André Gorz is an obvious point of reference to assist in an understanding of the work society, given that across several texts he develops an account of both the ideology of work and the mechanism by which paid work integrates individuals into capitalist society. But beyond the arguments that Gorz explicitly makes, this chapter has focused on Gorz's curious lack of attention to the relationship between the role of work in enabling functional integration and the ideology of work. In particular, I considered why Gorz might affirm the social role that heteronomous work plays in terms of integration, even though this prevents him from challenging a central element of the ideology of work as a social obligation. Again, the point of this exercise is not merely hermeneutic. Rather, I suggest that Gorz's arguments and the assumptions that underpin them can help us understand the inner workings of the work society:

in particular, that it rests on an individualist social ontology and that the resultant society, understood as an association, constantly risks disintegration back to its constituent parts and needs a justifying principle to maintain its cohesion.

Of course, this ontology need not lead to paid work acting as the mechanism of integration. However, turning to Freud, I showed a view of civilization and culture that is inextricably linked with work. If society is thought of as the product of work and justified to its members in terms of the benefits this work in common can offer, then it is easy to understand why work would constitute a social obligation. Moving beyond the work society thus entails not simply attaching a different meaning or value to work, but also rethinking community at the level of ontology. Chapter 5 is devoted to these considerations, but before then, chapter 3 serves as a more empirically grounded account of the pitfalls and possibilities of the contemporary work society, with particular attention to the regime of flexibility.

3

FLEXIBILITY

In October 2011, a report commissioned by Downing Street arguing that the UK government should ban unfair dismissal compensation to boost economic growth sparked outrage among unions and senior members of the Liberal Democrats. In response to the furor, the prime minister's official spokesperson stated that the government was "going to review [existing employment law] so that employers and employees can ensure they have maximum flexibility whilst protecting fairness and providing a competitive environment that we need for enterprise and growth."[1] Earlier that year but on the other side of the Atlantic, the State of Wisconsin passed a law dramatically restricting the collective bargaining rights of most state, county, and municipal workers. The office of the recently elected Republican governor, Scott Walker, explained that the reform had addressed the state's fiscal crisis by reducing "government spending, while giving government increased flexibility to provide services."[2]

These statements provide just two examples of the pervasiveness of flexibility within contemporary political and economic discourse. In fact, according to Nancy Fraser, "flexibilization" (the process of rendering institutions and individuals flexible) is a "ubiquitous buzzword of globalization."[3] As the two examples suggest, flexibility serves as a guiding principle of almost unquestionable value, thanks to its connotations of freedom and efficiency. Like most buzzwords, moreover, "flexibility" draws its rhetorical power from the ease with which different actors can assign meanings to it that align with their own interests.[4] The apparently amorphous character of flexibility, however, should not lead us to dismiss it as just another piece of management-speak, lacking substance or effect. On the contrary, this chapter shows that flexibility lies at the center of the neoliberal organization of work and labor markets and its construction of subjects as workers.

In this chapter, I respond to Fraser's invitation to analyze flexibility as an "emerging new mode of regulation" and to identify its "characteristic ordering mechanisms and political rationality."[5] In particular, I draw out two distinct modes of flexibility: under the guise of deregulation, the first reduces the influence of collective institutions like the state and unions on the organization of paid work, thus increasing the control that employers have over this domain and in the process transforming the terrain of class struggle; the second actively empowers individual employees by granting legal rights and promoting workplace norms, which in turn enable various forms of flexible working arrangements. By eroding the strength of collective protections and voice available to workers, the decollectivizing mode of flexibility effectively compels us to adopt an individualistic ethic of self-responsibility and entrepreneurialism or risk unemployment and social marginalization. The second mode of flexibility, on the other hand, provides (some) individual workers with an appealing measure of control over their employment, which can significantly soften tensions between the demands of paid work and other aspects of life, including family, community, and leisure. While this analysis suggests antagonism between the two modes of flexibility, however, at the level of ideology they act in a more complementary fashion.

Whatever the material effects of the first mode of flexibility on the working conditions of employees, its claim to liberate workers from the yoke of the Keynesian welfare state and unions helps construct an image of society founded on (naturally) free individuals. Any deficit of justice, equality, or freedom that remains is now seen as inherent to the "natural" order, beyond the reach of politics, and inevitable. The second mode of flexibility, meanwhile, helps shore up this negative conception of freedom with the promise (though not always the delivery) of individual empowerment through greater "work-life balance." By appealing to and basing itself on the deeply entrenched value of freedom, flexibility as a mode of social organization draws widespread support among employees who yearn for greater control over work. Meanwhile, as the broader political project of neoliberalism subsumes greater swaths of life under the logic of the market, the figure of the flexible worker, in all its entrepreneurial glory, becomes increasingly normative. In sum, this chapter shows that the discourses and practices of flexibility help construct an individualistic social formation, thus providing further support for the arguments I developed in the previous chapter about the individualist social ontology that prevails in the work society.

This chapter aims to disrupt the hegemony of flexibility by elucidating its political construction and by drawing attention to the double-edged character of the social transformation it has wrought; as such, it does not present a simple case for or against flexibility, but instead aims to complicate our understanding of it. Flexibility undoubtedly offers opportunities for some individuals to exercise a degree of control over the place (both literal and metaphorical) of work in their lives, and I will argue that, to move beyond the work society, we need to capitalize upon this emancipatory potential. But since these benefits are somewhat familiar and self-explanatory, I devote the greater portion of the following analysis to its less conspicuous yet nonetheless problematic implications. In particular, I show that flexibility has played a key role in the transformation and maintenance of the contemporary class structure by marginalizing collective institutions and inducing instability and precariousness for many less privileged workers, thus diminishing their capacity to act according to their own values, needs, and desires. Moreover, the enhanced control that more privileged workers enjoy over work comes at the price of a subtle mode of domination that operates by compelling a disciplined devotion to the expectations of employers and the market. As a result, work threatens to envelop life in a way that subverts flexibility's promise of providing individuals with greater freedom in relation to employment. Finally, to the extent that flexibility helps alleviate the tension between paid work and unpaid care needs, it dovetails with the neoliberal approach to care, which treats care as an individual responsibility. Moreover, I will argue that, by helping maintain the household as the privileged site of care, flexibility is complicit in the gender division of labor and assists in the transmission of privilege from one generation to the next.

A Short History of Flexible Labor Markets

Much like neoliberalism, flexibility takes shape in concrete political, institutional, and cultural settings, with the result that flexible labor markets, firms, and workers may look rather different from place to place.[6] Nevertheless, just as a narrow focus on local neoliberal strategies risks overlooking the more generic features of neoliberalism as an "extralocal project,"[7] so emphasizing the resilience of national industrial-relations institutions to common economic pressures tends to underestimate the degree to which those institutions are being transformed in a broadly neoliberal vein.[8] In what follows I map the general contours of flexibility in the North Atlantic zone,[9] focusing particularly on the United Kingdom and the United States, with the recognition that the conclusions I draw may have limited generalizability to other regions of the globe.

Faced with the almost chameleon-like figure of flexibility (one might even say that flexibility has heeded its own exhortations), I begin by examining what this concept opposes or is intended to replace. Proponents of flexibility most commonly place it in opposition to rigidity; hence attempts to achieve labor-market flexibility typically arise following a diagnosis of friction between the mobility of capital and so-called rigidities of labor.[10] The term "Eurosclerosis" evocatively expressed concerns about labor-market rigidity in the 1970s and 1980s, "conjuring up the image of an elderly man suffering from a tightening of the arteries, a stiffening of the sinews and a failure to summon up the blood."[11] Although the more appealing values of stability and security do stand in some tension with flexibility (especially from the perspective of the worker who may face dismissal, reduced wages, or altered working times, all in the name of the flexible labor market and flexible firm), rigidity functions as the key counter-concept to flexibility within mainstream academic and policy discourse.[12]

An early version of the flexibility/rigidity opposition appeared in the mid-1970s in the context of wages, wherein wage flexibility was seen as preferable to the so-called downward rigidity of wages, which referred to the refusal or unwillingness of workers to accept the lower wages upon which companies claimed their continuing profitability depended. This form of rigidity, according to its critics, stemmed from the Keynesian welfare state, which intervened in the economy by deficit spending and the commitment to full employment, and unionism, which was blamed for keeping wages unsustainably high.[13] The welfare state and organized labor have long been close allies, as the role of labor parties in the development of the US welfare state, especially during the 1960s, attests. If overweening and mutually reinforcing collective institutions were dragging down national economic competitiveness, as the Republican Party and its corporate allies began arguing in the 1970s,[14] then the remedy was their dismantlement under the auspices of flexibility.

Discourses and practices concerning the flexibility of the labor market as a whole then appeared in the 1980s and 1990s,[15] broadening the initial focus of wage flexibility to include hiring arrangements, working conditions, and working time—in other words, to address all aspects of the regulation of labor supply, whether enacted by statute or by collective bargaining.[16] In this sense, flexibility is of a piece with the neoliberal ideology of deregulation, as I discuss at greater length later. A report by the International Monetary Fund (IMF) includes six policy areas in its composite indicator of labor-market flexibility, demonstrating the continuing antagonism between flexibility, on the one hand, and unionism and state intervention into the economy, on the other. Here, minimum-wage requirements, hiring and firing regulations, centralized collective-wage bargaining, mandated cost of hiring (including all social security and payroll taxes and the cost of other mandated benefits like health care), mandated cost of work dismissal (including advance notice and severance), and conscription all constitute impediments to labor-market flexibility.[17]

At the same time as flexibility became the remedy for high unemployment, members of the new right, civil libertarians, traditional liberals, and even left-wing radicals on both sides of the Atlantic were also criticizing the powers of regulatory states and the corporatist relations between government, business, and unions on the basis of a desire to restore "control to the citizen as a free individual."[18] Particularly in the United States, supporters of what Thomas Frank calls "market populism" assailed

Keynesians and unionists as elitists who were trying to act outside of the market, the institution they identified with the will of the people.[19]

The call to make labor markets flexible thus appeals to both economic and philosophical arguments: flexibility will increase efficiency, productivity, and competitiveness, but also freedom, by "liberating" firms and individuals from the "dead weight" of regulations. The ideology of flexibility, moreover, claims to redress the presumptively illegitimate intrusion by the state and unions into the economic realm. Yet in spite of the hostility that flexibility shows toward regulation at the ideological level, the relationship between flexibility and regulation is more harmonious at the level of practice. In the following section I show how governments in the United States and the United Kingdom have used regulations (among other means) to constrain and diminish the power of unions in pursuit of labor-market flexibility. As will become evident, the granting of individual employment rights also helps to establish flexible working arrangements.

Flexibility as Decollectivization and Individualization

To gain a deeper understanding of the process of flexibilization, it will help to first consider the development and transformation of the broader neoliberal project. Rather than unfolding according to a singular logic, during the years of Margaret Thatcher and Ronald Reagan neoliberalism involved the rollback of the welfare state and the reduction of the influence of labor unions, while from the 1990s and into the 2000s, it featured the rollout of the state by constructing individualistic labor-market regulations as well as interventionist and at times paternalistic social policy to address some of the negative consequences of the earlier mode.[20] Building on this insight, I argue that flexibilization proceeds according to two distinct logics: decollectivization, which deploys regulatory and other means to reduce union strength, restrict collective bargaining, and limit recourse to strikes; and individualization, which actively empowers individual workers by granting new employment rights and protections and promoting flexible working arrangements. Recent developments in both countries following the 2007–8 economic collapse indicate a revival of decollectivization as well as a reversal of some of the individual employee gains made during the 1990s. While the individualizing mode of flexibility stands in tension with the idea of labor-market flexibility as expressed by the IMF report discussed earlier, the two modes nonetheless support one another in the construction of an individualistic social formation, which simultaneously demands and praises a self-entrepreneurial relation to work.

When Thatcher and Reagan assumed their offices in 1979 and 1981, respectively, they encountered quite differently structured labor markets, with the "voluntarist" system of industrial relations in the United Kingdom involving significantly less regulation by the state than was the case in the United States. While Conservative governments carried out six rounds of legislative reform during the 1980s,[21] Reagan and subsequent presidents left federal industrial-relations law largely unaltered.[22] Nonetheless, under Reagan the political balance of the National Labor Relations Board (NLRB) shifted in the direction of management, which helped to establish a regulatory framework more favorable to employers than union organizers. In particular, the NLRB increased employers' latitude to interrogate and even fire union supporters and to disseminate misleading or speculative information about unionization. Employers also benefited from a diminished obligation to bargain in good faith and the deregulation of reprisals against strikers.[23]

One key difference between US and UK labor law in the latter half of the twentieth century concerned the legal status of the closed shop, which makes union membership a condition of employment and thereby ensures that all employees at a given workplace are dues-paying members of a union. Whereas closed shops had been abolished in the United States under the 1947 Taft-Hartley Act, when Margaret Thatcher came to office in 1979 they were still legally permitted in the United Kingdom. Successive legislative restrictions on closed shops, ultimately leading to their abolition in 1992 under the Trade Union and Labour Relations (Consolidation) Act, was thus a key regulatory strategy to weaken organized labor in the United Kingdom.[24] The establishment of the "right not to belong to a union" in the United Kingdom represents a similar strategy of decollectivization to so-called right-to-work laws in the United States. The Taft-Hartley Act permits states to enact legislation prohibiting compulsory payment of fees to the legally recognized union at a given workplace. Withholding payment of fees to a union that is required to represent all workers (whether members of the union or not) within a bargaining unit not only creates a classic free-rider problem, it also reduces union funds and thus strength. While the majority of right-to-work laws were passed in the 1940s and 1950s,[25] in December 2012 Michigan became the twenty-fourth state to enact such legislation, demonstrating the continuation of the decollectivizing mode of flexibility. Speaking in support of the legislation, Michigan's governor, Rick Snyder, explained that workers "deserve the freedoms to make decisions for themselves."[26] In 2015, Wisconsin became the twenty-fifth state to adopt right-to-work legislation, although not without legal challenge from plaintiffs, who successfully argued before the 7th U.S. Circuit Court of Appeals in July 2017 that the law was unconstitutional and violated labor law.[27] Right-to-work movements have also sprung up in Missouri (which adopted a right-to-work law in 2017), New Hampshire, and Ohio.[28]

A second feature of decollectivization can be seen in the recent attacks on the right to collective bargaining, most notably in Wisconsin, where in early 2011 the Republican governor, Scott Walker, introduced Senate Bill 11 to the state legislature. According to the Governor's Office, Walker chose to address Wisconsin's fiscal crisis by reducing "government spending, while giving government increased flexibility to provide services."[29] The bill, eventually signed into law in June 2011, sought to achieve this flexibility in part by restricting the collective bargaining rights of most state, municipal, and county employees to the subject of base-level wages, requiring annual certification elections of unions that already represent collective bargaining units, limiting the term of collective bargaining agreements to one year, and prohibiting the deduction of mandatory dues and services fees from employees' salaries.[30]

One can glimpse the rationale for Governor Walker's opposition to unions and collective bargaining in his office's analysis of the reforms: collective bargaining is a "burden" to efficiency, an obstacle to managing staff on the basis of "merit and performance," and even the cause of teacher layoffs due to the fact that it made salaries and benefits "untouchable."[31] These criticisms resonate with the individualistic thrust of much antiunion rhetoric: talented individuals are being stifled, held back, and even denied employment because of the overly rigid and collectivist outlook of unions and fare better when the employer-employee relation is individualized. Three years after the reforms, the *New York Times* reported that the membership of Wisconsin's Council of the American Federation of State, County, and Municipal Employees had fallen 60 percent, while its budget had plummeted from $6 million per year to $2 million. As the article noted, with severely limited powers, what reason did workers have to continue paying dues to their union?[32]

A third key plank of the decollectivizing mode of flexibility involves the handling of strikes by the state and employers. By firing the striking air traffic controllers' union (PATCO) and replacing them with nonunion workers in the first year of his presidency, Reagan set a powerful example to employers about how to deal with restive employees.[33] Although the right to permanently replace lawfully striking workers had existed ever since a 1938 Supreme Court decision,[34] in the wake of Reagan's handling of the PATCO strike the permanent replacement of striking workers proceeded at an accelerated rate.[35] Similarly restricting recourse to industrial action in the United Kingdom, Thatcher defeated the National Union of Mineworkers in 1985[36] and introduced complex and technical industrial-action balloting rules, beginning with the Trade Unions Act of 1984.[37] Employers exploited these rules as a delaying tactic in legal challenges against strikers, notably in the 1989 dock strike. During the four weeks that it took the House of Lords to uphold the legality of the industrial action, the original strike ballot had expired, necessitating a new election, by which time the action had lost momentum.[38] Once again, this element of decollectivization has been resumed in recent years: between 2009 and 2010 no fewer than five injunctions were granted or confirmed against UK strikes due to "balloting or procedural defects," with courts making increasingly narrow readings of the procedures unions must follow in order to call lawful strikes.[39]

By creating conditions hostile to union organizing, collective bargaining, and industrial action, the decollectivizing mode of flexibilization diminishes the collective power of workers to advance their interests and helps increase the discretion of employers to manage workplaces. In the next section I consider various facets of this increase in employer discretion, but before that I examine the second mode of flexibility, which has involved the rollout of pro-individualistic regulations. In many cases, these work against labor-market flexibility as defined by the IMF index considered in the previous section. At the same time, some rights empower individual employees in such a way as to offer them new forms of flexibility. Indeed, in the context of a significantly weakened labor movement, New Labour introduced a raft of regulations to protect individual workers, such as a statutory minimum wage, enhanced protections against unfair dismissal, and the "first statutory entitlement to paid holidays in the UK," even for part-time workers.[40]

Moreover, the Labour government enhanced maternity and paternity leaves and, in 2002, granted parents the right to request flexible working practices from their employers.[41] Similar laws have also been adopted in San Francisco and Vermont, and in 2014 President Obama issued a presidential memorandum giving the roughly two million federal employees the right to request flexible working arrangements.[42] Finally, the Schedules That Work Act, introduced in the House of Representatives in July 2014 and in the Senate in July 2015, would give employees

> the right to request that his or her employer change the terms and conditions of employment relating to: the number of hours or times the employee is required to work or be on call; the location; the amount of notification he or she receives of work schedule assignments; and minimizing fluctuations in the number of hours the employee is scheduled to work on a daily, weekly, or monthly basis.[43]

I will consider this bill in more detail, but for now suffice it to say that the act presents itself as "a first step in responding to the needs of workers for a voice in the timing of their work hours and for more predictable schedules."[44]

Although these are all rights granted to individual employees, it is worth noting that unions influence the extent to which employers comply with them, so that "collective procedures guarantee individual rights."[45] In this sense, the weakening of unions under the first mode of flexibility might diminish the effects of the pro-individualistic mode of flexibility. The climate of austerity, moreover, proved hostile to these rights, as in 2012 the British coalition government lengthened from one to two years the "qualifying period of continuous employment needed . . . to acquire the right not to be unfairly dismissed."[46] In the name of reducing the risks of hiring, the coalition government effectively doubled the period of "at will" employment.[47]

Finally, it is worth noting that the relatively recent rollout of individualistic regulations in the United Kingdom contrasts with the United States, where for at least thirty years the state has played a strong role in the enforcement of basic individual employment rights. The origins of this regime can be found in equal-opportunity legislation dating back to the civil rights movement, and in particular, Title VII of the Civil Rights Act of 1964. Subsequent legislation has expanded protection against work-place discrimination for women, people with disabilities, the aged, and sexual minorities. During the 1980s and 1990s, moreover, legislation at the federal, state, and local levels granted workers' rights to family leave and living wages.[48] Perhaps most notable in this regard is the Family and Medical Leave Act of 1994, which guarantees employees twelve weeks of unpaid leave for family and medical reasons. Other federal legislation enacted in the 1990s provides minimum health and safety standards and regulates pension and other employee benefits plans.[49] These statutory protections arguably impede labor-market flexibility, yet rights to family leave increase the flexibility of individual employees.

In this section I have cataloged a range of actions taken by govern-ments both to constrain the scope and power of unions and to expand the rights of individual employees. Although these two modes can operate in harmonious ways, especially in their construction of an individualistic social formation, they can also clash: to some extent, individual rights benefit from collective protection, while an increase in the discretion of employers as a result of the first mode can stand in tension with the em-powerment of individual workers carried out by the second.

Flexible Organizations and Working Practices

Although the macroeconomic policy goal of flexibility is central to the construction of the free labor market, I turn now to consider how flexibil-ity can operate at the level of the firm or organization. Having a flexible or "deregulated" labor market does not necessarily equate to flexible work-ing arrangements, for these also depend on the techniques and practices managers use to organize workplaces as well as the individual rights of workers to various forms of flexibility with respect to their employment.

From the outset it is worth stressing that flexibility encompasses dif-ferent sets of arrangements for employers and employees. As I showed previously, the neoliberalization or flexibilization of industrial relations in-volves the removal of constraints on how employers manage workplaces, whether these constraints came originally in the form of laws or collective regulation.[50] An increase in employer discretion thus facilitates flexibility understood as the ability to hire and fire employees as needed (numerical flexibility) and to adjust compensation levels in ways not fully determined by collective bargaining or statute (financial flexibility). A diminution of collective regulation also enhances the ability of employers to change the content of jobs and move employees from one task or department to another (functional flexibility). Finally, "temporal flexibility" refers to the ability of employers to alter the total working time of their workforce not by changing the number of employees as in numerical flexibility, but by varying the hours the same number of employees work according to fluctuations in demand.[51]

These four managerial capacities have themselves been altered by the emergence of what Guy Standing calls "global managerialism." As he sees it, "Technological changes, economic reforms and structural changes have allowed many more managerial options, in terms of organizational structures, relations of production, locational choices and speeds of relocation." This means that the bargaining power of managers has significantly increased, as they can easily shift locations as needed. Taking this into account, I add a fifth form of flexibility, which Standing calls "organizational flexibility."[52] These five faces of flexibility help generalize insecurity and precariousness within the labor market, with insecure, low-paid, and irregular work "spreading relative to . . . regular, unionized, stable, manual or craft-based" employment.[53]

This brief overview of flexibility in the context of management shows that the term has multiple connotations, and the effects of flexibility from the vantage point of individual workers are similarly diverse. Focusing specifically on temporal flexibility, one scholar divides working practices into three groups: "employer-friendly," "employee-friendly," and "neutral." According to this classification, employer-friendly practices, such as involuntary part-time or temporary work, zero-hours contracts, and on-call arrangements, aim primarily to increase company profits.[54] The development of scheduling software has assisted in this goal by allowing employers, particularly in the retail and services sector, to precisely plan staffing levels in accordance with predicted demand, thus reducing labor costs. Such technology reportedly led one company, Jamba Juice, to save millions of dollars a year. But it also can result in irregular and unpredictable shift patterns for employees, increasing stress and uncertainty about the future and potentially limiting employees' freedom to use nonwork time in ways that they choose, whether it is the pursuit of an acting career or active involvement in the community.[55] A sign of the growing discontent with this situation: the Schedules That Work Act, mentioned in the previous section, would extend the protection already offered by laws in several states by ensuring predictability in scheduling and providing compensation for last-minute changes to shifts.[56]

Unlike employer-friendly flexibility, "employee-friendly" arrangements, such as flexible start and finish times, job shares, and sabbaticals, potentially enhance work-life balance.[57] A busy parent juggling childcare and paid work may benefit enormously from exercising some control over the hours of his or her employment, but so too might the employee who wants to take a sustained period of time off work for travel or the commuter who simply wants to beat the rush-hour traffic. The widespread appeal of flexibility is suggested by a survey of UK professionals, who listed flexible working as the number-one benefit they sought, and by another report in the United States, which found that 83 percent of hourly paid workers saw flexibility as "an important factor in deciding to take the job."[58] Of course, employee-friendly practices can also benefit employers as a whole by increasing the supply of labor and making more skills and expertise available at a lower cost.

While employee-friendly practices are said to improve work-life balance, "neutral" practices are generally employee-friendly *and* offer the chance of enhanced profits, since more contented employees tend to be more productive, committed, and healthy.[59] There is reason to suspect that many employee-friendly practices might fall into this category, for although one can imagine managers reluctantly conceding a limited number of strictly employee-friendly working arrangements to well-organized employees, perhaps in exchange for other concessions on the part of workers, it seems unlikely that they would do so if this posed a serious threat to the company's profitability. Articulating this view, an investigation into the transformation of work by Britain's Equal Opportunities Commission argues that increased flexibility "must deliver a sustainable 'win-win-win' for employees, employers and their customers and be seen, not as a concession to personal needs, but as a tool for improving business performance." According to this logic, adapting working arrangements to personal needs is only permissible when it also benefits the employer (and customers).[60]

Another key aspect of flexible working involves the ability to choose where to perform one's work, a freedom greatly enhanced by advances in information and communication technology. A report examining IBM employees found that flexible working arrangements increased the number of hours per week by nineteen that employees could work before they experienced work-life conflict comparable to that of their colleagues who worked only at the office.[61] This finding suggests that teleworking can offer an effective means of reducing stress levels and other work-related health problems. More broadly, the ability to work from home (or anywhere with an Internet connection) can be particularly beneficial to parents, for example, who may be allowed to leave the office early to collect children from school and who then finish their day's work at home in the evening. Yet this example also points to the possibility of employers using teleworking to increase working time beyond standard office hours. When this happens, work has "invaded personal space, instead of helping to free people's time."[62] As I discuss later, even employee-friendly forms of flexibility blur the distinction between the formerly discrete realms of work and private life, such that one is potentially never fully away from work, never off the clock.[63] While this loss of a clear separation from work may be a price worth paying for many workers, it nonetheless points to the need to approach even employee-friendly practices with a critical eye and to avoid treating them as an unqualified expansion of freedom.

However conducive to helping employees meet their other responsibilities and needs, flexibility with respect to time and place of work essentially leaves intact the conventional model of paying workers for their time. Underlying this approach is the traditional control model of management, or Douglas McGregor's Theory X, which "assumes that people have to be forced to work by constant management control." A more radical transformation of work, endorsed by Alison Maitland and Peter Thomson, for example, involves a corresponding shift in assumptions about how best to manage employees. According to Theory Y, "People are self-motivated and can be left to manage themselves." This means that, rather than focusing on time and place of work, managers pay attention to the results employees achieve for the company or organization.

An example of such a system is the Results-Only Work Environment, which has been rolled out in both the private and public sectors (Best Buy, Gap, and the White House Office of Personnel Management have all adopted it). As Maitland and Thomson summarize the case for this type of approach, "Assume people are responsible, give them the freedom to manage themselves, treat them like adults and watch them flourish." While Maitland and Thomson refer to their preferred mode of organization as "future work" and usefully point to the constraints of more conventional forms of flexibility in terms of their commitment to a command form of management, it could be argued that "future work" merely represents a more fully developed form of flexibility than arrangements like flexitime and teleworking. This flexibility plus comes to closely resemble a form of self-employment, wherein workers decide for themselves how to deliver the contracted work and are often paid on the basis of results rather than working time. This in turn means "running yourself as an enterprise and charging your customers for your services."[64] The idea of self-entrepreneurialism, as I will explore further in the next section, is a central plank of the neoliberal ideology of the free individual.

Finally, just because one has the option to work flexibly does not mean that it will always be prudent to exercise that choice. For example, in a study of temp workers in Sweden and Britain, researchers found that the attraction of temping lay in the potential freedom it offered "to travel, to study, or to take time off from working-life to be with one's children," but that the risk of not receiving future assignments if they turned down offers meant that workers "want to work as much as possible while they can, and to postpone ideas of making the promises of flexibility come true."[65] Similarly, taking maternity or paternity leave means potentially risking one's reputation as a committed employee and stalling one's career advancement. More broadly, risk and uncertainty play a central role in neoliberal discourse and policy programs, ranging from the supposedly perilous economic consequences of failing to deregulate labor markets to the need for individuals to constantly work on themselves to ensure continuing employability in an ever-changing economy. As I will show, this disciplines individual workers to think in terms of "harnessing the uncertainties of working in a global market in order to reduce their individual risks and maximize their personal rewards."[66] The pressure to remain competitive in both the workplace and the broader labor market can thus constrain the capacity of employee-friendly flexible working practices to expand the freedom individuals enjoy in relation to paid work.

The Construction of the Flexible Worker

The ideology of flexibility centers on a strong conceptual opposition between the individual and the collective, which implies that individuals need to be liberated from "bad" rigidities associated with collective institutions to reduce unemployment and stimulate economic growth. Beyond showing these economic justifications for the dismantlement of collective institutions, moreover, I noted the libertarian and populist criticisms of the welfare state and unionism as threats to individual freedom and control. To the extent that the ideology of flexibility seeks to establish a socioeconomic order in which individuals are free from the influence of collective institutions, it resonates with the classical liberal tradition within which the buyer and seller of labor power are idealized as free and equal individuals.[67] This fiction has been perpetuated since the late nineteenth century by the understanding of corporations as legal persons and intensified in recent years by the US Supreme Court's recognition of them as persons with First Amendment rights to free speech in *Citizens United v. Federal Elections Commission* (2010). Corporations are also, to some extent, anthropomorphized by the identification that is often made in popular culture between them and their CEOs.[68] To complete the circle, as I will show shortly, the flexible worker is encouraged to see him- or herself as the owner of human capital—that is, as an entrepreneur. In the kaleidoscope of neoliberalism, corporations appear as persons, persons appear as corporations, and in the process the viewer risks losing sight of the vast power imbalances and antagonisms between the two.

Although the ideology and policies of labor-market flexibility capitalize on the deeply held value of individualism, they attack collectives in a selective manner, targeting unions and some of the regulatory powers of the state while leaving intact, and even augmenting, the power of employers, including corporations and public bodies (as in the case of Wisconsin). In such an environment, individuals may be "liberated" from unions and the state, but they are arguably more vulnerable than ever to the vicissitudes of capital and the market, given their diminished collective protections and voice.

As has been shown, flexibility does not only connote an opposition to the welfare state and to unionism; it also contrasts with a rigid set of expectations on the part of employers concerning the place and time at which work is performed. Indeed, an important refinement to the analysis of labor-market flexibility offered previously acknowledges that governments have also granted rights such as a legal entitlement to family leave to individual employees, which in turn facilitate some flexible working arrangements. Yet here it is also important to note that the culture of a workplace, as well as broader narratives concerning risk and success within the economy and society, condition employees' exercise of those rights.

Drawing these threads together, I show that flexibility constructs and naturalizes the "flexible worker" as one who enjoys a liberation from earlier effects of political intervention and power: the Keynesian welfare state and its corresponding goal of full employment, unions, and the Fordist mode of accumulation, which requires "conformist discipline" to factory-centered conditions of industrialization.[69] This account describes the flexible subject in terms of what it is free from, but what characteristics and attributes, if any, does the flexible worker possess?

As I show in the remainder of this section, the flexible worker embodies an active form of adaptability that aligns with a spirit of self-entrepreneurialism: he or she acts as his or her own manager by determining the place and time of work and by completing tasks in an environment of autonomy and trust. Smartphone and laptop at the ready, the flexible worker is willing and able to work evenings and weekends, at home or in the office. In fact, these once discrete space-times become blurred for the flexible worker, so that work is potentially everywhere, all the time; in such an environment, the looming danger is that one may choose when and where to work without ever really being off the clock. Moreover, the flexible worker relentlessly develops and capitalizes upon his or her skills and attributes, preparing for new opportunities by scouring job listings even when already employed and by taking evening classes to gain career-advancing qualifications.

While some people may accept or at least tolerate this condition if they perceive it as affording them greater consumption or leisure opportunities, it would be a mistake to see it as purely optional.[70] Rather, the individualized, competitive, and precarious nature of the flexible labor market compels the individual to cultivate a spirit of self-entrepreneurialism and adaptation to the demands of employers and the market to remain employable, while the goal of employability as well as the persistence of the work ethic in turn puts pressure on the pursuit of valuable unpaid activities, such as care and community work.[71] Work thus envelops life in a way that subverts flexibility's promise of providing individuals with greater control over employment and an expansion of freedom as the capacity of agents to act according to their own values, needs, and desires.

In elaborating this account of the flexible worker, I begin with an examination of adaptability, which, as will be shown shortly, is closely related to the discourse of employability and to the notion of the enterprising self. An instructive source on the subject of adaptability is Tom Rath's *Strengths Finder 2.0*, which sets out thirty-four "themes of talent." Readers are encouraged to take an online test to discover which talents apply to them, then to follow the book's advice on how to make the best use of them in their professional lives. Indeed, reading this book in one's "free" time exemplifies the spirit of self-entrepreneurialism that flexible workers must cultivate and the degree to which that time is not as free as one might tend to think.

One feature of adaptability as a "theme of talent" is an openness to the future, such that the adaptable person lives "in the moment" and sees the future not as a "fixed destination" but instead as "a place that you create out of the choices that you make right now." Even future plans are constantly subject to revision by the adaptable person: adaptability enables him or her to "respond willingly to the demands of the moment even if they pull you away from your plans." It is worth noting that the only agency in the previous quotation is that of the adaptable person, since the things that might derail one's earlier plans are rendered impersonal by the phrase "the demands of the moment." No mention is made of what, or more precisely who, makes these demands and why, and thus from the perspective of neoliberal philosophy, this lack of intentional agency removes these abstract forces from the domain of coercion. Again, "You are, at heart, a very flexible person who can stay productive when the demands of work are pulling you in many different directions at once."[72] Here we see not only an obfuscation of the power relations in the workplace ("the demands of work" as opposed to the "demands of the employer"), but also the attribution of adaptability to the very core ("heart") of a person's being.

Elsewhere, when Rath does mention the agency of others, it is to acknowledge that too much adaptability can leave a person vulnerable: "Though your Adaptability serves you well, don't compromise your long-term success by bending to every whim, desire, and demand of others." In this advice one catches a glimpse of the downside of too much adaptability and flexibility: a self-sacrificing approach to coworkers and managers that ultimately risks thwarting personal advancement. Moreover, successful workers actively monitor their own adaptability to avoid this risk: "Use smart guidelines to help you decide when to flex and when to stand firm."[73] Despite this warning, Rath doesn't give specific reasons as to why excessive adaptability might thwart one's long-term success (nor does he say explicitly of what the latter might consist), but two possibilities suggest themselves.

First, managers may interpret a surplus of adaptability as evidence of subservience or a lack of ambition, thus rendering the employee a less suitable candidate for promotion in the eyes of employers looking for someone proactive and ready to take the initiative. Bending to literally "every whim, desire, and demand of others" would, of course, leave little or no scope for choosing the shape of one's own future; rather, it would place this entirely in the hands of others. This form of adaptability equates to docility and resonates with the traditional feminine role of selflessly serving the needs of fathers and husbands. Of course, for some roles, particularly those in low-level service work, this is precisely the characteristic some employers are looking for, because too much initiative and ambition will likely breed dissatisfaction and high staff-turnover rates. But, if one wants to get ahead, and in many white-collar jobs this is increasingly required simply to stay employed,[74] adaptability as docility will likely be a barrier to success.

In contrast with docile adaptability, adaptability that would be more conducive to long-term professional success entails a degree of self-awareness and reflexivity in that the subject conceives of his or her life as a project to be worked on and approaches his or her skills and attributes as resources or human capital to be exploited (by the self and by others). This contemporary preoccupation with one's employability results in a *"reflexive exploitation,* the ongoing reflection on the self as object of exchange, a kind of ongoing self assessment."[75] For example, it is a commonplace that successful job applicants know how to "sell" themselves by framing their skills and experience as commodities that employers need or value. This reflexivity contrasts with the passive form of adaptability I identified previously, in that the excessively adaptable worker fails to appreciate the possibilities for capitalizing on his or her talents. Indeed, he or she may fail to conceptualize those talents as resources or elements of human capital at all. Employers may also take such qualities for granted, particularly if they are seen as natural to the worker. This is, of course, a particular barrier to the recognition of women's reproductive labor, broadly construed.

A second but closely related possible pitfall of "bending to every whim, desire, and demand of others" is that one might grow dependent on particular employers and managers rather than developing transferable skills that will better advance one's career in other firms and organizations as the demand for labor and skills changes over time. Thus, the subject must "desire what employers in the abstract desire," even though one can never be quite sure what that is.[76] Regular perusal of job vacancies, for example, enables the flexible worker to stay abreast of the demands and expectations of employers and teaches which new qualifications would assist in career advancement as well as how to package experience and skills in an effective and appealing manner. It is easy to see how this drive for employability can all too easily become a fear-driven and cynical opportunism, which is arguably now a professional requirement of post-Taylorist society.[77]

This brief exploration has shown that adaptability, and hence flexibility more broadly, seems to call for what Nikolas Rose calls a "life of incessant job seeking," constant training, and the "continuous economic capitalization of the self."[78] The notion of capitalizing on one's talents and skills underscores the point that much of the responsibility for remaining in employment in a flexible labor market falls on the individual. This process begins even before full-time entry into the labor market as students bear an increasing share of the costs of financing their own higher education, despite the fact that we are continually told that economic growth depends on a well-educated workforce.

Once at work, employees have increasingly had to manage their own career development as a result of firms' reduced training budgets, part of the overall goal of flexibility and the attempt to remain competitive, as well as their own unpredictable job prospects.[79] Moreover, flexible working arrangements are often justified on the grounds that they enable workers to further their education without leaving employment.[80] And organized labor's weak position in relation to capital leaves the individual(ized) worker with few options but to be enterprising, in the sense that he or she must now cherry-pick the "ripest" of his or her available "use-values of subjectivity, attitudes, experiences, skills, human qualities and characteristics."[81] Indeed, books like *Strengths Finder 2.0* help people to identify and then capitalize upon their talents, their stock of human capital, that they may not even have realized they had.

It is worth noting that the idea of human capital and the related view of workers as self-entrepreneurs are conceptual innovations specific to neoliberal thought. The rationale is simple: people work for wages, wages are a form of income, with the income in question a return on the capital workers possess—namely, "all those physical and psychological factors which make someone able to earn this or that wage."[82] Foucault thus argues that, rather than seeing *homo oeconomicus* as a partner in exchange as classical liberalism had done in the nineteenth century, under neoliberalism *homo oeconomicus* is "for himself his own capital, . . . for himself his own producer, . . . for himself the source of [his] earnings," and in this sense "an entrepreneur of himself."[83]

This was a "new identity for the employee, one that blurred, or even obliterated, the distinction between worker and manager."[84] In fact, the portmanteau "entreployee" aptly conveys the sense in which the employee within neoliberal capitalism is "himself an entrepreneur." This blurring of the roles of worker, entrepreneur, and manager can be registered on multiple levels. First, as I have already shown, people are now all understood to be the owners of our their human capital and, in that sense, entrepreneurs. Furthermore, a distinguishing feature of neoliberal capitalism is the employee's self-motivation and readiness to deploy his or her own "abilities and emotional resources . . . in the service of individualized projects."[85] At the extreme, these characteristics merge into the conditions of "future work" discussed previously, whereby the individual runs him- or herself as an enterprise by determining his or her own working time and being paid on the basis of delivering goods and services as contracted.[86]

These trends have taken shape under conditions of post-Fordist production in which shorter production runs involve placing more decision-making into the hands of employees. The employee as reflexive actor is less constrained by the rules and resources of the shop floor than was the case in the Fordist production regime such that he or she "makes decisions as to alternative rules and resources" and "is responsible for the continuous transformation of both shopfloor rules and (in process and product) resources."[87] Similarly, the organization of work around the model of the project and team means that workers cooperate with one another for fixed periods of time before being assigned to another project.[88]

Of course, these accounts are highly stylized, and it is necessary to make the usual caveats concerning generalizations. Yet broad shifts in workplace relations corresponding to the regime of flexible production also mesh with well-documented developments in management theory, particularly the so-called human resources movement. This school of thought began in the 1960s in response to problems associated with Taylorism, including wildcat strikes, mass absenteeism, and sabotage, and sought to improve worker satisfaction and motivation by increasing the scope for autonomy, responsibility, and variety.[89] In particular, semiautonomous teams would "divide the work between themselves as they thought best, vary the rhythm of work throughout the day and monitor the result."[90]

Moreover, since at least the late 1980s, managerial discourse has tended to understand the world as complex and ambiguous and has accordingly emphasized the need for "looser organizational forms which are more able to 'go with the flow'" and the "production of subjects who can fit these forms."[91] The Equal Opportunities Commission's report on flexibility exemplifies a commitment to this approach by arguing that empowering workers by extending trust "to employees at all levels and in all types of work" and by moving away from command-and-control management benefits business and improves "worker engagement and productivity."[92] This move away from command-and-control management can be seen in the way values like commitment are prized over obedience and in the expectation that employees not merely submit to the authority of managers, but actually adopt their perspectives.[93] Similarly, as presentation, communication, and appearance have become key elements of much paid work, especially in the services sector, work has taken on a strongly performative character, with employees largely disciplining and managing themselves in this dimension of their work.[94] As the demands of work are experienced less as an imposition from outside the worker, they penetrate more deeply into the individual's consciousness, with the result that the flexible worker becomes an agent of his or her own subordination through an ongoing process of self-disciplining.

Although the ideology of flexibility tends to gloss over class differences, it is worth noting that employee-friendly forms of flexibility remain the preserve of more privileged members of the workforce. For example, employee control over working time in the United States is correlated with race and educational attainment, such that a significantly greater share of whites (29 percent) report such practices than blacks (20 percent) and Hispanics (18 percent). Moreover, having a bachelor's degree or higher makes a worker more than twice as likely to report flexible working practices than one with less than a high school diploma (38 percent compared with 15 percent).[95] Since flexibility of the employee-friendly variety means greater autonomy at work, access to these forms of working arrangement is a key factor in determining a person's occupation-based social status. Iris Marion Young, for example, argues that the privilege of professionals includes "considerable day-to-day autonomy."[96] The college professor who must attend meetings and classes but can manage the rest of his or her work time as desired stands in stark contrast with the retail assistant or cleaner who must report for work at times (and a place) often outside his or her control. Employee-friendly flexible working arrangements are not merely practical benefits; they also confer status and a positive sense of self on those who enjoy them, since they visibly and palpably lessen the degree to which work is experienced as an external imposition onto a person's life.

At the same time, even if flexibility may have lowered the rate of unemployment in countries like the United Kingdom,[97] there is consensus among scholars that this has come at the price of the "deterioration in wages, growing insecurity and increasing poverty."[98] This analysis also finds support in Robert Perucci and Earl Wysong's argument that the United States went from being a middle-class society in the mid-twentieth century to a "bifurcated and polarized two-class society" today, due in part to a pattern of shrinking benefits (like health care, pensions, life insurance, and vacation time) and to the growing contingency workforce, characterized by low wages, low prestige, and minimal job security.[99] These trends can be linked back to the decollectivizing mode of flexibility, and with the shifting of responsibility for employment to the individual previously discussed, it becomes easier to blame economic hardship, underemployment, and unemployment on the "bad choices" and behavior of those individuals. David Harvey notes that while on the whole the neoliberal experiment has not brought the promised levels of economic growth, some countries (including the United States and the United Kingdom) have done spectacularly well at the expense of others, and within those more prosperous nations neoliberalism has indeed been a success from the vantage point of the upper classes. The standard explanation for any deterioration of conditions among the lower classes, however, is failure, "usually for personal and cultural reasons, to enhance their own human capital (through dedication to education, the acquisition of a protestant work ethic, submission to work discipline and flexibility, and the like)."[100] Success in such a precarious environment demands the cultivation of employability and the spirit of self-entrepreneurialism discussed in this section.

One final consequence of the individualizing effects of flexibility concerns the view of society as an association of individuals, which I discussed in the previous chapter. The notion that individuals are to be blamed for their own lack of success in employment lends an air of legitimacy to the fact that paid work functions as a mechanism of inclusion in society. In other words, if one assumes that joblessness stems from individual characteristics like a lack of discipline or laziness, then this makes the marginalization and exclusion of unemployed persons from society seem more acceptable—"they brought it upon themselves"—than if the causes of unemployment are understood in a more structural manner. Note, however, that a structural explanation of unemployment is not the same as challenging the notion that paid work should form the basis of citizenship: for example, it may simply result in new efforts to make sure all can be employed, as was discussed in Gorz's argument for the reduction and redistribution of work.

Flexibility and Care

In this section I will examine how flexibility relates to the feminization of work, but also how it responds to the deficit of care resulting from women's increased labor-force participation. It is worth noting that the first is related to the second, in the sense that the feminization of work often refers precisely to women's greater involvement in paid work. For example,

Hardt and Negri describe the feminization of work as having three components: more women are taking part in paid labor, work is becoming flexible, and all work is taking on many of the characteristics of work traditionally performed by women. With respect to flexibility in particular, they note that "part-time and informal employment, irregular hours, and multiple jobs . . . are now becoming generalized even in the dominant countries."[101] Similarly, Guy Standing suggests that the labor market has been feminized in the sense that insecure, low-paid, and irregular employment, traditionally associated with women, has spread relative to the more stable, regular, unionized jobs traditionally filled by men.[102]

Importantly, though, Hardt and Negri note that the term "feminization" must be "said with a bitter irony, since it has not resulted in gender equality or destroyed the gender division of labor."[103] For his part, Standing observes the "sense of irony that, after generations of efforts to integrate women into regular wage labor as equals," the result has been for men's experiences of work to become more like those of women rather than the other way around.[104] In this regard it is interesting to note that, in her seminal essay "After the Family Wage," Nancy Fraser argues that the achievement of gender equity requires making "women's current life patterns the norm." Clearly, though, she does not mean the feminization of labor as Hardt and Negri and Standing describe it. Rather, Fraser insists that a postindustrial welfare state should allow everyone to combine paid work with unpaid care work. In her estimation, this would require not only the redesign of welfare institutions "so as to eliminate the difficulty and strain" currently felt by women trying to juggle paid and unpaid work, but more broadly the deconstruction of gender so as to dismantle "the gendered opposition between breadwinning and caregiving."[105]

As the discussion of flexible working arrangements has suggested, the appeal of flexibility to employees owes much to its promise of softening the conflict between the spheres of "work" and "life," where the latter often, but not always, means unpaid care work and other domestic responsibilities. In this regard, I argue that employer-friendly flexibility is best understood as a privatized response to the contemporary deficit or crisis of care, which has its roots in shrinking public support for care work and the expansion of women's labor-force participation.[106] Flexible working practices thus offer a partial and individualistic solution to the problem of how to meet our responsibilities for care alongside the need for paid work, thus helping legitimize the work society.

Although the crisis of care has multiple causes, the growing participation of women in the labor force is particularly salient for our purposes. Nancy Fraser argues that this trend was an unintended consequence of second-wave feminism's critique of "androcentric state-organized capitalism."[107] To be clear, second-wave feminists "sought to transform the system's deep structures and animating values—in part by decentering wage work and valorizing unwaged activities." Yet in a spectacular "cunning of history," Fraser argues that neoliberalism resignified the various elements of second-wave feminism's critique of androcentric state-organized capitalism. In particular, neoliberalism drew upon the critique of the family wage to help "intensify capitalism's valorization of waged labour."[108] Moreover, by the time of her 1994 essay "After the Family Wage," Fraser would observe the dominance of the universal breadwinner model in the "political practice of most US feminists and liberals," which is to say, a widespread acceptance of the view that women's employment is the route to gender equity.[109]

One of Fraser's main criticisms of this model as a viable feminist alternative to the family wage was that, while the "ideal typical citizen" is the "nominally gender neutral" breadwinner, in fact it is the "male half of the old breadwinner/homemaker couple, now universalized and required of everyone." Care work, by contrast, has "no social value" in this model and is "what must be sloughed off to become a breadwinner."[110] Indeed, in a 2014 interview, Fraser observes that the universal breadwinner model has been achieved by "highly educated, middle/upper-class women" who "compete with men, on male terms, in highly competitive professions." Their professional success then depends on delegating care responsibilities to "a class of much poorer women."[111]

In the context of women's increased labor-force participation, flexibility thus promises work-life balance by enabling employees with dependents to continue providing some care alongside their paid work. To the extent that flexibility helps maintain care within the private household, it dovetails with neoliberalism's individualizing logic of care, which Joan Tronto argues centers on the value of personal responsibility.[112] As Evelyn Nakano Glenn argues, moreover, thinking of the family as the "institution of first resort for caring" (rather than viewing it as a "public social responsibility") helps perpetuate the gender division of labor.[113] Indeed, women continue to perform a disproportionate amount of care work, even when they work full time.[114] This means that flexibility is also complicit in the gender division of labor, since it allows the existing privatized and gendered regime of care to continue alongside the universal obligation to earn. Flexibility thus allows the market economy to continue relying on "altruistic, collective, behaviour in the household" to produce labor power as a commodity,[115] but in a manner that ostensibly better supports a commitment to gender equality than the regime of the patriarchal family wage.

While more affluent workers can rely on the services of paid professionals to take up the slack in their care work, one should not lose sight of the benefits that they too derive from flexible work arrangements. In a competitive society, Tronto explains, caring well means giving one's children "a competitive edge against other children." Access to flexible work arrangements would enable a parent to attend a child's school, for example, thus facilitating the performance of intensive mothering.[116] The problem here is that flexible working practices, as part of the broader neoliberal individualizing approach to care, simply reproduce existing structures of privilege, especially when one notes that more privileged workers tend to have access to greater control over the time and place of employment.[117]

My purpose in this section, as in the chapter as a whole, has not been to offer an indictment of flexibility. Rather, I have tried to show that flexibility constitutes one element of the broader approach of neoliberalism to care, which places the burden of responsibility on individual households. Flexibility is not the only such measure: in the absence of free or heavily subsidized care for dependents, paying a professional for their services also counts as a personal responsibility and, importantly, one that not all can afford to fulfill. While I am not arguing against flexibility per se, then, it is worth considering what sort of policies and broader social transformations could help us meet our care needs in a more equitable way.

For example, Glenn and Tronto broadly agree that care should become a social or public concern, which is not to say that everyone necessarily must perform it—rather, that society needs to stop approaching it as a private matter for which individuals are responsible. Glenn thus suggests that we need to think of access to care as a right and the performance of it as "a social contribution on a par with other activities that are valued," such as paid work. In addition, addressing the care deficit quite clearly entails the reduction of working time.[118] Only insofar as it involves part-time work does flexibility achieve this goal. As is well known, however, part-time work is associated with the mommy track, wherein working mothers experience limited career progression and underutilization of skills.[119] Indeed, the most common form of flexibility for women in the United Kingdom is part-time work, with one study reporting 49 percent of women engaged in this type of work and only 13 percent of men.[120] Similarly, the rate of part-time employment of women in the United States is nearly twice that of men.[121] Once again, the deeper and more intractable problems to address are therefore an individual and collective commitment to the norm of full-time work as well as the gender division of labor. While flexibility has obvious appeal and emancipatory potential, caution is necessary so that access to it does not limit our commitment to tackling these more challenging issues.

This chapter has highlighted the double-edged character of the social transformation that flexibility has helped to initiate. On the one hand, flexibility can enhance the freedom that individual workers experience in relation to paid work, to some extent ameliorating the sense of alienation that many feel toward employment and offering the possibility of a more rewarding and healthy work-life balance. In this respect, the promise of flexibility to inject freedom into various levels of the organization of work helps sustain the wage relation by lessening feelings of alienation and general dissatisfaction with employment. In this way, flexibility works hand-in-hand with the work ethic, particularly its postindustrial variant that promises self-realization. On the other hand, access to employee-friendly flexibility is uneven and implicated in the contemporary class structure, while employer-friendly flexibility has heightened insecurity and precariousness. Furthermore, even when the second mode of flexibility expands the freedom individuals enjoy with respect to work, the accompanying self-management, blurring of work and private life, and imperative to maintain and increase one's employability inaugurate a new mode of domination that allows work to subtly subsume more and more of life to its demands. When the pursuit of employability entails the capitalization of one's skills and attributes, moreover, one may reasonably fear for the continuing existence of endeavors and social relations performed for their own intrinsic value, rather than instrumentally for profit or the enhancement of employability.

Looking to the future, employee-friendly flexible working arrangements may yet be extended to a broader cross-section of the workforce. Presumably, the impetus for such a transformation would come from a coalition of forward-looking managers (some of whom already recognize the economic benefits of employee-friendly flexibility), government, and workers themselves. As access to this form of flexibility becomes more evenly distributed across different occupations, one might even imagine a softening of the class and status hierarchy. The provision of an unconditional basic income adequate to a decent standard of living offers an effective and just way of compensating for the insecurity engendered by flexibilized labor markets.[122] The basic income is also a fitting complement to flexibility's promise of freedom and empowerment, since its rejection of the conditionality of benefits upon the performance of work could free people up to pursue a range of activities outside of paid employment, potentially replacing the work society with a "multi-activity society."[123] I will explore these issues at greater length in the following chapters.

In light of recent developments in both the United States and the United Kingdom, however, there are reasons to expect further decollectivization and an increase in employer discretion with respect to the organization of work. While more privileged workers may continue to enjoy flexible working arrangements, the erosion of union strength and dismantlement of individual employment rights would leave those lower down the socio-economic ladder with even less power to negotiate favorable terms and conditions of work with employers. Aside from these practical problems, it is also worth asking how the domination that I have identified with the second mode of flexibility can be overcome or at least softened.

To the extent that the basic income would provide individuals with economic security regardless of whether they are or have been gainfully employed, its introduction might make both paid work and the self-entrepreneurial spirit more a matter of choice than of necessity.[124] To be sure, much would depend on the details of the scheme and the "*nature of the ideological social environment in which it was implemented.*"[125] As I shall argue in the next chapter, in a society that, like Britain or the United States, attaches great social significance to paid work, the removal of the brute economic necessity to capitalize upon one's skills and attributes may not suffice to make self-entrepreneurialism purely optional. If so, further enhancing freedom in relation to work requires not only the introduction of a basic income, but also a movement to reconfigure the social meaning and value of work (also known as "the refusal of work"). Indeed, while this chapter has emphasized the ways that economic insecurity undercuts the emancipatory potential of flexibility, the blurring of work and private life also reflects the prime importance placed on paid work to individual and collective life. Making the most of flexibility therefore also means challenging the work ethic in its various forms.

4

Unconditional Basic Income

Awareness and discussion of the unconditional basic income (UBI) has been growing in recent months and years, spurred on by high-profile experiments in Finland and the Canadian province of Ontario, the (failed) referendum on the introduction of the UBI in Switzerland in 2016, and numerous other small-scale experiments around the world, including in the Netherlands, Italy, and India. These experiments and citizen initiatives make eye-catching headlines, such as "Free Cash in Finland. Must Be Jobless," "The Case for Free Money," and "Free Money Is Not So Funny Anymore: Confessions of a (Former) Skeptic of Basic Income."[1] But if the basic income is an idea whose "time has come" (a phrase that recent articles on the subject use remarkably frequently), what is the relationship between the basic income and the work society, and can it help address the problems with work that I have identified in previous chapters of this book? The answer to these questions depends, at least in part, on the arguments that are made in support of the UBI.

Of course, one cannot know with certainty what effects the introduction of a policy like the UBI might have on levels of unemployment, the construction of subjects, and the broader prospects for the expansion of freedom and justice. As Fitzpatrick points out, *"The character, significance and effects of a BI would depend substantially upon the nature of the ideological social environment in which it was implemented."*[2] But this does not mean that we should steer clear of these questions before there is a fully implemented UBI scheme in place to analyze. On the contrary, analysis of arguments in support of the basic income can reveal possible trajectories of social and political change, which not only enables a more nuanced understanding of the discourse on the UBI, but also helps clarify what is at stake in how one argues for it.[3]

In what follows I offer a reading of the basic income as a political demand that seeks to transform the welfare state, analyzing it first in relation to unemployment insurance and then to means-tested benefits. To be sure, the unconditionality of the basic income marks a break with the existing provision of benefits on the basis of means-tests and prior contributions, but this chapter demonstrates some surprising continuities between the UBI, the contemporary welfare state, and the work society. In particular, many advocates of the UBI propose it precisely as a scheme that would promote employment and thus remain attached to what I call the "fantasy of the work society."

For example, according to the Finnish Ministry of Social Affairs and Health, "The primary goal of the basic income experiment is related to promoting employment."[4] Indeed, one of the key questions that the experiment will seek to answer is whether "the social security system [can] be reshaped in a way that promotes active participation and gives people a stronger incentive to work."[5] Some advocates of the basic income cite the so-called Mincome program tested in Manitoba, Canada, during the 1970s,[6] as well as more recent studies of no-strings-attached cash transfers in developing countries,[7] as evidence that an unconditional basic income would have a negligible effect on working hours. Indeed, without a cultural shift in the meaning of work and a transformation of society that would provide access to the nonmonetary goods currently monopolized by paid employment (self-respect, social esteem, a sense of purpose, social connections, and so on), one might wonder why people would work significantly less if they received a basic income.

To be sure, a basic income motivated by the goal of increasing employment and introduced within a society still committed to the central value of paid work may offer benefits in terms of distributive justice. But arguments for the basic income that emphasize its capacity to boost employment and the employability of individuals mark a strong continuity with the existing logic of welfare in the sense that they mesh with the goals of "activating" the unemployed as well as enhancing the flexibility of labor markets and individual workers. Moreover, such arguments do not tackle the distortion of social esteem, whereby activities associated with middle-class white men garner the greatest recognition. Finally, treating the basic income as a solution to unemployment reaffirms the value of paid work and therefore cannot significantly challenge a value system that inadequately esteems socially vital but unpaid activities. In this respect, the UBI may not be as alternative, or deliver the degree of freedom from work, as it first appeared.

As I will show, however, not all arguments for the basic income display this overinvestment in the fantasy of the work society. On the contrary, some proponents remain open to the radical contingency of social relations, particularly the work society, and suggest the basic income as a non-reformist reform that could be part of more fundamental social change. A UBI justified and pursued in these terms does harbor the possibility of moving beyond the work society, but as I discuss in the final section of this chapter, one cannot assume that even this more radical perspective would deliver an unmitigated expansion of freedom. Rather, I suggest that we need to remain alert to the possibility that the new spaces for production and cooperation proposed by theorists in this camp could themselves undercut freedom and equality.

In sum, despite the simplicity of the basic income as a demand, the following analysis reveals a veiled struggle between its advocates over fundamental social, economic, and political questions. While arguments for the UBI couched in terms of the work society may ultimately attract more support than those that look to radical social change, an uncritical stance toward the meaning and value of paid work limits the emancipatory potential of the basic income. In other words, although the basic income pursued within more conservative horizons might enable important material redistribution, only a position open to the radical contingency of the social can tackle injustice and domination rooted in cultural norms that perpetuate the ideology of paid work.

Preliminary Notes: Historical Alternatives
and the Welfare State

Although the breadth of support that the UBI garners lends an intriguing air to debates about it,[8] here I want to emphasize the strong resonance between the demand and critical theory's project of searching for and analyzing historical alternatives. For example, Nancy Fraser treats the basic income as a possible instance of nonreformist reform in that it could "set in motion a trajectory of change in which more radical reforms become practicable over time";[9] Erik Olin Wright classifies the UBI as a socialist reform,[10] while Robert Van der Veen and Philippe Van Parijs argue that it could facilitate the transition to communism from within capitalism, thus bypassing the intermediary stage of socialism.[11] As I will show, although claims that the UBI may improve the functioning of capitalist labor markets stand in tension with these more radical aspirations, the basic income nonetheless fulfills the two criteria Marcuse sets for a historical alternative: it is within reach of contemporary society, and it expresses a "real need of the underlying population."[12] Evidence for the satisfaction of the latter condition is painfully easy to adduce in contemporary British and US society, but the second deserves more attention, not least because of what it reveals about debates surrounding the UBI itself.

How can one know whether the UBI is within reach?[13] One might be tempted to base an answer on the affordability of the basic income: if it turned out that the basic income was unaffordable, this might suggest that, at least for the time being, it does not constitute a bona fide historical alternative worthy of the attention of those committed to freedom and social justice. Here, however, it is easy to lose oneself in a thicket of technical details. For example, if one follows Kathi Weeks in stipulating that the basic income should be "sufficient to meet basic needs" and "large enough to ensure that waged work would be less a necessity than a choice,"[14] one must still ascertain what those needs are and how much they might cost to satisfy.

Another way to approach the question of affordability involves calculating the possible size of the basic income based on current social spending. As Fitzpatrick claims, however, even when one adds the revenue forgone due to tax allowances, credits, and contribution rebates to existing social security spending, the resulting basic income would still be insufficient to live on by itself.[15] Although the Swiss referendum on the UBI did not specify the amount that citizens would receive, the figure of 2,500 Swiss francs (roughly $2,500) was widely circulated, a sum that Philippe Van Parijs estimates would constitute 38 percent of Swiss GDP per capita and would likely require new forms of taxation to finance.[16] Moreover, depending on the exact amount paid, the UBI could disadvantage those in greatest need of financial support, since they could have received larger transfers under the existing system of means-tested and contributory benefits, given that not everyone receives them.[17]

While these considerations suggest that a sufficient UBI would require a politically unpopular increase in taxation, this does not necessarily mean that the basic income falls out of reach, for one cannot rule out the possibility that advocates might mobilize adequate support to bring about such a change in the tax system. Moreover, exactly what would constitute a sufficient basic income depends largely on the cost of living and on the extent of what Gorz calls "non-monetary exchange and self-providing."[18] The point is that in a highly commoditized society the level of the basic income would need to be significantly higher to meet basic needs than in one where individuals meet many of those needs through "collective facilities and services."[19] Although, of course, both an increase in taxation and a proliferation of "non-monetary exchange and self-providing" do entail a degree of social change, I shall treat them as within reach of contemporary society, given that each represents an intensification or radicalization of existing practices and norms rather than the creation of entirely new ones.[20]

To treat the basic income as an alternative, moreover, suggests the need to analyze what exactly it would transform or replace, hence my framing of it as a political demand that addresses the welfare state. For the sake of analytical clarity I take a selective view of the latter, specifically focusing on those benefits that relate most directly to the basic income. For example, since most advocates of the UBI do not propose substituting it for existing in-kind transfers such as education or health care, I will not consider this form of social welfare in the following analysis. Moreover, because the majority of proposals would pay the basic income to those beyond the retirement age and would allow them to supplement this income with private or public pensions, employment, and personal savings, I will not consider the case of pensions.[21]

To be sure, the introduction of the UBI in a country without universal health care, such as the United States, would pose a different set of challenges than the same task in, for example, the United Kingdom, with its National Health Service. One might also speculate as to whether the introduction of the basic income could produce the conditions necessary for the creation of a universal health care system, or whether, on the contrary, the absence of the latter suggests an unfavorable sociopolitical environment for the adoption of the basic income in the first place. Notwithstanding the importance of these issues, however, since the UBI would not replace existing in-kind benefits, I need not consider them in any detail here.

In addition to these considerations, since a key goal of this chapter is to enrich our understanding of the political meaning and value of paid work and to explore whether and how the introduction of the basic income might prove transformative in this regard, it makes both practical and conceptual sense to analyze those benefits most closely related to employment. Thus, I will focus primarily on two types of existing social transfers: contribution-based unemployment insurance and means-tested assistance (most commonly known as welfare).[22] While the method of delivery and eligibility requirements of these benefits varies across Britain and the United States (and even among the states), as I will show, they embody the principle of conditionality—whether in terms of a person's past and present performance of work or on his or her assessed financial need and willingness to work. In this respect they diverge from the UBI, which is, by definition, unconditional from the point of view of both income and performance of or willingness to work.[23] Despite this difference, however, in the following sections I will amplify some less audible resonances between the existing schemes of unemployment insurance and welfare, on the one hand, and the basic income, on the other.

Laboring Under the Work Society: Unemployment Insurance and the Basic Income

In this section I will explore the relationship between the basic income and unemployment insurance, with a particular focus on the ideal vision of society that motivates each. To do so, I first offer a general overview of the main social, economic, and political functions of unemployment insurance, leaving until the next section a closer discussion of its more specific features. From the outset, it bears emphasis that unemployment benefits function not merely as a means of ensuring social protection, but also as a mechanism of labor regulation.[24] Taking inspiration from Karl Polanyi, for example, one can theorize unemployment benefits as a response to the social and economic effects of marketization and the fictitious commodification of labor. These threaten not only social reproduction in general, but also the production of human beings capable of selling their labor, who are, of course, vital to the functioning of the market itself.[25] One can therefore understand unemployment insurance (alongside unions, education programs, immigration policies, and in some cases, centralized wage bargaining) as an institutional arrangement designed to coordinate the supply and demand of labor and to mitigate the negative social, economic, and political consequences of temporary imbalances between the two.[26]

Indeed, from the 1930s to the mid-1970s, Keynesian macroeconomic theory provided the dominant explanation of unemployment as a result of disequilibrium between the supply and demand of labor.[27] Moreover, the introduction of national compulsory unemployment insurance schemes from the beginning of the twentieth century reflected the understanding of unemployment as an accident or risk that "affects a given population with a certain probability and inevitability" and in this respect marked a break from "the moralizing, fault-finding" approach to unemployment characteristic of the nineteenth century.[28] Perhaps misleadingly, full employment did not preclude so-called frictional unemployment,[29] which occurred, for example, during "retooling or model-year changeovers"[30] and was understood as temporary and involuntary rather than as stemming from the fault or choice of individual workers.

Insofar as unemployment insurance serves to support temporarily jobless workers rather than try to tackle the root causes of unemployment, it clearly expresses a reformist tendency. And in helping normalize short spells of unemployment by providing a measure of income security, the introduction of social insurance in Britain also militated against attempts by socialists to raise awareness of the political constitution of unemployment as rooted in class interests.[31] This domesticating function of unemployment insurance seems particularly apt to what Nikolas Rose calls the "single matrix of solidarity," which he presents as a hallmark of governing from the "social point of view." Within this matrix, social citizenship gave a "politico-ethical form" to the relation between individuals and the "organically interconnected society."[32] Thus, social insurance functioned as an identification project in the sense that it embodied "an image of the socially identified citizen" who "understood [him- or herself] to be a member of a single integrated national society," albeit in a fashion that excluded women and racial minorities, as I discuss further below.[33] Here, though, I want to dwell on the vision of a single integrated national society. The Lacanian concept of fantasy proves a fruitful theoretical resource not only for understanding this notion, but also for interpreting support for the basic income.

A useful point of entry is offered by Ceren Özselçuka and Yahya Madra, who argue that the discourse and practice of the "modernist-corporatist vision of economy," including the policy of full employment and the establishment of paternalist welfare states by the New Deal in the United States and Labour governments in the United Kingdom, were informed by a "fantasy of social order and harmony."[34] According to Jason Glynos, "The logic of fantasy names a narrative structure involving some reference to an idealized scenario promising an imaginary fullness or wholeness (the beatific side of fantasy) and, by implication, a disaster scenario (the horrific side of fantasy)."[35] The idealized scenario that full employment and the welfare state served to shore up clearly overlaps with the basic tenets of the work society, in which paid work functions as an economic, ethical, and moral duty of individuals as well as the primary lever of social inclusion. Given that some degree of frictional/involuntary unemployment was expected within the terms of Keynesian economic thought, the provision of unemployment insurance did not unsettle that fantasy, especially since, as I will show in the next section, the design of these schemes would not permit contributor-claimants (permanently) to opt out of work. The shift away from Keynesian macroeconomics in the mid-1970s, high unemployment, increasingly stringent eligibility requirements, and a "process of implicit disentitlement due to the trend away from regular, full-time employment" have meant, however, that "even in industrialized countries, insurance benefits now reach only a minority of the unemployed."[36]

Furthermore, although the unconditionality of the basic income seems at odds with the very notion of the work society (since it would enable people to choose not to work), advocates of the basic income often cite structural features and limitations of the contemporary labor market as arguments in its favor, thus pointing to a continuity with the logic and function of unemployment insurance. For example, the Basic Income European Citizens' Initiative claims that by "supporting the reduction and redistribution of working hours," the basic income "will facilitate a new form of full employment."[37] Similarly, according to the Basic Income Earth Network, the most prominent basic income advocacy group, the basic income promises to reconcile two of the central objectives of social and economic policy—namely, "poverty relief and full employment."[38] Finally, Claus Offe writes that the "basic income is pointless in functional terms . . . if conventional policies of pursuing the goals of 'full' employment and equitable distribution can actually deliver on their promises; but the converse is also true."[39] In other words, the basic income can and does draw support from the failure of labor market and welfare policies to achieve full employment.

How exactly the basic income might boost employment, however, demands closer scrutiny. For example, Van Parijs acknowledges that, given the limitations of tackling unemployment either by pursuing economic growth or by cutting wages, we must give up on the idea of full employment if this means "a situation in which virtually everyone who wants a *full-time* job can obtain one that is both affordable for the employer *without any subsidy* and affordable for the worker *without any additional benefit*." But like the Basic Income European Citizens' Initiative, he then goes on to suggest that a reduction in the working week could have a positive effect on unemployment as long as this is combined with "explicit or implicit subsidies to low-paid jobs," either to employers or to employees. Employer subsidies might include abolishing their social security contributions for lower earnings, while the basic income amounts to an employee subsidy in that it would allow workers to take jobs at lower wages than they could otherwise afford or would be willing to accept.[40] Another means by which advocates of the basic income suggest that it would function as an employment-boosting policy concerns its promise to enhance the flexibility of both the labor market and of workers and to increase incentives to participate in paid work. Since these claims mark an additional line of continuity with the activating logic of workfare, which encourages the unemployed to become active and enterprising selves, I will give more detailed attention to it in a later section of this chapter.

We are now in a better position to grasp the implications of justifying the basic income in terms of the goal of boosting employment. Once again, the poststructural use of Lacan's concept of fantasy proves illuminating, but to see how, it will help to explicate the theory in more detail. In general terms, a Lacanian theory of ideology holds that fantasy mediates "the subject's relation to the norms and ideals governing a social or political practice."[41] Within the logics approach to critical explanation developed by Jason Glynos and David Howarth, the fantasmatic logic can thus help account for why certain political demands and practices grip or interpellate subjects.[42] Thus, to understand the grip of the UBI on its supporters, one can analyze the fantasmatic logic as promising an explanation that goes beyond the rational persuasiveness of arguments in favor of it.

It is particularly important to note that, when a subject engages with demands, practices, or norms in a way that is "governed quite stringently by the logic of fantasy," the corresponding "mode of enjoyment" is ideological. How does the notion of ideology relate to fantasy? Recall that fantasy involves an "idealized scenario promising an imaginary fullness or wholeness." Since poststructural social ontology postulates the "impossibility of closure," a subject's mode of enjoyment takes an ideological form to the extent that it maintains "the illusion of closure." Here ideology does not refer to epistemological misrecognition (as in false consciousness), but to ontological misrecognition, wherein the subject mistakes the contingent as necessary, natural, or essential.[43]

As Glynos and Stavrakakis note, "It is the imaginary promise of recapturing our lost/impossible enjoyment that provides the fantasy support for many of our political projects, social roles, and consumer choices." Indeed, the authors note that "romantic nationalist histories . . . are frequently based on the supposition of a golden era."[44] When supporters of the basic income invoke increased levels of employment as a justification, a similar phenomenon reveals itself: the idealized scenario of the work society sustains the grip of the basic income as a practice that promises to "restore" society to its imaginary fullness of social order and harmony. This mode of enjoyment is ideological because it ignores what Ernesto Laclau calls the "impossibility of society" or, more precisely, the impossibility of ever decisively eradicating antagonism and politics.[45]

This diagnosis is significant because it suggests that, although the basic income violates the principle of contribution enshrined in the social insurance model, like the latter, it can be understood as consonant with the fantasy of the work society. Carole Pateman notes that "because the direction of change depends, among other things, on the reasons why the change is advocated and what it is expected to achieve, the manner in which the theoretical case is made for a basic income or a stake is crucial."[46] In like manner, I suggest that motivations for supporting the basic income—in this case, the fantasy of the work society—would have a significant bearing on the direction of change. What might follow from the establishment of the basic income within an ideological mode of enjoyment?

Philippe Van Parijs makes clear that the purpose of the basic income (in his view) isn't to "discourage as much as possible waged labour or a career-dominated existence, but to do as much as can be done in order to provide everyone with a genuine opportunity to make different choices."[47] Elsewhere, he suggests that "if the motive in combating unemployment is not some form of work fetishism—an obsession with keeping everyone busy—but rather a concern to give every person the possibility of taking up gainful employment in which she can find recognition and accomplishment, then the UBI is to be preferred."[48] These points suggest that when supporters of the basic income appeal to its ability to deliver higher levels of employment, they do so out of an awareness of the key role that paid work plays in the granting of recognition and social esteem. Claus Offe suggests that the libertarian idea that those who live only from their basic income could perform freely chosen activities misses the point that "dominant institutions and values have decimated options for making oneself useful and feeling appreciated *other* than through gainful kinds of activities."[49] While this claim about social recognition is undoubtedly correct, it does not consider the significance of arguing for the basic income in terms of its ability to boost employment. I suggest that such arguments do not seek to challenge the existing meaning and value of work and that they therefore remain stuck in the mode of overinvestment.

Admittedly, a basic income motivated by the goal of expanding employment and introduced within a society still committed to the central value of paid work might address the unjust and disabling effects of the current distribution of material goods, a possibility that appears particularly attractive from a feminist perspective. Carole Pateman, for example, suggests that "an unconditional basic income, set at a modest but decent subsistence level, would provide women with [economic] independence for the first time in history, and thus be a major step forward to their full social and political participation and full citizenship."[50] Although one could readily translate this claim into Nancy Fraser's norm of participatory parity, Fraser in fact points out that, to avoid simply consolidating a "Mommy track" and thus "reinforcing . . . the deep structure of gender maldistribution," the basic income would need to be combined with "comparable worth and high-quality, abundant child care."[51] Similarly, Ingrid Robeyns suggests that, furnished with a basic income, some women may "work less on the labor market" given "the gendered nature of decision-making within families." She further claims that "a basic income would do nothing to change the traditional gender division of labor."[52] As these comments show, the basic income may be a necessary but insufficient condition for bringing about a more just distribution of material goods.

In making this claim, I do not mean to suggest that the unjust distribution of goods exhausts all that is problematic about the (gender) division of labor: issues surrounding decision-making and the cultural value of labor also deserve mention. Thus, just as Nancy Fraser contends that successful welfare reform must involve "struggles for cultural change aimed at revaluing caregiving and the feminine associations that code it,"[53] I suggest that the UBI as a distributive policy would need a corresponding cultural project to tackle the existing grammar of recognition, particularly the principle by which a person receives social esteem on the basis of his or her contributions to society through paid work.

While one might not object in principle to some connection between social esteem and social contribution, in practice paid work associated with women and people of color receives less social esteem than typically male pursuits, while an even lower regard is held for unpaid work performed in the home or the community.[54] Without a transformation in the meaning and value of paid work, moreover, it is not difficult to imagine the continuing impetus to cultivate employability and self-entrepreneurialism, even if this stemmed less from material necessity than is presently the case. I return to this point in the discussion of the activating logic of workfare. In sum, while one can begin to notice a recurring theme in the somewhat speculative character of these claims, they nonetheless point to ways in which the basic income pursued within the framework of the work society could fall short of hopes for more radical social change.

While arguments for the basic income that appeal to its employment-boosting potential signal an ideological mode of enjoyment, this does not exhaust the range of possible relations to it as a political demand. In contrast to the ideological mode of enjoyment, Glynos presents the ethical mode of enjoyment, "which signals a commitment to recognizing and exploring the possibilities of the new in contingent encounters."[55] As with the ideological mode, an ethical mode of enjoyment may or may not lead to the contestation and transformation of sociopolitical norms and practices. For example, an ethical mode of enjoyment in relation to the norms governing the food provided at schools means that subjects are "attuned to the contingency and creative potential of social reality," but this may or may not result in a change at the level of the culinary practices themselves.[56] When an "ethical mode of enjoyment" accompanies a "public contestation and transformation of social norms," however, this gives rise to the possibility of "political resignification."[57]

This suggests a continuum of relations to the demand for a basic income, from overinvestment in the fantasy of the work society at one end to a more radical posture that welcomes the openness and contingency of social relations at the other. In other words, all advocates of the basic income must be willing to abandon the principle of contribution (otherwise the income is not unconditional), but one can range them on a spectrum running from a commitment to the work society at one end to advocacy for the refusal of work at the other. I have already discussed examples of the former position, but what of the ethical mode of enjoyment? I suggest that Kathi Weeks exemplifies the latter position, not only because she explicitly calls for the refusal of work as a movement to reconfigure the social meaning and value of work, but also as she formulates the basic income as "a perspective and a provocation, a pedagogical practice that entails a critical analysis of the present and an imagination of the future."[58]

Similarly, when Gorz dismisses the question of the affordable level of the basic income and instead stresses the cultivation of "non-monetary exchange and self-providing,"[59] it is clear that his relation to the basic income is not in the manner of those who support it out of a commitment to full employment and that such an approach harbors a greater potential for "political resignification." Finally, the German group Freiheit Statt Vollbeschäftigung (Freedom Not Full Employment) explicitly opposes the goal of full employment on the basis, among other reasons, that it "ties up citizens in mind-numbing, undignified work," given that their labor is increasingly redundant due to automation.[60]

Social Citizenship: Unemployment Insurance and the Basic Income

In the previous section I showed that social insurance functioned as an identification project. Given the acceptance of low levels of temporary unemployment even within a Keynesian economic program that strived for full employment and bolstered by the view of (industrial) work as a "service and a duty to the nation," unemployment insurance thus came to function as a "badge of the social citizen."[61] This right of social citizenship rested on a person's status as a worker and was in this respect distinct from the stigmatizing mark of public assistance,[62] which I will discuss in the next section.

When one notes that "social benefits are rights that attach by virtue of status—the status of citizenship,"[63] the characterization of unemployment insurance as a right of social citizenship seems to imply an unconditionality resembling that of the basic income. Indeed, Tony Fitzpatrick suggests that the unconditional basic income would be a "fundamental right of citizenship."[64] It is worth pointing out, however, that since its inception, unemployment insurance has operated through a series of exclusions, effectively distinguishing the "legitimately" unemployed, who were eligible for benefits, from those not working due to sickness, old age, or "personal causes."[65] Thus, both the US and British versions of unemployment insurance are far from unconditional, since eligibility depends on having worked for a specified period and/or making a minimum level of contributions through payroll deductions, provisions that Walters notes of the British system were made to guard against "loafers" claiming benefits.[66]

Moreover, the fact that both systems place a limit on how long recipients can draw benefits makes unemployment insurance ill-equipped to deal with frequent and long-term joblessness.[67] This, in turn, leaves unemployed persons who fall short of eligibility requirements increasingly reliant on the less socially acceptable means-tested benefits, commonly known as welfare.[68] In other words, as much as social insurance has played a role in constructing the socially integrated national citizen, this identity has been far from universally available or inclusive. As Carole Pateman points out, the social citizen referred, in essence, to the male breadwinner. As she notes, the "Anglo-American social insurance system was constructed on the assumption that wives were not only their husbands' economic dependents but lesser citizens whose entitlement to benefits depended on their private status, not on their citizenship."[69]

How can a right that one is said to enjoy on the basis of citizenship, such as unemployment insurance, be at the same time conditional on the performance of work? In "Citizenship and Social Class," T. H. Marshall approaches citizenship in terms of civil, political, and social elements. "In early times," as Marshall somewhat vaguely puts it, "these three strands were wound into a single thread," meaning that what are now understood as civil, political, and social rights "were blended because the institutions [connected to them were] were amalgamated." Moreover, in feudal society, enjoyment of rights derived from a person's status, which was "the hallmark of class and the measure of inequality." Not only did the passage to modernity involve the differentiation of these rights and the institutions that provided them, according to Marshall, but there also emerged a new understanding of citizenship, which he defines as "a status bestowed on those who are full members of a community."[70]

While there is "no universal principle" determining the specific content of the rights and duties with respect to which "all who possess the status [of citizenship] are equal," Marshall suggests that "societies in which citizenship is a developing institution create an image of an ideal citizenship against which achievement can be measured and towards which aspiration can be directed." The growth and flourishing of the institution of citizenship in Britain since the seventeenth century is thus "an urge towards a fuller measure of equality, an enrichment of the stuff of which the status is made and an increase in the number of those on whom the status is bestowed."[71]

The essential character of a citizenship right, in Marshall's account, is the fact that any "full members of a community" can lay claim to it. While this invocation of full membership implies a corresponding incomplete membership, Marshall does not indicate who would fall into each category and why. In an early section of the essay Marshall indicates that social rights include the right to a "modicum of economic welfare and security." Later Marshall qualifies this definition, however, stating that

"social rights imply an absolute right to a certain standard of civilisa-
tion which is *conditional only on the discharge of the general duties of
citizenship.*"[72] Again, Marshall is vague on what these duties involve, but
as discussed previously, within the work society one fundamental duty
of citizenship is the pursuit of gainful employment. Presumably, because
paid work is widely recognized as constituting a general duty of citizenship, basing eligibility for unemployment insurance on the claimant's past
employment history does not introduce additional obligations. Indeed, the
right to protections against unemployment was simply one side of the citizenship coin; on the other side was the duty to perform paid work (when
able to do so).

Clearly, the introduction of the basic income would constitute a step
forward in this process of expanding citizenship, since it rejects the eligibility requirements, and hence the exclusions, of unemployment insurance. Indeed, this forms a key plank of a feminist defense of the basic
income, as discussed previously. Nancy Fraser argues that the Polanyian
figure of the double movement (referring to the forces of marketization,
on the one hand, and social protection, on the other) requires the addition
of a "missing third"—namely, emancipation. She points out that social
movements since the 1960s have turned "a withering eye on the cultural
norms encoded in social provision" and "unearthed invidious hierarchies
and social exclusions."[73] One might argue, then, that the demand for the
basic income brings social protection together with emancipation, in opposition to marketization.

To say that the UBI "would introduce the principle of citizenship into
the social security system for the first time" not only identifies the exclusionary and discriminatory effects of unemployment insurance, which
arise out of the fact that it operates on the basis of desert;[74] perhaps more
radically, treating the basic income as a citizenship right entails a detach-
ment of the duty to engage in paid work from the very definition of citizenship. This is, of course, one of the primary objections to the basic income,
which finds expression in the condemnatory phrase "something for nothing" and which already bedevils the provision of existing means-tested
benefits. Elizabeth Anderson, for example, worries that the unconditionality of the basic income "promotes freedom without responsibility, and
thereby both offends and undermines the ideal of social obligation that
undergirds the welfare state."[75] The fact that the unconditionality of the
basic income conflicts with the underlying principles of the contemporary

welfare state does not provide a normative argument against it, but this criticism does nonetheless draw attention to a deeper problem for the basic income in terms of the sustenance of social solidarity.

For example, Claus Offe argues that, to ensure that the basic income does not become "excessively demanding in moral terms and politically precarious as a consequence," beneficiaries must be seen as capable of doing "something useful 'in return.'"[76] Some authors have been tempted to try to overcome this potential deficit of reciprocity by making receipt of a minimum income dependent on the performance of certain socially useful activities. In *Critique of Economic Reason*, for example, Gorz argues against an unconditional basic income, not out of commitment to the work ethic per se, but "to maintain the indispensable dialectical unity between rights and duties." According to Gorz, the enjoyment of rights without the fulfillment of duties poses a problem at the level of social recognition and inclusion in the sense that "if [society] asks nothing of me, it rejects me."[77] To address this concern, he therefore proposed that everyone do 20,000 hours of work in their lifetime in exchange for the right to an income.

But it is worth pointing out that once one imposes such requirements, the basic income ceases to qualify as unconditional. Furthermore, Gorz himself would later present compelling arguments against making receipt of the basic income conditional on, for example, "work in the third sector of activities which meet needs that cannot be paid for," on the grounds, inter alia, that this would lead to the absurd conclusion of "compulsory voluntary work." It would, moreover, draw a potentially limitless list of activities "within the ambit of instrumental reason and administrative standardization."[78] As I discuss later, however, this does not mean that the duty or expectation to engage in socially useful activities would or should simply disappear.

Welfare, Social Exclusion, and the Basic Income

If the introduction of the basic income would constitute an expansion of social citizenship beyond the exclusionary boundaries of social insurance, the establishment of workfare programs in the 1990s has already transformed the meaning of social citizenship "from status to contract"[79] and thus points to a movement in the opposite direction. Although workfare systems vary in their specific practices, I follow Jamie Peck's distillation of its essence down to the "imposition of a range of compulsory programs and mandatory requirements for welfare recipients with a view to *enforcing work while residualizing welfare*."[80] On the face of it, whereas the UBI would represent the forward march of social citizenship, its introduction would break sharply from the existing systems of means-tested assistance organized according to workfarist principles. This is not only because these benefits are reserved to those with demonstrable financial need, but also because, since the introduction of workfare policies, eligibility has been made conditional on the performance of certain work-related activities. Although the introduction of the basic income would indeed radically reshape this landscape,[81] in this section I intend to excavate a subterranean continuity with workfare. More specifically, I draw out a set of arguments for the basic income that mesh with the workfarist logic of activating workers and turning them into self-entrepreneurial subjects. As in earlier sections of the chapter, therefore, I argue that the degree to which the work society retains hegemony would powerfully shape the effects of the basic income and, in particular, the construction of self-entrepreneurial subjects.

With the shift away from Keynesian economic theory toward supply-side economics since the mid-1970s, unemployment has increasingly been understood as the result of various rigidities and distortions (such as collective regulations and social-protection schemes) and as a reflection of the voluntary behavior of workers and employers.[82] In the previous chapter I analyzed the regime of flexibility as a project, partly motivated by concerns about high levels of unemployment, to remove rigidity from the labor market, organizations, and even individual workers. In that chapter I also explored the role of freedom within the ideology and practices of flexibility while giving an account of the construction of the enterprising self. Although means-tested benefits predate the emergence of the regime of flexibility, the logic of workfare, which lay at the heart of reforms on both sides of the Atlantic during the 1990s, converges in important ways with that of flexibility.

In particular, mounting concerns that existing welfare states were hindering the flexibility of labor markets, enabling a culture of dependency, and thereby causing slow economic growth and high unemployment, as well as fears about the socially disintegrating effects of long-term unemployment, led to the introduction of new eligibility requirements for means-tested benefits.[83] In Britain, the perception of society as fractured and divided as a result of geographically and socially concentrated unemployment provided the context for the Labour government's workfarist New Deal policies in the mid- to late-1990s.[84] According to Walters, the versatility of the New Deal lay in its ability to draw on both the discourse of social exclusion, which identifies structural factors leading to high unemployment among the young and old, the disabled, and single parents, and the conservative discourse of the underclass, which seeks to explain unemployment in terms of moral and behavioral pathologies.[85]

It is worth noting, moreover, that the label "underclass" came to the fore during the urban disorder that broke out in the United States in the mid-1960s. At this time, journalists and social scientists gave Gunnar Myrdal's purely descriptive term "under-class" a racial, behavioral, and above all, pejorative sense.[86] With these new connotations, "underclass" could convey the idea of dependency, a condition that, despite disagreeing about its causes, members of the political left and right could find common cause on the need to tackle.[87]

The broader discourse of social exclusion may place the "poverty and disadvantage of the so-called excluded . . . outside society," thus enabling "an overly homogeneous and consensus image of society"[88]—and here, once again, one is reminded of the illusion of closure and the fantasy of social order and harmony discussed previously—but it is important to note that the underclass was not thereby simply ignored. On the contrary, welfare reform targeted members of this group by tying the receipt of unemployment benefits to active job-seeking and a range of schemes to improve their employability as a means of tackling the problem of their social exclusion. As Nikolas Rose notes, in the welfare reforms enacted in Britain and the United States, "Problems of the excluded, of the underclass, are to be resolved by a kind of moral rearmament." Marking a shift away from the understanding of frictional unemployment as the involuntary predicament of responsible workers caught in the maelstrom of macroeconomic forces, this approach "presupposes that poverty is no longer a question of inequality among 'social' classes," but that full inclusion in the community requires the "moral reformation" and "ethical reconstruction" of excluded individuals.[89]

Here the parallel between support for the conditionality of welfare programs (both in terms of economic means and the requirement to take part in job seeking and training) and opposition to the unconditionality of the basic income comes into sharper focus. Enthusiasm for the disciplining effects of work has not only played a leading role in welfare reform, it has also provided fodder for arguments against the basic income. For example, William Galston suggests that proponents of the basic income have overlooked the "positive dimensions of work," particularly its ability to organize one's life and give "structure and meaning to what can otherwise become a formless and purposeless existence."[90] Of course, if work does in fact play these salutary roles, one might ask why the introduction of a basic income would radically diminish incentives to engage in it.[91]

Similarly, versions of the discourse of social exclusion and dependency find expression within both welfare and basic-income debates. For example, despite remaining critical of the 1996 Welfare Reform Act in the United States, Nobel Prize–winning economist Robert Solow argues that "the total or partial replacement of unearned welfare benefits by earned wages" would make welfare recipients and taxpayers alike "feel better"— the former because they would be "exhibiting self-reliance" and the latter "not merely because less is demanded of their limited altruism but also because they can see that their altruism is not being exploited."[92] As Amy Gutmann puts it, the aim of this "fair version of workfare" is to make mutual dependency replace complete dependency, for the former is the "normal condition of citizens in a liberal democracy."[93] These concerns echo Gorz's earlier opposition to the basic income, which was grounded on a commitment to ensuring each citizen's right "to 'earn their living' " and "not to be dependent for their subsistence on the goodwill of economic decision-makers," rights that Gorz argued were necessary to avoid a "splitting of society into one section who are by rights permanent workers and another which is excluded."[94] The notion that social harmony and order require the maintenance of the "indispensable dialectical unity between rights and duties"[95] thus clearly converges with the discourse of social exclusion that appeared in the context of welfare reform.

It is far from clear that existing workfare programs have succeeded in their goal of including marginalized members of society through the imposition of new eligibility requirements. On the contrary, as one element of neoliberal poverty management, welfare reform has arguably worsened the marginalization of poor people by "ignoring the distributive inequalities that shape markets."[96] Similarly, Rose argues that workfare programs have produced "a sector of the laboring population that is casualized, unprotected against risk, insecure and desocialized."[97] In short, decades after the introduction of workfare policies, many of the concerns that provided their initial impetus persist. Within this context, advocates of the basic income from a variety of political perspectives suggest that it may provide an effective instrument to increase the rate of employment. In the terms of the earlier discussion, I suggest that these arguments display an ideological mode of enjoyment in the sense that they treat the basic income as a policy tool to restore society to its former wholeness, rather than welcoming radical change.

For example, advocates of the basic income claim that its unconditionality (both in terms of willingness to work and financial means) may help undermine both the unemployment trap (whereby employment is disincentivized by a fall in income as a result of accepting a job) and the poverty trap (where the structure of tax and benefits results in falling net income even as gross income rises).[98] In addition, it is claimed that some individuals may be more, not less, likely to participate in paid work, given the "exit option that the basic income provides."[99] Related to this, advocates suggest that the basic income would reduce "the risks associated with moving between jobs and occupations" while also making it "easier for people to take work sabbaticals in order to upgrade their skills."[100] Finally, some argue that the basic income promises to "enable wages to fall to their market-clearing levels" because, unlike the current system, which "consists largely of *replacements* for lost earnings and/or a loss of earning-power, the unconditional nature of BI means that it is a *floor* for wages." In other words, rather than offering benefits that allow people to "price themselves out of the market," thus pushing up labor costs, the basic income would effectively subsidize the market for low-paid jobs.[101] This in turn would make the economy more efficient and flexible, thus increasing employment and growth.[102]

In briefly reviewing these claims, I should make clear that what calls our attention is not their empirical or theoretical validity. To be sure, it is difficult, if not impossible, to know in advance what the precise impact of a basic-income scheme would be on the unemployment rate. But even if one could reach a definitive conclusion as to the merits of these arguments, I want to highlight the fact that the UBI attracts support on the basis of claims about its putatively employment-boosting capacity. These points thus provide further evidence for my earlier argument about the ideological mode of enjoyment in relation to the work society. While the basic income can be part of a more radical agenda of social change, as in the later work of Gorz and Weeks, for example, a commitment to it on the basis of its ability to enhance opportunities and incentives to work suggests a continuity with earlier attempts to tackle unemployment and the social ills it allegedly produces, albeit via a route that travels in the opposite direction to the heightened conditionality of benefits eligibility.

To reiterate, the unconditionality of the basic income stands in opposition to what Claus Offe calls "administrative 'activation,'" whereby the unemployed person is integrated "into the labor market by means of negative administrative and economic sanctions."[103] But, as suggested previously, without altering the grammar of social recognition and contesting the meaning and value of paid work, one might expect a continuation of pressures to cultivate one's employability and to become effectively self-enterprising. Although workfare currently involves a coercive element, these programs also treat the unemployed as "clients" as a means of securing their "commitment" and avoiding the appearance of an "external authority" imposing its schemes on the "recalcitrant individual."[104] For example, one of the four purposes of the US Temporary Assistance for Needy Families program includes the promotion of job preparation,[105] while in the United Kingdom the coalition government established the Work Programme in 2011 to create a "structure that treats people as individuals" and to "tailor the right support to the individual needs of each claimant."[106] In this way, the contemporary government of unemployment interpellates the individual as "an active agent in their own economic governance through the capitalization of their own existence,"[107] such that he or she is effectively governed as a *"self-employee."*[108] Given the active role of the subject, it might even be appropriate to refer to these practices as instances of ethical self-formation, which in Mitchell Dean's terminology "concerns practices, techniques and rationalities concerning the regulation of the self by the self, and by means of which individuals seek to question, form, know, decipher and act on themselves."[109]

Just because the UBI would, by definition, be paid regardless of the activities a person engaged in, I suggest that this would not necessarily spell the end of governmental self-formation, in which "authorities and agencies seek to shape the conduct, aspirations, needs, desires and capacities of specified political and social categories, to enlist them in particular strategies and to seek definite goals."[110] Once again, the effect of the basic income on self-formation would depend to a large extent on the perseverance of the work society. For example, while the introduction of an unconditional basic income would dismantle administrative (or governmental) activation, Offe welcomes the fact that it would activate people "in the sense of creating space for doubtlessly 'useful' (though not marketed) voluntary activities in the family, the community, civil society organizations, and educational systems."[111]

Whether such spaces would spring up of their own accord or require more intentional orchestration one cannot know in advance. But Gorz suggests that to avoid being undermined and discredited, the basic income should be pursued alongside efforts not only to combine "the redistribution of work with the individual and collective control over time," but also to encourage "new socialities to blossom, and new modes of cooperation and exchange, through which social bonds and social cohesion will be created beyond the wage-relation." In fact, he claims that each of these policies "assumes its true meaning only when combined with, and supported by, the other."[112] In the next section, I consider the stakes for freedom when the basic income aligns with this more radical position with respect to the work society.

Freedom and the Basic Income as a Radical Demand

I make a first pass at this question by considering Van der Veen and Van Parijs's early article, in which they claim the basic income could facilitate a transition to communism from within capitalism. Here the authors consider four principles that could guide basic-income policy: (1) the maximization of economic growth, provided the basic income remains above a minimum level; (2) the maximization of the "absolute level of the universal grant" (which they label the Rawlsian principle); (3) the maximization of the basic income, relative to total taxable income (the so-called Marxian principle); and (4) the maximization of equality.[113] For my purposes, the Marxian principle is most relevant, since this aims to raise the tax rate to the maximum possible level (without it resulting in a fall in the absolute level of the basic income), so as to expand the realm of freedom through a reduction in working time and improvement in the quality of work. In other words, this principle implies the greatest separation from the terms of the work society, since the explicit goal is to reduce the amount of necessary labor time to a minimum.

In keeping with Gorz's proposals noted previously, Van der Veen and Van Parijs state that this "may mean that an increasing part of society's wealth is produced outside the formal sector, in the form of self-production, mutual help, volunteer work, etc." The authors point out that the benefits of this production may not be evenly distributed and that compared with Rawlsian or growth-oriented principles for guiding basic-income policy, it may not lead to the highest quality of free time. But they suggest that "if what really matters to us—as it arguably did to Marx—is the expansion of freedom, the abolition of alienation, we need not be bothered by the persistence of substantial inequalities, because everyone's fundamental needs are covered anyway."[114]

It is easy to see how the basic income, guided by this principle, would indeed provide greater freedom from work than most people currently enjoy. But what basis is there for optimism about the broader emancipatory possibilities that the basic income might open up? In *Real Freedom for All*, Van Parijs presents the basic income as policy that would help maximize "real-freedom-for-all."[115] Whereas formal freedom involves a structure of rights that includes the notion of self-ownership, Van Parijs presents real freedom as supplementing this conception of formal freedom with the requirement that "each person has the greatest possible opportunity to do whatever she might want to do."[116] In this respect, his definition of freedom closely resembles my own, which in chapter 1 I defined as the capacity of agents to act according to their own values, needs, and desires. It is hard to deny that the basic income would foster freedom so defined, but it is also important to note that Van Parijs recognizes that freedom is necessarily a "matter of degree" and that the "ideal of a free society must therefore be expressed as a society whose members are maximally free . . . rather than simply free."[117] This stipulation both avoids the clumsy interpretation of freedom as an ideal that can be achieved once and for all and, in a related manner, recognizes the contingent and potentially limitless character of a person's wishes.

Of course, in practical terms, much would depend on the level of basic income as to the degree of real freedom it could underwrite, but Van

Parijs's conceptualization of real freedom as distinct from formal freedom nonetheless provides an important corrective to the shortcomings of the latter, known at least since Marx's critique of liberal rights. Although I do not dispute the capacity for an adequate basic income to deliver substantial freedom from paid work and to pursue alternative activities, my earlier discussion of social recognition suggested that one should not expect the basic income alone to transform the achievement principle, whereby subjects receive social esteem based on their contributions to society in the form of paid work. Here I want to consider the prospects of freedom when the basic income accompanies a shift in the meaning and value of paid work. How might the UBI become entangled with freedom beyond the more obvious expansion of material opportunities discussed previously?

If the introduction of the basic income must accompany efforts to cultivate institutions and opportunities for cooperative production and exchange, then the power relations within and surrounding these spaces assume particular relevance to the question of how the UBI might expand freedom. Indeed, as Foucault points out, since social existence entails power relations, one faces the "permanent political task" of analyzing and bringing them into question, as well as the "agonism" between these power relations and the "intransitivity of freedom."[118] Given this, who exercises power over whom, in what manner, and for what ends, would have a crucial bearing on the assessment one could make of the claim that the basic income would expand freedom. Indeed, to the extent that the social relations present in a postwork society undercut equality, they would also undermine freedom, and by extension, justice. To see why, one needs to simply observe that inequality means relations of subjection and mastery and that these directly undercut freedom, understood as the capacity to act according to one's own ends.[119] Of course, one cannot know in advance all such possible threats to freedom and equality, but the manner in which a community cultivates, promotes, expects, and rewards the social contributions of its members stands out as worthy of note. I will explore these questions in greater detail in the next chapter.

To be clear, the foregoing considerations are not intended as an argument against the UBI. Instead, my point is that we need to be on our guard against a naive optimism about the capacity of the UBI to deliver freedom once and for all. But while these insights disclose ways in which the introduction of the UBI may represent less of a boon for freedom than one might have thought, I want to be clear that it nevertheless presents a significant opportunity to expand freedom in relation to paid work. Moreover, supporters of the basic income often point to the increased leverage workers would have over employers and the increase in the quality of working conditions that might ensue. Beyond the realm of paid work, the basic income would afford women the financial security and independence both to act as full citizens (as Pateman points out) and to contest, or if necessary leave, unhealthy relationships. Finally, the enhanced capacity to engage in acts of resistance granted by the basic income could even find expression in the spaces of voluntary cooperative production that I discussed previously and thus serve as a corrective to any instances of subjection and mastery that would undercut the UBI's promise of freedom and equality.

In the concluding passages of *The Protestant Ethic and the Spirit of Capitalism*, Max Weber offers a chilling assessment of his society's attachment to paid work: "The Puritan wanted to work in a calling; we are forced to do so." In other words, whereas the Puritan's subjection of life to the dictates of work could at least be justified by appeal to an understanding of work as a religious duty, the early twentieth-century worker found his or her life merely determined by the "tremendous cosmos of the economic order."[120] Weber ponders the future of the iron cage in which his contemporaries dwelled and, eschewing predictions, suggests that "no one knows who will live in [it] in the future, or whether at the end of this tremendous development, entirely new prophets will arise, or there will be a great rebirth of old ideas and ideals, or, if neither, mechanized petrification."[121]

If the notion of paying every member of society (or perhaps more correctly, of humanity) an income regardless of his or her economic contribution seems to suggest a cracking of the iron cage's bars, the preceding analysis has suggested the need for an alternative metaphor. Indeed, I have shown that some supporters of the basic income seek to justify it on the grounds that it would further the related goals of full employment, labor market flexibility, and the end of welfare dependency, all with the implicit purpose of restoring the work society to its former glory. True, the unconditionality of the basic income would seem to allow individuals to treat work once again as a "light cloak" (to paraphrase Weber's discussion of Richard Baxter), but my key contention is that this may be the case only if its introduction accompanies a reconfiguration of the meaning and value of work itself. For although questions of distribution and recognition clearly overlap, I have argued that merely providing people with an income without conditions does nothing to challenge the existing grammar of recognition in relation to paid activities or to tackle the marginalization and loss of social respect of those who do not engage in paid work at all. Indeed, when arguments for the basic income tout its ability to restore the work society, there is no reason to expect a disruption of social pressures and rewards to engage in paid work or the undervaluing of unpaid activities—whatever their social contribution—and those who perform them.

Although I share Weber's wariness of making predictions, like him I have tried to sketch possible trajectories of social and political change. Thus, it is possible that the implementation of the basic income might in fact release humanity from the iron cage of work if the terms of the work society itself come under sufficient scrutiny and criticism. As I have shown, while the basic income per se cannot perform this task, some supporters of it, from the later Gorz to Kathi Weeks, do add this ingredient to their work. Yet drawing on a Foucauldian reading of freedom, I have argued that, even in this more propitious soil, one should not assume some final attainment of freedom. Indeed, to do so would be to succumb to an ontological misrecognition similar to an overinvestment in the fantasy of work—that all antagonisms could definitively be reconciled, all imbalances of power removed, and all members of society at last could rest in freedom and justice. Instead, the fundamental contingency of the social suggests a variety of deployments of freedom, from the governmental to the ethical, and of course, with many shades in between. This observation does not amount to a case against the basic income. Rather, it points to the problematic claim that the basic income would simply expand freedom and suggests the need to remain cautiously optimistic about the spaces of cooperation and exchange that could take the place of paid work and monetized economic relations.

To return to the questions with which I began this chapter, while the basic income surely qualifies as a historical alternative in the sense that it would indeed alleviate "man's struggle for existence," this is perhaps to set too low of a bar, especially as I have shown that the basic income could represent just another strategy with which capitalist society can "deliver the goods." This chapter has thus tried to elevate a submerged struggle over the meaning and purpose of the basic income itself, a struggle that is inextricably linked with the work society. Those critical of the latter should therefore make extremely cautious alliances with basic-income supporters who see basic income as a means to restore the work society.

5

Community beyond Work

Beyond the simple refusal, or as part of that refusal, we need also to
construct a new mode of life and above all a new community.

MICHAEL HARDT AND ANTONIO NEGRI, *EMPIRE*, 204

Community cannot arise from the domain of work. One
does not produce it, one experiences or one is constituted
by it as the experience of finitude.

JEAN-LUC NANCY, *INOPERATIVE COMMUNITY*, 31

If not the work society, then what? In other words, if we are to go beyond the work society that I have analyzed in the preceding chapters,
what form might human coexistence take? Defenders of the work society deliver a kind of blackmail: either we organize our collective life substantially around work, or we stare into the abyss of social disintegration,
radical individualism, and the loss of advantages that come from living in
common. Having a (relatively) clear view of social relations after the work
society is thus important, not only to help orient and nourish the hopes of
those who are already on board with the critical aims of challenging the
work society, but also to enlist those currently more invested in the contemporary work society.

Kathi Weeks recognizes the importance of heading off complaints that
the refusal of work is naive and irresponsible, in particular by insisting

that it does not mean a refusal of all activity and labor. But Weeks deliberately refrains from offering a detailed vision of a postwork society, favoring instead what she calls two "utopian demands"—namely, for the unconditional basic income (UBI) and the reduction of work without loss of income. Weeks defends the value of utopian thought, but by comparison with the "traditional literary and theoretical utopias that offer detailed visions of alternative worlds" (such as Thomas More's *Utopia*) or the "utopian manifesto" (such as Marx and Engels's *Communist Manifesto*), she argues that "less can sometimes be more."[1] The demands Weeks proposes are undoubtedly provocative and do indeed point beyond the work society. Yet given the deep-seated connection between work, sociality, and indeed civilization more broadly, we need to confront head-on the question of collective life beyond the contemporary work society.

In the previous chapter I considered two broad sets of arguments for the UBI: those that justify it by appeal to the measure's ability to restore the work society, and those that see in it the potential to bring about a more radical social transformation. But I showed that, even when the UBI figures as a more radical nonreformist reform, there remains the risk that the new spaces for production and cooperation proposed by theorists in this camp could undercut freedom and equality. In this chapter I want to extend these reflections by examining two prominent accounts of postcapitalist society, one developed by André Gorz, the other by Michael Hardt and Antonio Negri. Of course, these represent just two of many such visions. Yet Gorz's sustained interest in work and the influence that Hardt and Negri have exerted on left political thought—for example, their *Empire* has over 12,000 citations, according to Google Scholar—make them obvious choices for analysis.

Moreover, both sets of arguments are broadly complementary, particularly in their critiques of capitalism and in the hopes they pin on contemporary immaterial production for the possibility of radical social transformation. Whatever the strengths and weaknesses of their analyses of contemporary capitalism, however, I will show in this chapter that both Gorz and Hardt and Negri do not sufficiently distance themselves from the work society, since they view community as the product of work. In Gorz's case, the connection between work and community in the multiactivity society that he proposes appears in the claim that cooperative activities would primarily forge the social bond and in the norm that everyone should participate in voluntary associations. Hardt and Negri also see community as the product of work: not just by explicitly proposing the construction of a new community, as the quotation that serves as one of the epigraphs to this chapter indicates; but also in affirming the multitude's (re)production and use of the common, broadly understood to include both natural resources and interpersonal skills, collective knowledge, and social relationships.[2]

As I will show, the crisis of contemporary capitalism that Gorz and Hardt and Negri diagnose stems from the fetters that it places on immaterial production. The postcapitalist societies that they envision would thus involve the full flowering of cooperative activities, unimpeded by the barriers and enclosures erected in the name of private property and the accumulation of capital. By promising to replace macrosocial, heteronomous, alienated labor with autonomous activities, and by incorporating an unconditional basic income, these accounts show how we might overcome the incursions on freedom that afflict the contemporary work society. Yet understanding social bonds and community as entities to be constructed by and through work makes it likely that the type of productive or reproductive activities that a person performs will continue to function as a mechanism of inclusion/exclusion. Moreover, such an approach does not help establish solidarity with individuals and communities who are not obviously within the same cooperative networks.

While their arguments and my critiques of them are not identical, neither postcapitalist vision sets out a genuinely postwork society. Indeed, to break fully with the work society requires a different approach to community. In the final section of this chapter I thus turn to the work of Jean-Luc Nancy, who develops an account of what is usually translated as the "inoperative community," but that I prefer to call the "unworked community." I suggest that we find in this account a more ethically satisfactory starting point for thinking and enacting a postwork community and that his related concept of literary communism shows how we can realize it.

Postmodern Capitalism and the Promise of Immaterial Labor

In *The Immaterial* Gorz proposes a new definition of wealth in response to his assessment that capitalism has now "arrived at a boundary beyond which it can exploit its potentialities to the full only by transcending itself in the direction of a different economy." I will examine this new definition of wealth in greater detail later. Here, though, I want to focus on the link between this new understanding of wealth and the form of production that characterizes contemporary capitalism. The particular development forcing the need for a "different economy" is the emergence of a postmodern form of capitalism in which "the heart of value-creation is immaterial work." As Gorz explains, immaterial work involves the mobilization and utilization of skills and experiences formed in the culture of everyday life and "tends, in the end to be indistinguishable from a labour of self-production," in the sense that it depends upon "continual innovation, communication and improvisation."[3]

In cognitive or knowledge capitalism, Gorz observes that the main productive force is knowledge and shared culture, which have no exchange value and are produced collectively and by largely unpaid activities. Moreover, the fact that this knowledge can be shared online, Gorz suggests, means that for the first time the productive force can potentially lie beyond private appropriation.[4] As a concrete example, Gorz points out that formalized knowledge contained in software can replace vast amounts of paid labor and thus "diminishes—or even reduces to zero—the monetary exchange-value of an increasing number of products and services."[5] While this emphasis on knowledge perhaps makes Gorz seem insufficiently attuned to the affective dimension of immaterial production (and which Hardt and Negri put on an equal footing with the cognitive), Gorz does describe immaterial labor as the provision of services, while he treats knowledge as referring to "a wide diversity of *heterogeneous* capacities, including judgment, intuition, aesthetic sense, level of education and information, ability to learn and to adapt to unforeseen situations."[6]

For Gorz, formalized knowledge heralds the affluent economy, the reduction of immediate labor, and the distribution of "fewer and fewer means of payment."[7] The affluent economy could transform in turn into a "no-cost economy" and promote "forms of production, cooperation, exchange and consumption based on reciprocity and pooled resources as well as on new forms of currency." Given this, "so-called cognitive capitalism *is* itself the crisis of capitalism."[8] Similarly, for Hardt and Negri, in the current biopolitical mode of production, capital exploits "common forms of wealth, such as knowledges, information, images, affects, and social relationships."[9] Yet "in contrast to cars and typewriters," they find that the products of immaterial labor "can directly expand the realm of what we share in common," since they are often themselves "immediately social and common."[10] Moreover, one of the openings for revolutionary change that emerges with the regime of biopolitical production derives from the way that the interdependence and reciprocity of capital and labor that characterized industrial production are broken. As they put it, "Capital still depends on biopolitical labor, but the dependence of biopolitical labor on capital becomes increasingly weak." While industrial production required management to enable cooperation and provide materials, "biopolitical labor tends to have direct access to the common and the capacity to generate cooperation internally."[11]

To be clear, while immaterial labor has become central to the valorization of capital in Gorz's estimation, he points out that this does not mean that so-called direct labor or material labor isn't still "indispensable and even dominant from the quantitative standpoint." What Gorz means, rather, is that "the provision of services—immaterial labour—is becoming the *hegemonic* form of labor, while material labour is relegated to the periphery of the production process or is quite simply outsourced."[12] This echoes Hardt and Negri's discussion in *Multitude*, where they describe immaterial labor as the hegemonic form of labor in the late twentieth century. For them, the hegemony of one particular figure of labor (earlier, it was that of the industrial worker) does not mean that it exercises quantitative dominance within the production process; rather, it "serves as a vortex that gradually transforms other figures to adopt its central qualities." Most importantly, this means that the fastest-growing employment sectors tend to be in the domain of immaterial labor—"food servers, salespersons, computer engineers, teachers, and health workers"—while even labor that produces tangible products has increasingly integrated aspects of immaterial labor, emphasizing "communication mechanisms, information, knowledges, and affect."[13]

For Gorz, as for Hardt and Negri, this "era of the general intellect" requires a new form of economic rationality that promotes "human development" and cooperation, because this, rather than the attempt to measure and maximize the individual performance of workers, now drives "optimum efficiency."[14] In other words, the self-production of immaterial labor prefigures the inversion of values that would stand at the center of

Gorz's much earlier notion of the "humanism of free activity,"[15] but the full potential of this labor can only be realized by surpassing capitalism's restrictive economic rationality. Indeed, Gorz points out, commenting on a passage from Marx's *Grundrisse*, that humanity would no longer be "in the service of the development of production but production in the service of human development, that is to say, of the production of the self." In a society based on this new definition of wealth, the goal would be to cultivate "our sensory, affective, expressive and bodily faculties," with the "full development of each" becoming the "common aim of all."[16]

Similarly, Hardt and Negri write that "the exercise of capitalist control is increasingly becoming a fetter to the productivity of biopolitical labor." To challenge the limits imposed by capital on the productivity of biopolitical labor, however, would require open access to the products of the common, autonomous organization of time, control over migration, and "reforms of the physical, social, and immaterial infrastructure," as well as "the power to construct social relationships and create autonomous social institutions." But the very reforms that would save capitalism, Hardt and Negri suggest, will also at some point spell its demise: "Pursuing its own interests and trying to preserve its own survival, it must foster the increasing power and autonomy of the productive multitude. And when that accumulation of powers crosses a certain threshold, the multitude will emerge with the ability autonomously to rule common wealth."[17]

One needs to be careful not to infer from this very brief discussion of Gorz and Hardt and Negri that they expect capitalism to transcend itself without the political struggle of human beings to resist and transform it. This, in fact, was a criticism that Gorz himself leveled against works by Hardt and Negri prior to the publication of *Empire*. In *Reclaiming Work*, he reads what he calls the "theorists of 'mass intellectuality,'" including Negri and Hardt, as claiming that "autonomy in work generates, in and of itself, the workers' capacity to abolish any limit or obstacle to the exercise of their autonomy." He calls these "theoreticist ravings," suggesting that they conjure up an "inherent revolutionary subject" from the production process, while "evad[ing] the most difficult task, namely that of creating the cultural and political mediations through which the challenge to the mode and goals of production will emerge."[18] For their part, Hardt and Negri return the "complement" in more subdued terms by writing of

Gorz's *Reclaiming Work* that his analysis "appropriates central elements" of autonomist Marxism "but ultimately fails to capture its power."[19]

This mutual criticism suggests a starker opposition than actually exists between Gorz, on the one hand, and Hardt and Negri, on the other, if one takes a broader reading of their respective works. Gorz's sensitivity to the development of "forms of production, cooperation, exchange and consumption based on reciprocity and pooled resources" reflects the potential that Hardt and Negri see within immaterial labor, but a further point of agreement with Hardt and Negri lies in Gorz's observation that the "economy of the immaterial" subjectivizes a capacity for autonomy that underpins the aspirations for multiactivity.[20] In other words, while employers need workers' autonomy, people are tending to claim more of it for themselves.

Moreover, when Gorz writes that "the power struggle then becomes inevitable and relates to the status of that autonomy and its scope—autonomy's *rights over itself*: the rights of persons to and over themselves,"[21] he anticipates a point that Hardt and Negri make in *Commonwealth* that class struggle today "takes the form of exodus," by which they mean "a process of *subtraction* from the relationship with capital by means of actualizing the potential autonomy of labor-power."[22] Finally, whatever the validity of Gorz's observations about Hardt and Negri's earlier works, Hardt and Negri insist throughout *Empire*, *Multitude*, and *Commonwealth* on the need for political agency to bring an end to Empire or what they later call the "republic of property." For example, in the second work of their trilogy, *Multitude*, they clearly state that "the multitude needs a political project to bring it into existence."[23]

In this section I have presented two prominent visions of a postcapitalist future. Both identify a crisis of capitalism whose resolution they claim would undermine capitalism itself and allow for the development of new forms of cooperative and autonomous labor. Given the interest garnered by Hardt and Negri's work, it is not surprising that criticisms of it abound. Here I want to briefly consider a worry about the optimism that Hardt and Negri display concerning the radical potential of immaterial labor, since this seems to apply equally to Gorz's arguments. Wanda Vrasti writes that the "very same affective and intellectual predispositions that would allow labor to spontaneously organize itself are also what tie individuals to the gratifying, expressive, and pleasurable promises of essentially precarious and exploitative economic arrangements." In other words, why assume that immaterial labor will lead to the demise of capitalism, rather than to a strengthened loyalty to it?

Vrasti is right in my view of the need to "examine how our deepest attachments to technological advancements, sprawling acts of charity, gratifying types of employment, self-actualizing forms of consumption, and exclusionary forms of attachment invest us in what remains an inherently domineering and destructive mode of social organization."[24] But neither Gorz nor Hardt and Negri see the transformation of capitalism as possible without a political struggle by a broad coalition of actors. Moreover, not all immaterial labor is necessarily "gratifying": many service jobs are underpaid, undervalued socially, and do not give significant scope for autonomy or personal development. And even when work is gratifying, I see no reason to assume that this gratification must liquidate opposition to the broader capitalist social formation. Solidarity with others who are less fortunate in their experience of work and a broader perspective on the harms perpetuated by global capitalism can and do motivate even relatively privileged workers to struggle against it, although again, as Vrasti points out, it is hasty to assume that immaterial labor in itself can form these movements, particularly out of very differently situated subjects.

But even if one casts away doubts over this sanguinity about immaterial labor and the difficulties of organizing a counter-power sufficient to lead the transformation (out) of capitalism, there exists a more fundamental problem with the visions that Hardt and Negri present of life beyond capitalism—namely, their understanding of community as an entity produced by work—that I identify in the next two sections. To be clear, I do not intend to challenge or criticize the persistence of work per se in these thinkers' visions of a postcapitalist future, since it seems to me fanciful and even perverse to imagine that we could ever meet all of our needs and wants without expending mental, emotional, or physical energy, that is, that we could be completely without work, or that we would even want to be. Rather, we need to explore what the remaining work would achieve, and in particular, how it stands in relation to community and social relations. Let me begin again with Gorz.

Beyond the Wage-Based Society: André Gorz

In texts spanning several decades, Gorz displays a consistent commitment to the expansion of individual autonomy by reducing, if not eliminating, paid work without the loss of income. In *Critique of Economic Reason*, for example, Gorz argues that work—defined as "an activity in the *public* sphere, demanded, defined and recognized as useful by other people and, consequently, as an activity they will pay for"—should be reduced and more evenly distributed across society, thus expanding the time and opportunities for all to engage in noncommodity activities, including the production of goods for personal or communal use and activities "which are themselves their own end."[25] Yet, Gorz also maintains that the sphere of heteronomous macrosocial activities should not be completely eliminated. As I showed in chapter 2, this position stems from his concerns that those without paid work will lose their social identity, but it also reflects his critique of the "utopia of work in Marx," which he argues presupposes a community marred by totalitarianism and the effacement of the individual.[26]

In this chapter I engage mainly with Gorz's *Reclaiming Work*, first published in 1997. This text marks a turning point in Gorz's thought: his attention to the immaterial economy, noted in the previous section; his embrace of the UBI after decades of opposition to it; and his growing optimism about the possibility of transforming all labor into autonomous activity, despite his earlier critique of the utopia of work. Moreover, despite the tension between Hardt and Negri and Gorz around *Reclaiming Work* noted previously, it is at this point that their respective positions begin to converge. Finally, although he explores the theme of immateriality more directly in later work, in this text he offers a particularly vivid portrait of the post-waged-based society.

To understand the meaning of the book's subtitle—*Beyond the Wage-Based Society*—I first consider the role of heteronomous macrosocial work within the multiactivity society proposed by Gorz. On one hand, Gorz still recognizes the value of heteronomous work, suggesting that cooperative circles "will be at the most developed in a context where . . . everyone 'works' intermittently in the system of macro-social exchange." On the other, not only does his support for an unconditional basic income (rather than one paid in exchange for the performance of a set number of hours of social labor, as he proposes in *Critique of Economic Reason*) suggest that he no longer views it as a social obligation in the interest of functional integration. In addition, he writes in an earlier passage that "wage-labour has to disappear and, with it, capitalism."[27]

With the reduction and eventual disappearance of wage labor, then, Gorz argues that "social time and space will have to be organized to indicate the general expectation that everybody will engage in a range of different activities and modes of membership of the society." Indeed, in the multiactivity society "the production of the social bond" would take place in "relations of co-operation, regulated not by the market and money, but by reciprocity and mutuality," and individuals should be able "to measure themselves against others, gain their esteem and demonstrate their value not mainly by their occupation and earnings but by a range of activities deployed in the public space and publicly acknowledged in other than monetary ways." It would thus be "the norm . . . for everyone to belong—or at least to be able to belong—to a self-providing co-operative, a service exchange network, a scientific research and experiment group, an orchestra or a choir, a drama, dance or painting workshop, a sports club, a yoga or judo group, etc."[28]

While Gorz emphasizes participation in voluntary cooperative associations as the lifeblood of community, at the time of *Reclaiming Work* he doubts that "the self-managed co-operative" could be "extended to planetary scale." Gorz thus follows Jürgen Habermas in maintaining the need for a distinction between the social system and the lifeworld: "The public services and administrations of complex modern societies cannot dissolve themselves entirely into the communicative and consensual cooperation between communities." At the same time, he envisions a "feedback loop, connecting the evolution of the system back to that of the life-world, each spurring on the other," which would mean that "micro-social ensembles can themselves assume a growing proportion of their mediations with the social whole."[29]

This collaboration between microsocial ensembles appears to find its fullest expression in an article published just before his death in 2007, in which Gorz presents a "concrete utopia" of "cooperative communal self-providing."[30] While Gorz recognizes that it is "not immediately realizable on a grand scale," he nonetheless believes that this utopia will "stand as an exemplary piece of social experimentation" if implemented somewhere and that this alone will illustrate the "possibility of a radically different world."[31] In particular, Gorz imagines the appearance of inter-connected workshops all around the world deploying the latest high-tech tools that can "manufacture almost any three-dimensional objects with a much higher level of productivity than industry and with a minimal consumption of natural resources." In this scenario, "the market and commodity relations" would be replaced "by negotiated agreement about what should be produced, and how, and to what end; of manufacturing all that it is necessary locally; and even of building large and complex plants through the cooperation of several dozen local workshops."[32]

Of utmost importance in signaling the break with a commitment to heteronomous wage labor, Gorz anticipates that under these circum-stances "work can now free itself from 'external necessities' (Marx), re-cover its autonomy and turn towards the effectuation of everything that has no price and cannot be bought or sold. It can become that which we do because we really want to do it, and because we find our fulfillment in the activity itself as much as in its outcome."[33] This utopia does not, therefore, spell "the end of work," but the "end of the tyranny exerted by commodity relations over work in the anthropological sense."[34]

While Gorz earlier doubted the possibility of transforming all labor into autonomous activity, the thought that wage labor distorts true work appears throughout his writings. For example, in *Capitalism, Socialism, Ecology*, Gorz distinguishes between true and false work, where the lat-ter describes work in the sense of "currently existing jobs and occupa-tions" and the former can be seen in Hegel's definition of the human being externalizing itself and should be thought of as the "non-alienated, au-tonomously determined activity by which a subject transforms and ap-propriates the sensible world." Moreover, true work, Gorz insists, is a "historical-fundamental need: the need the individual feels to appropriate the surrounding world, to impress his or her stamp upon it and, by the objective transformations he or she effects upon it, to acquire a sense of him- or herself as an autonomous subject possessing practical freedom."[35] One key advantage of the multiactivity society or of cooperative commu-nal self-providing, from Gorz's perspective, is therefore that they would allow for the blossoming of true work. Indeed, the title *Reclaiming Work* (which perhaps suggests greater optimism than the original title, *Misères du présent, richesse du possible*, which literally translates as "Woes of the Present, Wealth of the Possible") indicates precisely this hope.

In *Reclaiming Work*, *The Immaterial*, and *Ecologica*, Gorz thus shows increasing optimism about the transformation of labor into autonomous activity, but no longer fears that this would come at the price of a total community that subsumes the individual, as he had in his critique of the utopia of work. Some of the shift in Gorz's position with respect to the possibility of overcoming alienated labor can be explained in terms of new technologies that lessen the advantages of industrial production. The fact that he takes the free software networks as "prefigurations of another possible world" and understands them as a form of "anarcho-communism"[36] also shows how much Gorz no longer assumes that communism involves a tightly integrated community that snuffs out individual autonomy.[37] Despite these implications of a looser model of community than that of the utopia of work, though, I want to dwell on the norm of participating in voluntary associations and the related idea that it is through these associations and cooperatives that the social bond would mainly be produced and that people would prove their value to themselves and others.

Gorz is clear that the point of these voluntary associations would not be to "select, eliminate or rank individuals, but to *encourage each member to surpass him/herself ever anew in competitive co-operation with the others, this pursuit of excellence by each being a goal common to all*."[38] While it is conceivable that a person may not belong to any such groups—Gorz says that the norm should be "at least" for everyone "to *be able* to belong"—the strength of the social bond that ties individuals would seem to depend, in Gorz's account, precisely on the degree to which people do participate in them. Failure to do so would not result in loss of the basic income, but it presumably would produce, and perhaps also reflect, degrees of social marginalization and disrespect.

The key point of my critique is that a community in which the creation of the social bond and recognition depend not on commoditized activities but nonetheless on work in the broader sense does not decisively break with the basic terms of the work society. While Gorz's argument no doubt reflects many people's experience of the socializing effects of work (whether paid or not), one needs to consider whether this is an ethically satisfactory way to ground community. Here I have in mind the idea that inclusion in a community matters both to a person's self-esteem and in terms of the treatment, including care, assistance, and solidarity, that he or she can expect from others. Although few would claim that one has no obligations whatsoever to those outside of one's own community, as the social bond appears less strong or tangible, the sense of duty typically weakens.

One presumably unintended implication of Gorz's suggestion that the social bond should be created mainly through cooperative activities is that this suggests a lack of relation, or at best a weak tie, between those who do not cooperate in some shared enterprise. In other words, a person who does not participate in any associations whatsoever—perhaps due to chronic illness or disability—remains at the margins of community life. Perhaps he or she will continue to enjoy social citizenship on the basis of birth or even domicile and thus be able to claim fundamental entitlements from the state. And perhaps caring neighbors will help out with domestic tasks and provide opportunities for socializing. But when this person fails to conform to the norm of participating more actively in associational activities and thus to prove his or her worth to the community, there is the real possibility that he or she will suffer disrespect and a lack of consideration from others. In this respect, the multiactivity society carries forward one of the chief problems of the existing work society, albeit with an expanded list of activities through which the social bond is established and recognition earned. It is also possible that certain activities would be valued more highly than others as a means of establishing and maintaining one group's privilege and power, as is currently the case in the domain of paid work.

Another unwelcome implication of Gorz's theory of the construction of social bonds through cooperative activities is that even if you do work, if you do not take part in any of the same associations as I do, or simply do not recognize that you do, then there appears to be no social bond, or at best a weak one, between us. The existence of a macrosociety (as Gorz envisioned in *Reclaiming Work*) might enable abstract solidarity between members of different communities that make up the broader society, but not only is this solidarity weaker in Gorz's account, it would also be exclusionary in the absence of a genuinely global society. The point here, analogous to the earlier one about the person who does not work in any socially recognized way, is that theorizing the social bond as constructed by cooperative activities provides only a weak foundation for solidarity with, and mutual recognition between, people who do not take part in common associations.

None of this is to say that Gorz is opposed to internationalism or that he suggests that one's duties to others stop at national borders. In fact, as I showed earlier, his concrete utopia has an international dimension, while in *The Immaterial* he considers the possibility of global change and the creation of another world by the alter-globalization movement, comprising "academics, writers, artists and scientists, linked with and radicalized by oppositional trade-unionists, post-industrial neo-proletarians, cultural minorities, landless peasants and unemployed and insecurely employed people."[39] But again, my concern here is that Gorz does not challenge, but rather, he affirms a central tenet of the existing work society, whereby work (however broadly construed) constitutes the primary lever of social integration.

You might respond to this argument with an air of fatalism: isn't it inevitable that when people work together they will develop a deeper concern for each other's well-being than for people whom they have never met? If people understand themselves as coparticipants in even large-scale forms of cooperation, won't the sense of common purpose and experience of similar conditions inevitably make them more sympathetic toward each other than toward people who have no such entanglements? Maybe so, but there is a choice about whether to affirm this tendency or to resist it. My wager is that by positing as a norm belonging to various cooperatives and by theorizing the social bond and recognition as the product of these interactions, the Gorzian multiactivity society does not do enough to challenge this tendency. As I will show, Hardt and Negri offer more resources for this task, especially in their concept of love, but I will argue that even their approach remains insufficient.

Instituting the Common: Hardt and Negri

Hardt and Negri's assessment of the possibilities opened by immaterial labor in many ways parallels Gorz's later analysis of cognitive capitalism. As I will show in this section, their own vision of a postcapitalist future, while sketchy, also resembles in many ways Gorz's utopia of "cooperative communal self-providing." What Hardt and Negri contribute most to this postcapitalist vision, however, are their accounts of biopolitics, the multitude, and love. Let me first examine the concept of biopolitics, which they most clearly articulate in the third work of their trilogy, *Commonwealth*. Like other theorists who have worked in the field of biopolitics, most notably Giorgio Agamben and Roberto Esposito, Hardt and Negri take their inspiration from Michel Foucault. They find two distinct powers of life in Foucault's work, which they term "biopower" and "biopolitics," suggesting, however, that he uses this terminological distinction inconsistently. Very briefly, whereas what they call "biopower" refers to the "power over life," "biopolitics" refers to the "power of life to resist and determine an alternative production of subjectivity."[40]

It is in the sense of biopower that Hardt and Negri write in *Empire* that all aspects of society, including reproduction, are "subsumed under capitalist rule," meaning that "reproduction and the vital relationships that constitute it themselves become directly productive."[41] Lest this sound like total domination, Hardt and Negri draw on Foucault's notion of the "recalcitrance of the will and the intransigence of freedom" that he identifies within every power relationship. Since, as Foucault puts it, "power is exercised only over free subjects," there is an irreducible potential for resistance within even the most oppressive of social relations.[42] Given this, one can understand biopolitics as an event that disrupts the continuity of history and the normative system, as well as being a moment of "innovation, which emerges, so to speak, from the inside." In other words, biopolitics involves the production of new subjectivities and new relations to self and others that challenge the existing power over life exercised by capital.[43]

As I showed earlier, for Hardt and Negri class struggle today "takes the form of exodus," by which they mean "a process of *subtraction* from the relationship with capital by means of actualizing the potential autonomy of labor-power." Like the refusal of work of the autonomist Marxists, "exodus" does not mean the rejection of productive activities, in this case the "refusal of the productivity of biopolitical labor-power." Instead, with "exodus" Hardt and Negri have in mind the more limited "refusal of the increasingly restrictive fetters placed on its productive capacities by capital."[44] Indeed, given that the biopolitical event involves a rebellious "production of life,"[45] for Hardt and Negri there can be no question of abandoning the terrain of biopolitics. To understand how the biopolitical event can arise, as well as to understand more fully the idea of biopolitical production, we need next to examine Hardt and Negri's concept of the multitude, which both uses and creates the common.

The first point to note about the multitude is that Hardt and Negri define it by contrast with a people, which "*is in fact a product of the nation-state.*"[46] They observe that Thomas Hobbes was aware of this distinction, writing in *De Cive* that "the people is somewhat that is one, having one will, and to whom one action may be attributed; none of these can be properly said of the multitude."[47] Thus as Hardt and Negri put it in clearly Deleuzian terms, "A multitude is a multiplicity, a plane of singularities, an open set of relations, which is not homogeneous or identical with itself and bears an indistinct, inclusive relation to those outside of it."[48] I will return to the contrast between the people and the multitude when I consider the relationship between Hardt and Negri and Nancy. To give greater specificity to the multitude now, however, it is worth asking who constitutes it.

Hardt and Negri explain that the multitude is the "common name of the poor."[49] By "poor," however, they refer not to people who fall below a certain threshold of income and wealth. Rather, they use the term as the "only non-localizable 'common name' of pure difference in all eras." Thus "the poor is destitute, excluded, repressed, exploited—and yet living! It is the common denominator of life, the foundation of the multitude."[50] The multitude today then can be understood as a "set of free subjectivities" whose productive power based on autonomous cooperation is controlled and exploited by capital.[51] This autonomy is both the source of profit and the greatest risk faced by Empire: its autonomy cannot be destroyed because of its productivity, but if the multitude were to develop into an "autonomous mass of intelligent productivity, into an absolute democratic power," this would spell the end of "capitalist domination of production, exchange, and communication."[52] Later in *Empire* Hardt and Negri anticipate the objection that the multitude constitutes neither "a properly political subject" nor "a subject with the potential to control its own destiny." Their response to this reveals the connection they make between the multitude and freedom: "The revolutionary past, and the contemporary cooperative productive capacities through which the anthropological characteristics of the multitude are continually transcribed and reformulated, cannot help revealing a telos, a material affirmation of liberation."[53]

Having seen that the multitude therefore harbors the potential for revolutionary action, what can be said of the type of society that might replace the current one? Although they do not claim to be able to offer a blueprint for an alternative to Empire, insisting instead that the "genius of collective practice will certainly be necessary today to take that next concrete step and create a new social body beyond Empire," in this text Hardt and Negri do propose postmodern republicanism, the "effective notion" of which should be constructed "on the basis of the lived experience of the global multitude."[54] Moreover, when considering how the multitude might organize itself to act against Empire, Hardt and Negri suggest three elements of a "political program for the global multitude," which can help shed light on the direction of change that they envisage.[55]

First is the demand for global citizenship, which means that "all should have the full rights of citizenship in the country where they live and work." Underlying this is the multitude's "*general right to control its own movement*," which means deciding when, where, and indeed whether to move. It is worth dwelling on the implications of couching this demand in terms of work. As they explain, the demand merely reflects the fact that capital has itself demanded ever-greater geographical mobility of the global multitude. Given that "capitalist production in the more dominant regions . . . is utterly dependent on the influx of workers from the subordinate regions of the world," the demand for global citizenship can be understood as a revamping of the "modern constitutional principle that links rights and labor" for the postmodern era. While it might seem that Hardt and Negri come perhaps perilously close to affirming this principle, the second demand for the global multitude, namely "*a social wage and a guaranteed income for all*,"[56] suggests otherwise, since by definition it would guarantee an income regardless of a person's paid work.

Indeed, their case for a guaranteed income (and Gorz agrees on this point) rests on the impossibility of measuring working time and individual output and from the increasingly blurred line between production and reproduction. As they put it, the social wage extends to the "entire multitude, even those who are unemployed, *because the entire multitude produces*, and its production is necessary from the standpoint of total social capital."[57] This particular claim helps understand the logic of calling the income a "social wage," since in effect it remunerates every member of the multitude for his or her (re)production, which itself simply reflects his or her participation in the social relations and practices that make up the multitude. In other words, since biopolitical production has a cognitive, affective, and thus necessarily social-relational dimension in both its inputs and its outputs, it would be perverse to try to disaggregate individual contributions and use these as the basis for wages. Hardt and Negri put this point most succinctly in *Commonwealth*: "Wealth is produced across a widely dispersed social network, and therefore the wage that compensates it should be equally social."[58] They thus write that "once citizenship is extended to all, we could call this guaranteed income a citizenship income, due each as a member of society."[59]

Finally, in keeping with their analysis of biopolitical production as centering on "knowledge, information, communication, and affects," the third demand that Hardt and Negri propose for the global multitude is the right to reappropriate these means of production, which means "having free access to and control over" them.[60] As I have shown, overcoming the limits imposed by capital on the productivity of biopolitical labor would involve implementing measures that harbor the potential to release the multitude from the control of capital. "The commons is the incarnation, the production, and the liberation of the multitude."[61] The three demands that I have reviewed in this section can be read as responses to the primary strategies of capitalist control that currently hinder the productivity of the multitude.

In reverse order, the third demand for the right to appropriate the means of production seeks to address the privatizations of the common that limit access to knowledge, such as paywalls around academic journals. Second, the demand for a social wage would allow everyone control over his or her time and thus addresses the imposition of labor precarity as a strategy of capitalist control, which is counterproductive precisely because "the production of ideas, images, or affects is not easily limited to specific times of the day." Finally, the demand for global citizenship brings control over migration to the multitude, thus breaking down the barriers that currently impede productivity, given that interactions with cultural and social others "in a situation of equality" drive the productivity of the multitude.[62] In addition, Hardt and Negri emphasize the need for reforms that would ensure the "physical, social, and immaterial infrastructure" required for biopolitical production, as well as "the power to construct social relationships and create autonomous social institutions," for example, through deepening democratic participation "at all levels of government to allow the multitude to learn social cooperation and self-rule."[63]

If a concern with Gorz's account of the construction of the social bond through work is that it risks marginalizing those who do not work and fails to build solidarity between those who do not cooperate in the same associations, at first glance it appears that roughly the opposite charge could be leveled against Hardt and Negri's concept of the multitude—namely, that it is excessively, or perhaps rather impossibly, inclusive. In *Multitude*, Hardt and Negri anticipate the objection, which they identify as broadly deconstructionist in orientation, that "every identity . . . even the multitude, must be defined by its remainder."[64] One way of phrasing this objection, suggested by Jean-Luc Nancy in a short article critical of the concept of multitude, is that it is not possible for the multitude to say "we."[65]

Here Nancy recognizes the concern of the alter-globalization activists with the idea of the people as a closed identity, but goes on to outline three problems with their recourse to the multitude as an alternative concept. First, he observes that the demands of the movement arise from minorities that identify as communities, whereas the multitude "disperses everything in singularities." Second, he wonders whether "this dispersion into multitudes" is not a direct effect of the global capitalism, which the activists oppose. Third, he suggests that while "multitude" implies the multiplication of individuals or small groups, it lacks the sense of an increase of force and implies a kind of wandering.

Instead of the multitude, Nancy thus proposes the idea of "the people," which has two meanings that he thinks elevates it above the multitude: the people are defined by their opposition to the powerful and names those who are "excluded, oppressed, exploited" but demand their rights (as in the plebs). While this is an idea of the people "never resting on an essence defined a priori"—and as I will show in the next section, this is a signature of Nancy's thought—it nonetheless "allows for a certain common enunciation, that a 'we' can be spoken." Unfortunately, the way that Nancy poses the people as an alternative to the multitude does not suggest a close reading of *Empire*, since in that text, as we have seen, Hardt and Negri specify that the multitude comprises the poor, who are the "destitute, excluded, repressed, exploited." In this regard at least, Nancy's "people" seems less distinct from the multitude than he suggests. In any case, Nancy's intervention here is valuable because it helps flesh out the type of interpretation of the multitude that Hardt and Negri want to avoid: that its all-encompassing quality means that it cannot recognize the persistence of multiple self-identified communities and that it is a weak and ineffective agent of change.

In response to the deconstructionist objection that the multitude seems to permit no remainder, Hardt and Negri compare the multitude to "the unlimited and indefinite nature of distributed networks." This allows them to imagine the existence of "points or nodes outside a network," at the same time as stipulating that "none are *necessarily* outside. Its boundaries are indefinite and open."[66] In more practical terms this means that while "no one is necessarily excluded," neither is inclusion guaranteed, because "the expansion of the common is a practical, political matter."[67] It is also important to note that, later in the same text, Hardt and Negri describe *the* multitude as an assemblage of numerous multitudes. They thus write that "multitudes intersect with other multitudes, and from the thousand points of intersection, from the thousand rhizomes that link these multitudinous productions, from the thousand reflections born in every singularity emerge inevitably the life of the multitude."[68] In other words, while *the* multitude names the living tissue or "social flesh" formed of innumerable singular productions, Hardt and Negri also conceive of multitudes in the plural, where each would presumably have its own "indefinite and open" boundaries.

As with Gorz, labor is central to the production of community in Hardt and Negri's work. For example, they write that the "notion of labor as the common power to act stands in a contemporaneous, coextensive, and dynamic relationship to the construction of community"[69] and that "from the *sociological standpoint*, the constituent power of the multitude appears in the cooperative and communicative networks of social labor."[70] Moreover, for them, "the common" means not only the "common wealth of the material world" but "also and more significantly those results of social production that are necessary for social interaction and further production."[71]

This approach to community and the common suggests a similar criticism to the one that I have developed with respect to Gorz—namely, that only those who take part in these networks can count as full members of the community. Although the sprawling and inclusive nature of the multitude goes some way to alleviating that concern, the fact that inclusion is not guaranteed but a political matter leaves open the possibility of exclusion on the basis of a person's contribution to the common. Hardt and Negri's attempt to redefine love as a political concept itself offers a check on this kind of exclusion, but I will argue that what is ultimately needed is a different conception of community than the one implicit in either Gorz or Hardt and Negri.

Although love appears in both *Empire* and *Multitude*,[72] the concept receives its fullest treatment in *Commonwealth*, in which they devote a whole section to it. To put it succinctly, for Hardt and Negri, love is "the production of singularities and the composition of singularities in a common relationship." This means that love "does not simply happen to us," rather "it is an action, a biopolitical event, planned and realized in common." To the extent that love produces subjectivity, Hardt and Negri also view it as "producing a new world, a new social life."[73] It is clear, then, that love significantly overlaps in Hardt and Negri's thinking with their concept of labor, defined as the "common power to act."[74] Indeed, based on their understanding of biopolitical production, they see love as an "economic power" in the sense that it involves "the production of affective networks, schemes of cooperation, and social subjectivities." The slight difference between the two concepts derives from their interpretation of Baruch Spinoza's understanding of love as "*the increase* of our power to act and think, together with the recognition of an external cause." As they go on to put it, "Through love we form a relation to that cause and seek to repeat and expand our joy, forming new, more powerful bodies and minds."[75] In other words, love is the decision to enhance the productive power of our minds and bodies through encounters with other singularities in the common.

Hardt and Negri's great insight in this section concerns the vulnerability of love to corruption and exploitation, which they label "evil." "The primary locus of this corruption is the shift in love from the common to the same," or the corruption of love as a "process of unification." Indeed, this idea of love as unification is the predominant form that love tends to take in popular culture, they observe. Even love of thy neighbor, if understood narrowly, can function as a corrupt form of "identitarian love" because it calls on you to "love those most proximate, those most like you." Similarly, love for your family, race, and nation all imply loving most those "most like you, and hence less those who are different."[76]

Although they do not make the point here, another form of identitarian love would be loving less those whose activities fail to register as work according to prevailing definitions, or those who do not work in the same associations as you.

As an antidote to identitarian love, Hardt and Negri propose a more "generous interpretation of the mandate to love thy neighbor," which would replace "neighbor" with the other and which thus becomes "love of the stranger, love of the farthest, and love of alterity."[77] Since they conceive of "evil as a corruption of and obstacle to love," this makes evil "secondary to love," which in turn means that one needs not limit oneself to containing or restraining evil, but instead can more actively combat it on the "battlefield" of love.[78] Counteracting corrupt forms of love therefore requires "promoting the encounters of singularities in the common."[79] It is also important to add that the common "composes the interaction of singularities in processes of social solidarity and political equality."[80] In its radical expression, love therefore calls on us to embrace encounters with others in solidarity and equality, fortifying the common and thus eventually freeing the multitude from control by capital and Empire. Hardt and Negri thus present love as the means to bring life to their political project of instituting the common and of establishing a global democracy of the multitude.[81]

While I agree that the politicization of love would encourage us to keep expanding the common and to deliberately encounter the other in terms of solidarity and equality, the trace of productivism in its justification limits the ability of love to counter the potential for exclusiveness that arises when community is understood as constructed by work. To be sure, loving the other does suggest a more proactive stance to seeking opportunities for interaction than Gorz's stipulation that anyone should be free to take part in cooperative self-organized activities.[82] This amounts to the difference between not deliberately excluding anyone who wants to take part in a cooperative scheme and actively recruiting new members to it out of love for the other. However, it is possible to understand the limitations of Hardt and Negri's concept of love by recalling their interest in Spinoza's definition of it as "the increase of our power to act and think." While all encounters of singularities might, however intangibly, increase our overall power to act, the possibility remains of at least the perception that some activities will be more productive than others in this regard.

Since everyone is unavoidably part of various affective networks, use a common language, and so forth, it would perhaps be impossible for anyone living not to take part in biopolitical production. But even if everyone alive is minimally included because no one can escape biopolitical production, by approaching community as the product of work, activities deemed to offer greater gains in the overall capacity to act of the multitude are likely to be valued more highly. This in turn could lead to a situation in which those with skills or traits that are particularly in demand—for example, the ability to relate to others and put them at ease or to communicate fluently and creatively—would enjoy greater privileges and power in their own community as well as greater ease of mobility to others. In a word, because the community is understood to be the product of work, it would be difficult to avoid the creation of social hierarchies and marginalization on the basis of the perceived value of particular contributions, the definition and ranking of which is, of course, far from objective.

To be clear, I am not suggesting that Hardt and Negri would endorse this outcome, or that the open-ended nature of the multitude together with the concept of love could not temper it to some degree. But what these arguments underscore is that regarding community as the product of work makes it difficult to completely disable the functioning of work as a mechanism of inclusion and exclusion. In the next section I therefore turn to the work of Jean-Luc Nancy in search of an alternative account of community. As I will show, his idea of the unworked community suggests the opposite relation to work and community than the ones considered thus far.

Community beyond Work

Throughout many of his writings, Nancy tackles head-on the dominant approach of "thinking community as an essence," which means to think of it as "a *common being*."[83] According to Nancy, such an approach to community, apparent not only in totalitarianism but also haunting "democracies and their fragile juridical parapets,"[84] destroys the true meaning of community as the sharing of the lack of "*such a substantial identity*" by singular-plural beings.[85] Indeed, Nancy writes that "immanence, communal fusion, contains no other logic than that of the suicide of the community that governed it." Death shows the truth of this claim: if one understands "decomposition leading back to nature" as what brings about immanence in death, one sees that in such a situation there "is no longer any community or communication: there is only the continuous identity of atoms."[86] Of key significance, whereas this thinking of community in terms of a common being understands community as a "work," Nancy gives an ontological account of community by showing that being is necessarily in common.[87]

If Nancy sets himself the task of thinking community anew, this reflects his awareness that the emblem of communism "is no longer in circulation."[88] Without another conception of community having taken its place, this leaves only what he calls elsewhere the "liberal response to the social." Just as "so-called real communism" repressed "the question of being-in-common" with the idea of a common being, so too the "liberal response to the collapse of communism" represses being-in-common, but in this case by "designating the 'social' and the 'sociological' as relatively autonomous spheres of action and knowledge."[89] Thus while "the testimony of the dissolution, the dislocation, or the conflagration of the community" is the "gravest and most painful testimony of the modern world,"[90] the end of "real communism" also represents an opportunity: rather than taking the meaning of community for granted and focusing on the means necessary to reach it, one now can and must ask, "What is community?"[91]

In his reflections on Maurice Blanchot's *Unavowable Community*, a text published in response to the "Inoperative Community," Nancy explains his choice of the term *désœuvrée* as reflecting his rejection, shared with Blanchot, of the idea of community as the work of a common being, whether a "community of a people itself understood as a spiritual or natural entity or equally communism understood as the force of collective self-production."[92] "All our political programs," writes Nancy in "The Inoperative Community," "imply this work: either as the product of the working community, or else the community as work." The problem with this view of community as work, however, is that community takes on a "unicity and a substantiality" that effaces its "properly 'common' character." Instead of a "being-together," community becomes "a being *of* togetherness."[93]

I do not mean to suggest that Gorz and Hardt and Negri approach community in precisely this manner. Indeed, Gorz's concerns about the utopia of work, especially regarding the suppression of individual liberties at the hands of the collective, to some extent overlap with Nancy's account of the totalitarianism of the community conceived as a common being. As I've shown, aware of the limitations and risks of the total identification of the individual with a particular community, Gorz thus counsels that the community must be part of a broader macrosociety. Similarly, Hardt and Negri emphasize the inclusiveness and multiplicity of the multitude. Yet what Gorz and Hardt and Negri do share with the view of community that Nancy wants to challenge is an understanding of it as a work. Indeed, Nancy insists that "one does not produce [community]"; rather, "one experiences or one is constituted by it as the experience of finitude," where finitude for Nancy means the "infinite lack of infinite identity" and a sharing of this lack.[94]

In place of the community of work, Nancy thus calls for the unworked community. While the title of his essay "La communauté désœuvrée" is commonly translated as "The Inoperative Community," I prefer a more literal translation as the "unworked community" because *désœuvrée* in Nancy's use connotes not so much the absence of work but the fact of being unworked.[95] Nancy understands Blanchot's concept of unworking as referring to "that which, before or beyond the work, withdraws from the work, and which, no longer having to do either with production or with completion, encounters interruption, fragmentation, suspension."[96] In Nancy's particular use of the concept in relation to community, "unworking" thus means resisting the "fulfilled infinite identity of community, . . . its 'work,' " so that we can base community instead on finitude, the "infinite lack of infinite identity," and a sharing of this lack.[97] In other words, Nancy proposes the "communionless communism of singular beings," which takes place "in the unworking and as the unworking of all its works."[98]

In his essay "Literary Communism" (included in *The Inoperative Community* volume) Nancy links unworking to communication, writing, and ultimately literary communism. Whether one refers to the works of individuals (although, of course, he recognizes that "one never writes alone"[99]) or to the works that "the community as such produces: its peoples, its towns, its treasures, its patrimonies, its traditions, its capital, and its collective property of knowledge and production"[100]—in all cases the unworking is the same: the work is "offered up for communication," which means specifically that it is "presented, proposed, and abandoned on the common limit where singular beings share one another." The truth that the unworking of the work communicates does not lie in its completion, substance, or unity as a work. Instead, this communication involves an "exposition" that takes place both within and beyond the work: the exposition of beings to one another in the production of the work, and the exposition "through which the work is offered up to the infinite communication of community." In sum, when one offers up the work for communication, it "trace[s] and retrace[s]" the limit where singular beings share and expose themselves to one another.[101]

To illustrate the character of communication that the work takes on once it has been "abandoned as work," Nancy quotes at length a passage from Marx's *Contribution to a Critique of Political Economy*, in which he describes the social labor of women and men spinning and weaving to meet the family's needs within the "rural patriarchal system of production."[102] Here Marx points out that both forms of labor constitute social labor, and both of their products constitute social products. Yet this clearly cannot be because spinning and weaving have taken "the abstract form of universal labour" or because the products assumed "the form of a universal equivalent," as they would in the capitalist mode of production. What, then, gives these forms of labor and their products a social rather than a merely private character? In Nancy's reading of Marx, it is the fact that they are part of a mode of production based on "community" (Nancy interpolates the term into his quotation of Marx). As Marx writes, "The product of labour bore the specific social imprint of the family relationship with its naturally evolved division of labour. . . . It was the distinct labour of the individual in its original form, the particular features of this labour and not its universal aspect that formed the social ties."[103]

Nancy acknowledges Marx's "retrospective illusion in this interpretation" but suggests that its value lies in the fact that it offers a thought of community as "the socially exposed particularity, in opposition to the socially imploded generality characteristic of capitalist community." In this formulation we find an echo of the relation that Gorz, in *Critique of Economic Reason* and to some extent *Reclaiming Work*, wants to maintain between grassroots community and macrosociety. But Nancy is clear that this is "a thinking, not merely an idyllic narrative ready to be transformed into a future utopia."[104] In other words, one should not read him as in any way advocating a return to Marx's depiction of primitive communes or even of recuperating their essence as a model for microsocial activities that could then be strung together into a larger macrosociety. Rather, Nancy considers this community to demonstrate the character of communication that works might assume as a result of their being unworked.

Key to unworking, as I have shown, is communication, which Nancy also calls "literature," hence the concept of literary communism. Importantly, this includes not just writing, but also voice, music, painting, dance, and thought.[105] I will consider later the resonance between these activities and immaterial labor in the later work of Gorz and Hardt and Negri. At this point, however, one needs to recognize that the process of writing means that singular beings "share their limits, share each other on their limits," and that they thus "escape the relationships of society ('mother' and 'son,' 'author' and 'reader,' 'public figure' and 'private figure,' 'producer' and 'consumer'), but they are in community, and are unworked."[106] Rather than writing establishing connections or bonds between people that might come to exist as a kind of common substance, it articulates singularities.[107] Literary communism thus means "thinking, the practice of a sharing of voices and of an articulation according to which there is no singularity but that exposed in common, and no community but that offered to the limit of singularities."[108] Bringing these threads together, realizing the unworked community entails engaging in various acts that resist the idea of the community as a collective work produced by its members and that instead expose the particularity of singular-plural beings. In sum, literary communism involves the political exigency to resist everything that would complete or finish off community, along with the inscription of that resistance.[109]

By now it has perhaps become apparent that Nancy has relatively little to say about the ideal organization or social function of work. But this is not to say that he has no position on political economy and capitalism more broadly. For example, in addition to criticizing the thought of community as an essence, Nancy highlights the tension between capital and being-in-common.[110] In particular, he claims that capital "negates community [of the kind that he is proposing] because it places above it the identity and the generality of production and products."[111] For this reason, neither real communism (which he calls "capitalist communism") nor advanced liberal society (which he less obviously labels a form of communist capitalism) aligns with the view of community intimated by Marx in the passage considered previously.[112] In a more nuanced fashion, he observes in *Being Singular Plural* that capital displays, in a distorted or alienated way, the "simultaneity of the singular . . . and the plural." This exposition is distorted because singular being is reduced to "the indifferent and interchangeable particularity of the unit of production," while the plural poses "as the system of commodity circulation."[113] As a result, being-together in capitalism "becomes being-of-market-value [*l'être-marchand*] and haggled over [*marchandé*]. The being-with that is thus exposed vanishes at the same time that it is exposed, stripped bare."[114]

Yet while Nancy is critical of capitalism, he offers little or no guidance about how to move beyond it. Indeed, Ignaas Devisch claims that although Nancy can and does raise the question of economics, his "choice in favor of social ontology" prohibits him from conducting intensive economic analysis.[115] Nevertheless, I suggest that Nancy's account of community can help one evaluate the alternatives proposed by other thinkers. Indeed, when he says that thinking better of capitalism demands that one thinks "how capitalism could, by itself, overcome itself,"[116] it is hard not to call to mind the work of Hardt and Negri and Gorz, which as I have shown, stresses the possibility of transforming capitalism from within. Although Nancy offers no specific "politics of work," literary communism shows how to resist the view of community as constructed through work, whether that work is controlled by capital or functions more autonomously, as in the post-wage-based societies of Gorz and Hardt and Negri.

In light of my discussion of biopolitical production and immaterial labor earlier in this chapter, it is perhaps difficult not to see the concept of unworking as itself a kind of work. However, not only should one view this as a risk to be averted rather than as something inevitable,[117] in addition, the advantage of Nancy's approach is that, since community is not conceived as a work, those who do not or cannot write in Nancy's sense of the term would not be excluded or marginalized. Rather, because literary communism involves the political exigency to resist everything that would complete or finish off community, not everyone need take part in this unworking. That is not to say that greater engagement in acts of literary communism would not be beneficial in keeping alive the more originary sense of community as being-in-common. But in my view, any such acts of writing can serve as an antidote to the problems I identified with Gorz's theory of the construction of the social bond.

In the previous section I argued that Hardt and Negri's emphasis on love as a political concept goes some way to mitigating these concerns. Since Nancy also engages with the topic of love, I conclude this section by considering how his thinking relates to Hardt and Negri's. As I showed earlier, Hardt and Negri propose a conception of love that breaks with both the idea of loving the same more than the other and with the idea of love as unification of parts into a whole. Instead, they propose love as the composition of singularities in the common. Even though the multitude is open-ended and dynamic, this use of love still stands in some tension with the way in which Nancy sees the relationship between love and community. Nancy stresses that "love does not *complete* community (neither against the City, nor outside of it, nor on its fringes)"—and it seems that this is more or less Hardt and Negri's approach to love—because then "it would be its work, or it would put it to work."[118]

Instead, for Nancy, as long as lovers are not unified according to the "politico-subjective model of communion in one" but instead expose their singular being to one another, they mark "the extreme though not external limit of community."[119] That is, even the love between individuals does not exist apart from community or somehow detract from it; rather, love involves the most intense experience of the sharing of finitude that defines community.[120] "Lovers expose, at the limit, the exposition of singular beings to one another and the pulse of this exposition: the compearance, the passage, and the divide of sharing."[121] One can thus understand literary communism in terms of "the sharing of the sovereignty that lovers, in their passion, expose to the outside rather than produce." Despite the affinity of love with community, it is worth noting that Nancy distinguishes between the speech of lovers and unworked communication as writing: while the former "seeks a duration for their joy that joy eludes, 'writing' . . . would on the contrary *inscribe* the collective and social duration of time in the instant of communication, in the sharing."[122]

Both Gorz and Hardt and Negri offer important insights into the type of society that might replace the contemporary capitalist work society. Their visions of the liberation from work are, I believe, valuable in provoking our political imagination and in guiding criticism of the present. But by continuing to see the social bond and community as constructed through (unpaid) work, and in Gorz's case, by explicitly tying performance of this work to social esteem, their alternative societies mark less of a break from the work society than we need. In chapter 2 I suggested that Gorz adheres to the value of heteronomous labor because his individualist social ontology leaves him in need of a mechanism that can bind individuals together into a society. While Hardt and Negri do not share this commitment with Gorz, their emphasis on biopolitical production and immaterial labor leads them also to a view of community as constructed through work.

As I have pointed out, my concern with these accounts is not that they fail to somehow banish work. Even if technology does reach a stage of development that allows us to meet all basic material needs without the expenditure of any human energy, it seems to me that some degree of work would still be needed to meet other needs and desires, particularly of an emotional nature. Even if we manage to program a machine to raise children effectively, would we want to delegate that work to a nonhuman? Rather, my concerns with Gorz and Hardt and Negri's postcapitalist visions are that they leave open the possibility that work will continue to act as a mechanism of inclusion and exclusion; that certain forms of work will be valued more highly than others as a way to establish or maintain social privilege and power; and that Gorz's focus on work as the basis of the social bond makes it difficult to establish solidarity with individuals and groups who do not participate in shared cooperative endeavors.

While Nancy's unworked community and literary communism are highly abstract, I believe that in them can be found the germ of a solution to these problems. Even though it is perhaps inevitable that cooperation with others will enhance a sense of duty to them, an account of community that deliberately emphasizes a lack of shared identity and shared lack of a substantial identity provides a powerful counterweight to such tendencies.[123] Moreover, literary communism—the idea of writing that takes various forms to resist the closure of the community—offers a concrete tool by which to achieve an unworked community or, as the title of this chapter suggests, a community beyond work. In case it is not sufficiently clear what would constitute an act of unworking, it is my hope that this chapter and the book of which it is a part can play this role. In the next chapter I will turn to the relationship between this unworked community and capitalism and consider what type of work might remain in it.

6

The Postwork Community

In the previous chapter I showed that two prominent accounts of post-capitalist society carry forward from the contemporary work society the notion that community is produced by work. This connection between work and community harbors the risk that work will still function as a mechanism of inclusion and exclusion, with the related possibility of a hierarchical sorting of different activities according to their perceived productivity, and that understanding work as constituting the social bond may hinder the experience and expression of solidarity with those outside one's own cooperative networks. Moving beyond the work society thus entails a new approach to community that can allow one to break the connection between membership and work regardless of whether the latter is paid or not.

While Nancy's account of community offers valuable resources for this task, I have yet to draw out its full implications for the organization and political significance of work in the postwork community. To that end, this chapter explores the relationship between capitalism and the postwork community and responds to a possible objection that such a community would amount to a free rider's paradise bereft of duties to others. As I will show, the postwork community entails overcoming capitalism but is compatible with—indeed, it entails—taking responsibility for the well-being of others, even though this can take the form of work. While the postwork community therefore does not prohibit a duty to perform work, this work should not and cannot function as a mechanism of inclusion. The chapter closes with some brief reflections on how we might move toward the postwork community, including a discussion of some of the major obstacles to doing so and how to overcome them.

Capitalism and the Postwork Community

Karl Marx insisted that the historical development of wage labor as a core feature of the capitalist mode of production rested on the expropriation of the commons and the virtual extinction of subsistence ways of life. This process of primitive accumulation involved transforming both "the social means of subsistence and of production . . . into capital" and "the immediate producers into wage-labourers."[1] While Marx's analysis of primitive accumulation as a historical episode helps us understand how wage labor became the predominant means of securing a living in capitalism, enclosure can be understood more abstractly as a continuous channeling of human activity "into forms that are compatible with the priority of capital's accumulation."[2] In other words, while primitive accumulation forced peasants off the commons and into the wage relation at the dawn of capitalism, various forms of enclosure continue to maintain the economic necessity of selling our labor power in contemporary society. To illustrate this point, I briefly consider four instances of enclosure that perpetuate the structural coercion to engage in paid labor.

First, although it is possible to use revenue from the earth's natural resources to fund an unconditional basic income, these goods largely remain in private hands, and those excluded from the wealth they provide must seek their livelihood through paid work.[3] Similarly, instead of establishing a universal entitlement to health care, in the United States it is treated as a commodity to be bought and sold, thus maintaining the economic necessity of paid work, whether as a means of earning money to pay expensive premiums or to qualify for employer-subsidized plans. Third, while the welfare state promises a common refuge from the battering winds of the competitive market, its boundaries have been drawn increasingly narrowly in the neoliberal era, and the adoption of workfare schemes has tied benefits directly to paid employment. And fourth, noncommoditized forms of social provisioning become harder to sustain under the time crunch of paid work and given the low social esteem that attaches to unpaid activities. This in turn creates a vicious circle in which the absence of noncommoditized goods and services increases the need for money and therefore paid work to purchase those commodities.

These contemporary forms of enclosure help one understand the material basis of the structural coercion to sell our labor power. One of the great virtues of the UBI—if provided at an adequate level—is precisely that it would remove this material coercion to take part in paid work. Of course, additional factors account for the lack of opposition to this coercion and even enthusiastic embrace of work: as I showed in chapter 2, not only the work ethic, but also the notion that society is formed by and for cooperation for mutual advancement and that work helps to construct a fair, stable, and harmonious community of integrated individuals. For this reason, I have argued that moving beyond the work society entails a new approach to community along the lines of the unworked community, so that work ceases to function as a criterion of social inclusion and belonging. The question that I have not yet addressed, however, is whether realizing this postwork community requires us to move beyond capitalism. In answering this question in the affirmative, I will distinguish between a left-liberal orientation to work (which would attempt to reduce the burden of paid work while leaving intact the capitalist mode of production) and the more radical and explicitly anticapitalist perspective that I propose.[4]

In chapter 1 I presented several problems with contemporary work. In addition to the structural coercion we face to sell our labor, these included incursions on freedom in the workplace, a lack of control over work, and the difficulties of pursuing nonwaged activities due to the time consumed by paid work. At first glance, it might appear that the introduction of the UBI and a shift in the social value of paid work could address these criticisms without the need to transform capitalism. Indeed, while the social obligation and material necessity to engage in paid work are certainly functional to capitalism, perhaps capitalism could survive without them.

True, absent the need to work to earn a living and social respect fewer people might willingly offer up their labor for sale as a commodity. But since the desire for luxury commodity consumption, social interaction, and personal fulfillment also motivate people to work for wages, it seems reasonable to assume that capital could continue to exploit these additional factors to ensure an adequate supply of labor.

Moreover, as UBI advocates often claim, workers receiving a UBI would have increased bargaining power, since they would be less dependent on earned income. This in turn would mean that employers would need to improve working conditions, especially in dangerous, stressful, or unfulfilling jobs, to make sure that they can retain necessary staff. In this scenario, people would have greater choice about whether and how to work and would be better positioned to find paid work with which they identify and that makes effective use of their talents and aspirations. In fact, this situation would allow for more entrepreneurial behavior, understood in Friedrich Hayek's sense of making "the best use of our abilities."[5] In sum, these reflections suggest that we could break the link between employment and citizenship, displace work from the center of our lives, and improve the quality of waged work, all without having to depart from capitalism.

However, another set of considerations demonstrates the misplaced optimism of this left-liberal perspective. First, if the economy remains predominantly capitalist (in the sense that most of the means of production is privately owned and the use of the surplus is not directed by the producers themselves), then one can expect limits to the control that workers could achieve over the organization of work.[6] In other words, managers will tolerate and even embrace increasing worker autonomy so long as doing so provides productivity or efficiency gains, but resistance will mount when autonomy proves detrimental to profits. Moreover, Gorz points out that the norm of full-time work helps maintain patterns of consumption beyond "felt needs." As he puts it, *"People must be prevented from choosing to limit their working hours so as to prevent them choosing to limit their desire to consume."*[7] Gorz's assumption here is that luxury consumption is particularly valuable to capital because it can be manipulated and because "wants and the desire for the superfluous are . . . potentially unlimited."[8] Employers will tend to resist a reduction of working time, in this analysis, because it would result in a drop in effective demand for luxury items.

While to some extent an unconditional basic income provided at such a generous level as to afford people the opportunity for some luxury consumption could overcome this problem, it is also questionable how much demand there would be for commodities if we were no longer dominated by the need to work for wages. For example, Gorz notices that consumer goods and services act as "incentive regulators" to ensure participation in heteronomous labor.[9] But the reverse is also true: the value of hard work helps sustain consumer culture because people treat themselves to luxuries as compensation for the travails of work. With greater freedom from paid work and more opportunities to participate in various voluntary activities, it's possible that people would succumb less readily to the marketing ploys of companies trying to inculcate new desires. Finally, the more people work for wages, the less time they have to take care of themselves, their families, their houses, and so on, and so the more they rely on goods and services offered as commodities in the market. The prospects for a significant reduction of working time and improvements to working conditions within capitalism thus appear less promising than they did at first glance.

Finally, and at a deeper level than the previous concerns, capitalism thwarts the enactment of the type of community that I have been defending because it both assumes and perpetuates an individualistic and egoistic form of coexistence in civil society. Even if it were possible to conceive of a form of capitalism in which no one had to work for wages and in which paid work had been displaced from its central position in life, the persistence of individualism and egoism directly contradicts the "social" social ontology that I have borrowed from Nancy and the ethics that flow from it. Moreover, to the extent that private property encourages us to think of ourselves as atomistic individuals with distinct claims to exclude others from goods, and to behave in ways that maximize self-interest, it keeps us trapped in a view of society as a voluntary association of individuals who enter into it for instrumental purposes. The logical implication of this view is obvious: the blaming and exclusion of those whose behavior is not perceived to make a sufficient or acceptable contribution to society.

It would be beyond the scope of this book to offer a fully developed alternative to capitalism, and like Marx and many after him, I doubt the wisdom of doing so even if it were possible. However, what I can say is that contemporary society already involves numerous forms of noncapitalist (re)production: for example, the unwaged care work of family and friends, volunteer work by neighbors to maintain local public spaces, use of common land and its resources, and "collective and cooperative enterprises."[10] In this regard the work of J. K. Gibson-Graham to "read the economy for difference" is exemplary in that it helps unseat the widespread assumption that the economy is (or could be) exclusively capitalist.[11] Careful examination of existing alternative economies and forms of cooperative work, as well as the cultivation of new ones, must be part of the establishment of a truly postwork community, with the caution that when community itself is thought to be the product of work we have not fully broken with the work society.

Gibson-Graham's work is also theoretically complementary to my own, given that their effort to articulate a discourse of community economy draws on Nancy and distances itself from theorizations of community economy that rest on a "*commonality of being*, an ideal of sameness, whether defined in terms of incubator capitalism, or a 'natural holistic community,' or self-reliant localism." Their concern is that such visions suppress economic difference and are not sufficiently attuned to an "*ethic* of being-in-common." Rather than elaborating an "ideal community economy," moreover, they prefer to "specify coordinates for negotiating and exploring interdependence."[12] This means negotiating "what is *necessary* to personal and social survival; how social *surplus* is appropriated and distributed; whether and how social surplus is to be produced and *consumed*; and, how a *commons* is produced and sustained."[13] These coordinates do not specify which particular arrangements should be made, but the postwork community, as I have shown, does involve an unconditional basic income as well as a rejection of the idea that membership depends on the performance of even unpaid work.

Notice, finally, that I am being deliberately ambivalent about whether paid work would have any place in the postwork community that I am proposing or instead all work would take the form of individual and cooperative noncommodity activities. The problem is less whether paid work will remain (in a much reduced and displaced form) or be eliminated altogether and more whether it takes place within a broader capitalist setting that not only threatens to resist the reduction of working time and autonomy at work but, at a deeper level, helps support a social ontology that results in the exclusion of persons deemed to make inadequate social contributions. In a noncapitalist postwork community, paid work might still have a future—such as the wages that members of a cooperative manufacturing shoes pay themselves according to their own democratic procedures—but like unpaid work, it must not form the basis of community or act as a mechanism of inclusion and exclusion.

Work in the Postwork Community

I have taken for granted that some amount of work will remain a feature of the postwork community, partly because it seems implausible that we would simply want to automate all work, even if the technology were available to do so. Not only may the results of automated production fail to fulfill expectations in terms of quality—earlier I used the example of care work, particularly parenting—but people may wish to continue working for the personal satisfactions and opportunities for social interaction that it offers. Assuming, then, that we will never be without some kind of work—understood here very broadly to mean simply the manipulation of matter, signs, and affect through the application of physical, intellectual, and emotional capacities—it behooves us to consider its political significance in the postwork community.

To do so, it will be helpful to begin by considering a possible objection: if we no longer view community as constructed by work and resist the idea that membership of it should be conditional on work, then doesn't this give free rein to individualism and egoism, the loss of any sense of social justice and responsibility for others, and even the collapse of social order and harmony? In short, isn't the postwork community a paradise for free riders? Clearly this concern echoes the defense of the contemporary work society and the individualist social ontology that underpins it: work integrates presumptively preformed and self-contained individuals into society understood as a cooperative association that exists to serve the interests of all its individual members. One way to respond to it, then, is to note the implications of adopting a more "social" social ontology. As I will show, this raises a further challenge, but not an insuperable one.

Rather than seeing community as constructed by the work of individuals, following Nancy I have suggested the need to understand community as part of our ontological condition as humans. Recognizing this relational social ontology, moreover, can help us see that "the suffering of any one, of each one, is a suffering which I share and, concretely, for which I have responsibility."[14] What would it mean to take responsibility for the suffering of others, or more broadly and affirmatively, to take responsibility for the well-being of others? One cannot avoid the conclusion that much or all of what it would take to fulfill this obligation would amount to one or more forms of work. This could consist of sending a letter to your representative or local newspaper, writing an article or blog post, or taking part in a mass mobilization or direct action. Perhaps it involves donating a part of your earned income to a nonprofit advocacy group. Or maybe you volunteer your time and energies to a charity or community organization. But if fulfilling the responsibility we have for the well-being of others involves work, doesn't the unworked community therefore involve a duty to work?

The short answer is "yes," but with two important qualifications, one practical, the other conceptual. First, note that this is not an obligation to do just any work, as is the case in the contemporary work society; rather the obligation is to take responsibility for the well-being of others, in a context in which the UBI is already provided at an adequate level. Now, clearly what counts as fulfilling this obligation will not only be highly contextual, it will also involve significant disagreement about how best to go about doing it, including the means taken and the particular issues and subjects to prioritize. I take it that this disagreement cannot be avoided, since the only possible way of doing so would be by appealing to an objective standard of well-being, which does not exist.

Yet precisely the persistence of this disagreement suggests that we should not let the obligation itself serve as the basis of membership of the community. To see why, consider that those with greater political power can (and in fact, currently do) exclude others from full membership of the community by devaluing their social contributions or by claiming that they do not make any contribution at all. In other words, given the indeterminacy and contestability of concepts like well-being and needs, the possibility remains that activities genuinely motivated by a concern for others will not receive the respect they deserve because they fail to conform to dominant standards of a proper civic duty. For example, labor activists presumably see their task in terms of improving the well-being of workers, but employers and representatives of capital often reach a different conclusion and have incentives to try to discredit such efforts.

Aside from this practical concern, it would be conceptually incoherent to treat the ethical duty to help others as a founding principle of the community and hence as a criterion of inclusion, since this would amount to another thought of community in terms of a common substance. Todd May argues that a community that sets antitotalitarianism as a founding principle would fall foul of Nancy's conception of community, because this principle acts as a common substance that defines the community.[15] For this reason, May argues that Nancy's response to the normative question of how to "conceive a community in a non-totalitarian manner" is "self-defeating."[16] What May identifies as a flaw in Nancy's argument is for my purposes a strength, however, because it shows that the principle of reducing suffering or of improving well-being cannot become the essence of a community, such that full membership depends on adhering to it. Committing to the value of helping others cannot be a precondition for membership of the postwork community, but that does not prevent people from holding these values and acting upon them. Indeed, doing so is what would help give full expression to the unworked community.

Moving to the Postwork Community

Without proposing a particular model for the postwork community, I hope nonetheless to have developed answers in this book to the question of what can and should come after the contemporary work society. But how can we get from here to there? We should be under no illusions about the immediate feasibility of the steps necessary to reach the postwork community: the expansion of employee-friendly forms of flexibility to increase control over work; the establishment of an unconditional basic income to remove the material necessity to work for wages, coupled with the cultural shift in the meaning and value of work necessary to realize the emancipatory potential of both flexibility and the UBI; a radical change in how we think about and enact community that embraces our ontological relationality; and last, a transformation out of capitalism.

One immediate obstacle to the expansion of employee-friendly flexibility is the weakness of the organized labor movement and the notorious difficulties of organizing workers in the sector within which more and more people work—namely, services. On the other hand, the recent campaign for the $15 per hour minimum wage that began with fast-food workers in New York and that has mobilized thousands of workers around the country and beyond to take part in one-day strikes and protests offers a glimmer of hope. California, New York State, and several cities have signed $15 minimum-wage laws, and the Democratic National Convention adopted a $15 federal minimum wage in its official platform in 2016. It is also important to note that Fight for $15 calls for union rights, criticizes the deportation regime and police brutality against African Americans, and seeks to defend health care. In these ways, although the focal point of the movement is higher wages, the breadth of commitments that it expresses, especially the support for unionization, suggests that these same energies might also help animate demands for greater employee control over work. Moreover, without attributing to the movement a commitment to any particular theory of community, its opposition to deportation suggests at least an affinity with the nonessentialist view of community that lies at the heart of the postwork community.

Another promising event of recent history is the Nuit debout protests staged in France during 2016, primarily in response to a proposed law that aimed to flexibilize the labor market. Beyond their opposition to this particular reform, participants criticized neoliberalism and institutional politics more broadly, while some made demands for the UBI, stressed the need to rewrite the French Constitution, and even proposed to abolish the private ownership of the means of production.[17] The immediate impact of the protests may have been limited—the government adopted the law anyway—but as with the Fight for $15 movement, they show the degree to which work remains deeply political and capable of arousing strong passions. On the other hand, although the popularity of Senator Bernie Sanders's democratic socialism gives reason for hope about the prospects of a renewed left in the United States, it is important to note that he has not questioned the value of paid work in contemporary society at all. On the contrary, Sanders explains that "democratic socialism means that our government does everything it can to create a full employment economy."[18] It is one thing to fight for higher wages and even greater control over work, another to question the value of work itself, and the left more broadly will need to learn to submit its traditional celebration of the dignity of work to greater critical scrutiny.

One of the biggest challenges facing social movements is the degree to which paid work consumes most people's time and makes sustained participation in politics difficult if not impossible. Indeed, one of the participants at an *atelier constituant* (constituent workshop) that took place in Paris as part of Nuit debout noted that "if you work eleven hours a day, it's impossible to be a fully engaged citizen. We need the right to reflect freely, individually as well as collectively, by guaranteeing the time and the material means of reflection in the Constitution."[19] In that sense, the UBI could act as a stepping-stone to much greater social transformation, as it would, if set at an adequate level, free up time for political participation of all kinds.

And yet, as I showed in chapter 4, for the UBI to assist in the development of a postwork community, arguments to justify it must not make appeal to its employment-boosting promise. This is a sticking point given the preeminence of work, which means that perhaps the most appealing or politically palatable arguments for the UBI adopt just this approach. Those who advocate the UBI must therefore carefully craft arguments for it that do not affirm the value of paid work, but that at the same time avoid the impression that the intended or likely result would be a society of layabouts. Moreover, while the breadth of the UBI's appeal can appear as a virtue, the risk of its cooptation by capital is very real: it must not merely serve to insulate workers from increasingly contingent and precarious employment that benefits mainly the superrich. There is also a risk that increased income will be absorbed by higher prices and that purchasing power and quality of life will not be significantly improved by the UBI.[20]

Finally, although the level of the UBI adequate to release people from the necessity to engage in paid work depends on the degree of noncommoditized production, this suggests the need for a larger UBI at first and the possibility of reducing it over time as alternative economies develop. Yet a smaller UBI will be more politically acceptable until the idea is more tested and has broader support. It becomes clear from all of these concerns that we should not treat the UBI as a panacea and that a broader social movement needs to challenge the meaning and place of work in people's individual and collective lives to ensure that its emancipatory promise is fulfilled, not subverted, as well as to defend the lives of the most vulnerable and marginalized.

This is where the difficult philosophical work of rethinking community becomes most important. Although Nancy's unworked community is highly abstract and unlikely to win large numbers of supporters outside academia, the idea of a nonessentialist community might become more accessible and appealing as people become more accustomed to living in plural and heterogeneous communities. Similarly, as the norm of stable, full-time employment becomes more and more anachronistic and as noncapitalist economic practices like cooperatives become more commonplace, perhaps the current hypervalorization of paid work will gradually diminish, and with this, a new way of thinking community will also emerge. Widespread resistance to the deportation of migrants and opposition to the anti-immigrant proposals of President Trump could prove particularly valuable in this regard, although a populist commitment to hard borders (which in part accounts for Trump's popularity) remains a stumbling block here.

Finally, I have shown that capitalism is incompatible with the postwork community and therefore must be challenged and overcome. To be sure, this constitutes another enormous and daunting task, but it is well to remember that capitalism is neither the only mode of production known to humans nor the only way of organizing economic activities at the present. As discussed previously, we need to build upon and expand existing noncapitalist practices. To use the language of Erik Olin Wright, we need to erode capitalism by "introducing the most vigorous varieties of emancipatory species of noncapitalist economic activity into the ecosystem of capitalism, nurturing their development by protecting their niches, and figuring out ways of expanding their habitats," at the same time taming it through regulation and redistribution. The "real utopias" that Wright suggests can link up the two approaches of eroding and taming capitalism include worker cooperatives, peer-to-peer production (such as Wikipedia), and the proposal for the UBI, which would both tame capitalism and erode it by nurturing noncapitalist activities.[21]

We should not delude ourselves that the transformation to a postwork community will happen overnight. Powerful forces will counteract emancipatory social change, and the ideology of work is deeply engrained even among self-identified leftists. Moreover, when more immediate concerns dominate media and political discussions—for example, the excessive use of force by police around the United States, particularly against people of color, the so-called refugee crisis, or the catastrophic effects of climate change—the thought of the postwork community can seem self-indulgent and woefully utopian. Nonetheless, this does not mean that the criticism of the work society and efforts to envision and bring about a postwork community should be postponed until a time when more urgent matters have been resolved.

Indeed, the problems just mentioned might be fruitfully analyzed and confronted in conjunction with a critique of the contemporary work society and the vision of an alternative. Not, of course, in a reductive manner that explains them in terms of the work society and that imagines they will automatically be overcome along with it; but instead, in a way that seeks out connections and points of instabilities. For example, how do differentially inclusive discourses and practices in the regulation of cross-border migration both flow from and help irrigate the work society? How might efforts to combat inequality and exclusion—whether of undocumented migrants or the largely racialized poor—reinscribe the value of paid work, and with it the legitimacy of the work society? Finally, how does the hypervalorization of work contribute to climate change, and how can a postwork community proceed in an ecologically responsible way? It is well beyond the scope of this chapter or book to offer more detailed reflections on these subjects. My goal instead is to stimulate further thought on the intersections between the work society and various forms of oppression and social injustice. Notwithstanding the urgency of other contemporary social problems, criticizing and overcoming the work society is not a luxury or of secondary importance. To put it bluntly, freedom and justice depend on it.

NOTES

1. The Ends of Work

1. "Donald Trump's News Conference: Full Transcript and Video," *New York Times,* January 11, 2017, accessed January 20, 2017, https://www.nytimes.com/2017/01/11/us/politics/trump-press-conference-transcript.html.

2. Lauren Appelbaum, "Sanders: Full Employment Needed for All," *RespectAbility Report,* July 8, 2015, accessed January 20, 2017, http://therespectabilityreport.org/2015/07/08/sanders-full-employment-needed-for-all/.

3. "PM's Speech on the Fightback after the Riots," Cabinet Office and Prime Minister's Office, August 15, 2011, accessed February 15, 2013, http://www.number10.gov.uk/news/pms-speech-on-the-fightback-after-the-riots/.

4. Max Weber, *The Protestant Ethic and the Spirit of Capitalism,* trans. Talcott Parsons (New York: Routledge, 2002), 123.

5. Daniel T. Rogers, *The Work Ethic in Industrial America, 1850–1920* (Chicago: University of Chicago Press, 1979), 13.

6. Zygmunt Bauman, *Work, Consumerism, and the New Poor* (Maidenhead, UK: Open University Press, 2005), 20.

7. Judith Shklar, *American Citizenship: The Quest for Inclusion* (Cambridge, MA: Harvard University Press, 1991), 82.

8. Kathi Weeks, *The Problem with Work: Feminism, Marxism, Antiwork Politics, and Postwork Imaginaries* (Durham: Duke University Press, 2011), 46.

9. Ibid., 60.

10. Ibid., 52.

11. Shklar, *American Citizenship*, 3.

12. David Roediger, *The Wages of Whiteness: Race and the Making of the American Working Class* (London: Verso, 2007), 67, 81.

13. Nancy Fraser and Linda Gordon, "'A Genealogy of Dependency': Tracing a Keyword of the US Welfare State," in *Justice Interruptus: Critical Reflections on the "Postsocialist" Condition*, by Nancy Fraser (New York: Routledge, 1997), 126–29.

14. See Ulrich Beck, *The Brave New World of Work* (Cambridge: Polity, 2000).

15. Quoted in Sandro Mezzadra and Brett Neilson, *Border as Method, or, the Multiplication of Labor* (Durham: Duke University Press, 2013), 249.

16. Hence the British acronym NEET, which refers to sixteen- to twenty-four-year-olds who are "not in education, employment, or training."

17. Shklar, *American Citizenship*, 3.

18. Weeks, *Problem with Work*, 8.

19. Ibid., 109.

20. Ibid., 54.

21. Here I take inspiration from various thinkers, including Socrates, Jean-Paul Sartre, and poststructuralist thinkers like Jason Glynos and David Howarth; see Socrates's "Apology," in *The Trial and Death of Socrates*, by Plato, trans. G. M. A. Grube (Indianapolis: Hackett, 2000), 39; Jean-Paul Sartre, "Existentialism Is a Humanism," 1946, trans. Philip Mairet, accessed October 8, 2013, http://www.marxists.org/reference/archive/sartre/works/exist/sartre.htm; and Glynos and Howarth, *Logics of Critical Explanation in Social and Political Theory* (London: Routledge, 2007), 14.

22. Nikolas Rose, *Powers of Freedom: Reframing Political Thought* (Cambridge: Cambridge University Press, 1999), 59.

23. Hannah Arendt, *The Human Condition* (Chicago: University of Chicago Press, 1958), 5.

24. In articulating this position, I take inspiration from a range of authors, including: Monique Deveaux, *Gender and Justice in Multicultural Liberal States* (Oxford: Oxford University Press, 2006), chapter 6; John Stuart Mill, *On Liberty* (Indianapolis: Hackett, 1978); Rose, *Powers of Freedom*; Philippe Van Parijs, *Real Freedom for All: What (If Anything) Can Justify Capitalism?* (Oxford: Oxford University Press, 1995); and Iris Marion Young, *Justice and the Politics of Difference* (Princeton: Princeton University Press, 1990).

25. Friedrich A. Hayek, *The Constitution of Liberty* (Chicago: University of Chicago Press, 1960), 12.

26. See Isaiah Berlin, "Two Concepts of Liberty," in *Liberty: Isaiah Berlin*, ed. Henry Hardy (Oxford: Oxford University Press, 2002).

27. Chris Bertram, Corey Robin, and Alex Gourevitch, "Let It Bleed: Libertarianism and the Workplace," *Crooked Timber*, July 1, 2012, accessed September 24, 2014, http://crookedtimber.org/2012/07/01/let-it-bleed-libertarianism-and-the-workplace/.

28. Ibid.

29. Étienne Balibar, *Equaliberty: Political Essays*, trans. James Ingram (Durham: Duke University Press, 2014), 49.

30. In articulating justice in this manner, I have drawn from the arguments of Iris Young and Nancy Fraser; see Young, *Justice and the Politics of Difference*, and Nancy Fraser and Axel Honneth, *Redistribution or Recognition? A Political-Philosophical Exchange* (London: Verso, 2003).

31. See Young, *Justice and the Politics of Difference*, 55.

32. André Gorz adopts this view of "true" work in *Capitalism, Socialism, Ecology*, trans. Martin Chalmers (London: Verso, 2012), 55.

33. Giorgio Agamben, "What Is a Destituent Power?," trans. Stephanie Wakefield, *Environment and Planning D: Society and Space* 32 (2014): 69.

34. Arendt, *Human Condition*.

35. Ibid., 124.

36. Ibid., 12.

37. John Rawls, *A Theory of Justice* (Cambridge, MA: Harvard University Press, 1999), 4.

38. Jean-Luc Nancy, "Literary Communism," in *The Inoperative Community*, ed. Peter Connor, trans. Peter Connor, Lisa Garbus, Michael Holland, and Simona Sawhney (Minneapolis: University of Minnesota Press, 1991), 72.

2. The Work Society

1. "Transcript: Vice President Biden's Convention Speech," *National Public Radio*, September 6, 2012, accessed March 12, 2013, http://www.npr.org/2012/09/06/160713378/transcript-vice-president-bidens-convention-speech.

2. Gorz, *Farewell to the Working Class: An Essay on Post-Industrial Socialism*, trans. Michael Sonenscher (London: Pluto, 1982), 126.

3. Gorz, *Critique of Economic Reason*, trans. Gillian Handyside and Chris Turner (London: Verso, 1989), 219–20.

4. Gorz, *Farewell to the Working Class*, 1, 48; Gorz, *Paths to Paradise: On the Liberation from Work*, trans. Malcolm Imrie (London: Pluto, 1985), 53.

5. Gorz, *Critique of Economic Reason*, 13.

6. Ibid., 215n33.

7. Finn Bowring notes that Gorz "attributes ethical primacy to the autonomy of the individual" and that "it is the incomplete bonds which bind individuals to the social order—and thus our sense of alienation from that order—which enable us to exercise autonomous action and judgement"; Bowring, "André Gorz: Autonomy and Equity in the Post-Industrial Age," *Sociological Review* 53, no. 1 (2005): 135, 138.

8. Gorz, *Critique of Economic Reason*, 69–70.

9. Ibid., 70.

10. Ibid., 220–21.

11. Ibid., 69.

12. Ibid., 221.

13. Gorz, *Paths to Paradise*, 35.

14. Gorz, *Farewell to the Working Class*, 135, 136.

15. Gorz, *Paths to Paradise*, 35.

16. Gorz, *Farewell to the Working Class*, 136.

17. Gorz, *Critique of Economic Reason*, 119.

18. Ibid., 65.

19. Ibid., 66.

20. Ibid., 70.

21. Gorz, *Capitalism, Socialism, Ecology*, 46; emphasis added.

22. Gorz, *Critique of Economic Reason*, 70.

23. Gorz, *Capitalism, Socialism, Ecology*, 56.

24. Gorz, *Farewell to the Working Class*, 46.

25. Ibid., 80.

26. Gorz, *Capitalism, Socialism, Ecology*, 56.

27. In elaborating this unofficial version of ideology I am drawing from poststructuralist political theory, which treats ideology as ontological, rather than epistemological misrecognition; see, for example, Jason Glynos, "The Grip of Ideology: A Lacanian Approach to the Theory of Ideology," *Journal of Political Ideologies* 6, no. 2 (2001): 191, http://dx.doi.org/10.1080/13569310120053858.

28. Karl Marx, *Grundrisse: Foundations on the Critique of Political Economy*, trans. Martin Nicolaus (New York: Vintage, 1973), 245.

29. Gorz, *Critique of Economic Reason*, 140.

30. Ibid., 137.

31. Ibid., 138–39.

32. Ibid., 139.

33. Ibid., 135, 156–57.

34. Gorz, *Reclaiming Work: Beyond the Wage-Based Society*, trans. Chris Turner (Cambridge: Polity, 1999), 87. In this passage Gorz is in fact suggesting why a basic income needs to be unconditional, but the point equally applies to his concerns about the commodification of helping and caring activities.

35. Gorz, *Critique of Economic Reason*, 139.

36. Ibid., 206.

37. Ibid., 14.

38. Ibid., 140.

39. Ibid., 20.

40. Ibid., 139, 143, 145.

41. Gorz, *Reclaiming Work*, 52.

42. Gorz, *Critique of Economic Reason*, 207.

43. Ibid., 206–7.

44. Ibid., 207.

45. Ibid., 142, 6.

46. Gorz, *Capitalism, Socialism, Ecology*, 35.

47. Weeks, *Problem with Work*, 67.

48. Evelyn Nakano Glenn, "Creating a Caring Society," *Contemporary Sociology* 29, no. 1 (2000): 88.

49. I am grateful to Amy Allen for suggesting this formulation of my argument.

50. Gorz, *Farewell to the Working Class*, 3.

51. Gorz, *Critique of Economic Reason*, 70.

52. Gorz, *Capitalism, Socialism, Ecology*, 44–45.

53. Bauman, *Work, Consumerism, and the New Poor*, 2.

54. Gorz, *Reclaiming Work*, 58.

55. Gorz, *Capitalism, Socialism, Ecology*, 47.

56. Gorz, *Critique of Economic Reason*, 215n33, emphasis added.

57. Ibid., 32.

58. Ibid., 39.

59. Ibid., 42.

60. Ibid., 215n33.

61. Gorz, *Reclaiming Work*, 118.

62. Gorz, *Capitalism, Socialism, Ecology*, 24.

63. Gorz, *Reclaiming Work*, 55; emphasis added.

64. Gorz, *Paths to Paradise*, 64.

65. Gorz, *Reclaiming Work*, 117.

66. Gorz, *Critique of Economic Reason*, 160.

67. Gorz, *Paths to Paradise*, 64.

68. Bowring, "Misreading Gorz," *New Left Review*, no. 217 (1996): 102.

69. Inspired by Jean-Luc Nancy, I can say that Gorz's individualist social ontology leads to a form of togetherness as association, which in turn opens "a questioning about its own possibility and its own consistency." In other words, thinking of society in this manner opens the question of how, as Nancy puts it, "to associate those who seem not to want it or even to

reject it. Society then is what its members—the socii—have to accept and to justify"; Nancy, "Communism, the Word," in *The Idea of Communism*, ed. Costas Douzinas and Slavoj Žižek(London: Verso, 2010), 147.

70. Gorz, *Strategy for Labor: A Radical Proposal*, trans. Martin A. Nicolaus and Victoria Ortiz (Boston: Beacon, 1968), 128.

71. Gorz, *Critique of Economic Reason*, 123.

72. I am grateful to Keith Moser and Dylan Evans for confirming my suspicions on this matter.

73. Gorz, *Critique of Economic Reason*, 123.

74. Ibid., 124.

75. Nancy, *Being Singular Plural*, trans. Robert D. Richardson and Anne E. O'Bryne (Stanford: Stanford University Press, 2000), 56.

76. See Carole Pateman, *The Sexual Contract* (Stanford: Stanford University Press, 1988), 103. She notes that in Freud's *Moses and Monotheism* Freud himself calls "the pact made by the brothers after the murder of the father 'a sort of social contract.'"

77. Herbert Marcuse, *Eros and Civilization: A Philosophical Inquiry into Freud* (Boston: Beacon, 1974), 92.

78. Gorz, *Critique of Economic Reason*, 160.

79. Sigmund Freud, *Civilization and Its Discontents*, trans. James Strachey (New York: W. W. Norton, 2010), 42, 44–45, 43, 44.

80. Ibid., 45.

81. Ibid.

82. Ibid., 63.

83. Ibid., 48.

84. Ibid., 49n5.

85. Ibid., 79.

86. Ibid., 82, 90.

87. Ibid., 111.

88. Marcuse, *Eros and Civilization*, 82.

89. Ibid., 12.

90. Max Hastings, "Years of Liberal Dogma Have Spawned a Generation of Amoral, Uneducated, Welfare Dependent, Brutalised Youngsters," *Daily Mail*, August 12, 2011, accessed February 15, 2013, http://www.dailymail.co.uk/debate/article-2024284/UK-riots-2011-Liberal-dogma-spawned-generation-brutalised-youths.html.

91. Freud, *A General Introduction to Psychoanalysis*, quoted in Marcuse, *Eros and Civilization*, 17.

92. Marcuse, *Eros and Civilization*, 81, 3, 3.

93. Pateman, *Sexual Contract*, 25.

94. Freud, *Civilization and Its Discontents*, 63.

95. Marcuse, *Eros and Civilization*, 5.

96. Ibid., 37, 45, 44.

97. Nancy, "The Inoperative Community," in *The Inoperative Community*, 19.

98. John Rawls, *Theory of Justice*, 4.

3. Flexibility

1. Hélène Mulholland, "Senior Lib Dem and Unions Condemn Proposal to Scrap Unfair Dismissal," *Guardian*, October 26, 2011, accessed October 27, 2013, http://www.theguardian.com/politics/2011/oct/26/unions-condemn-report-unfair-dismissal.

2. Office of Scott Walker, "Reforms and Results," 1–2, accessed September 17, 2012, walker.wi.gov/Documents/Act_10_Success_Recap.pdf.

3. Nancy Fraser, *Scales of Justice: Reimagining Political Space in a Globalizing World* (New York: Columbia University Press, 2009), 129.

4. Christina Garsten and Jan Turtinen, " 'Angels' and 'Chameleon': The Cultural Construction of the Flexible Temporary Agency Worker in Sweden and Britain," in *After Full Employment: European Discourses on Work and Flexibility*, ed. Bo Stråth (Brussels: P. I. E. Peter Lang, 2000), 163.

5. Fraser, *Scales of Justice*, 125.

6. Noel Whiteside, "Britain and France in Comparison," in Stråth, *After Full Employment*, 129.

7. Jamie Peck and Adam Tickell, "Neoliberalizing Space," *Antipode* 34, no. 3 (2002): 382, http://dx.doi.org/10.1111/1467-8330.00247.

8. Lucio Baccaro and Chris Howell, "A Common Neoliberal Trajectory: The Transformation of Industrial Relations in Advanced Capitalism," *Politics and Society* 39, no. 4 (2001): 521–63, http://dx.doi.org/10.1177/0032329211420082. The authors define the general characteristics of the neoliberal project as it relates to industrial relations and discuss the movement toward fewer constraints on how employers manage workplaces, whether these constraints came originally in the form of laws or collective regulation.

9. Peck and Tickell, "Neoliberalizing Space," 384.

10. Beck, *Brave New World of Work*, 85.

11. Guy Standing, *Global Labour Flexibility: Seeking Distributive Justice* (Basingstoke: Macmillan, 1999), 59.

12. Peter Wagner. "The Exit from Organised Modernity: 'Flexibility' in Social Thought and in Historical Perspective," in Stråth, *After Full Employment*, 37.

13. Ibid.

14. Frances Fox Piven and Richard A. Cloward, "The Decline of Labor Parties," in *The Breaking of the American Social Compact*, by Frances Fox Piven and Richard A. Cloward (New York: New Press, 1997), 21, 34.

15. Steve Fleetwood, "Why Work-Life Balance Now?" *International Journal of Human Resource Management* 18, no. 3 (2007): 393, http://dx.doi.org/10.1080/09585190601167441.

16. Wagner, " 'Flexibility,' " 38.

17. Lorenzo E. Bernal-Verdugo, Davide Furceri, and Dominique Guillaume, "Labor Market Flexibility and Unemployment: New Empirical Evidence of Static and Dynamic Effects," International Monetary Fund Working Paper 12/64 (March 2012): 4, *accessed April 24, 2012, http://*www.imf.org/external/pubs/ft/wp/2012/wp1264.pdf.

18. Peter Miller and Nikolas Rose, "Production, Identity, and Democracy," *Theory and Society* 24, no. 3 (1995): 453, http://dx.doi.org/10.1007/BF00993353; see also David Harvey, *A Brief History of Neoliberalism* (Oxford: Oxford University Press, 2005), 53.

19. Thomas Frank, *One Market under God* (New York: Anchor, 2000), 31.

20. See Peck and Tickell, "Neoliberalizing Space."

21. Chris Howell, "The Changing Relationship between Labor and the State in Contemporary Capitalism," *Law, Culture and the Humanities* 12 (2012): 3, 7–8, http://dx.doi.org/10.1177/1743872112448362.

22. Jack Fiorito, "The State of Unions in the United States," *Journal of Labor Research* 28, no. 1 (2007): 47, accessed October 29, 2013, http://connection.ebscohost.com/c/articles/2381 5043/state-unions-united-states.

23. Henry F. Farber and Bruce Western, "Ronald Reagan and the Politics of Declining Union Organization," *British Journal of Industrial Relations* 40, no. 3 (2002): 385, http://dx.doi.org/10.1111/1467-8543.00240.

24. Sandra Fredman, "The New Rights: Labour Law and Ideology in the Thatcher Years," *Oxford Journal of Legal Studies* 12, no. 1 (1992): 33–36, http://dx.doi.org/10.1093/ojls/12.1.24.

25. "State Right-to-Work Laws and Constitutional Amendments in Effect as of January 1, 2009 With Year of Passage," US Department of Labor, December 2008, accessed November 12, 2012, http://www.dol.gov/whd/state/righttowork.htm#.UKFCBIXOZV4.

26. Ashley Woods and David Sands, " 'Right to Work' Michigan: Gov. Rick Snyder Says New Legislation Gives Union Workers 'Freedom,' " *Huffington Post*, December 6, 2012, accessed December 18, 2012, http://www.huffingtonpost.com/2012/12/06/right-to-work-michigan-snyder-unions_n_2250601.html.

27. Timothy Mclaughlin, "U.S. Appeals Court Upholds Wisconsin 'Right-to-Work' Law," Reuters, July 12, 2017, accessed August 11, 2017, http://www.reuters.com/article/us-wisconsin-labor-idUSKBN19X34T.

28. Nicole Pasulka, "Right-to-Work Laws, Explained," *Mother Jones*, March 16, 2012.

29. "Reforms and Results," 1–2.

30. State of Wisconsin, 2011–12 Legislature, January 2011 Special Session, Senate Bill 11 (2011): 2, accessed September 17, 2012, docs.legis.wisconsin.gov/document/proposaltext/2011/JR1/SB11.pdf.

31. "Reforms and Results," 5–6.

32. Steven Greenhouse, "Wisconsin's Legacy for Unions," *New York Times*, February 22, 2014, accessed October 14, 2014, http://www.nytimes.com/2014/02/23/business/wisconsins-legacy-for-unions.html?_r=0.

33. Farber and Western, "Ronald Reagan," 392–93.

34. *NLRB v. Mackay Radio and Telegraph Co.*, 304 U.S. 333 (1938); see Fiorito, "State of Unions," 47.

35. Farber and Western, "Ronald Reagan," 394.

36. Clare Beckett, *Thatcher* (London: Haus, 2006), 76–77.

37. Nicola Countouris and Mark Freedland, "Injunctions, *Cyanamid*, and the Corrosion of the Right to Strike in the UK," UCL Labour Rights Institute On-Line Working Papers, *LRI WP* 1/2010, accessed October 27, 2013, http://www.ucl.ac.uk/laws/lri/papers/Injunctions_Cyanamid_the-corrosion-of-the-right-to-strike-in-the-UK.pdf.

38. Fredman, "New Rights," 35–36.

39. Countouris and Freedland, "Injunctions," 5, 7.

40. Chris Howell, "From New Labour to No Labour?," *New Political Science* 22, no. 2 (2010): 221–22.

41. The Employment Act (2002) provides this right for parents of children under six years old and of disabled children under eighteen years old. In 2007 this right was extended to parents of children under seventeen and of caregivers of disabled people over eighteen, while in 2009 all parents of children under seventeen could claim the right; see Advisory, Conciliation and Arbitration Service, "Acas Consultation on: Draft Code of Practice on the Extended Right to Request Flexible Working" (February 2013): 3, accessed October 27, 2013, http://www.acas.org.uk/media/pdf/2/r/Consultation_draft_COP_FW.pdf.

42. Greenhouse, "A Push to Give Steadier Shifts to Part-Timers," *New York Times*, July 15, 2014, accessed October 14, 2014, http://www.nytimes.com/2014/07/16/business/a-push-to-give-steadier-shifts-to-part-timers.html.

43. US Congress, "Summary: H.R.5159—Schedules That Work Act," n.d., accessed June 24, 2016, https://www.congress.gov/bill/113th-congress/house-bill/5159; "Summary: S.1772–14th Congress (2015–2016), n.d., accessed June 2, 2016, https://www.congress.gov/bill/114th-congress/senate-bill/1772.

44. US Congress, "S. 1772: Schedules that Work Act," Section 1, paragraph 9, accessed June 24, 2016, https://www.congress.gov/bill/114th-congress/senate-bill/1772/text.

45. Paul Willman and Alex Bryson, "Union Organization in Great Britain," *Journal of Labor Research* 28, no. 1 (2007): 102, http://web.ebscohost.com/ehost/detail?vid=3&si d=87414c4a-e116-4482-92ac-d14a909772d3%40sessionmgr10&hid=25&bdata=JnNpdG U9ZWhvc3QtbGl2ZQ%3d%3d#db=bth&AN=23815053.

46. Explanatory Note to the Unfair Dismissal and Statement of Reasons for Dismissal (Variation of Qualifying Period) Order 2012, accessed November 5, 2012, http://www.legis lation.gov.uk/uksi/2012/989/note/made.

47. Damian Grimshaw and Jill Rubery, "The End of the UK's Liberal Collectivist Social Model? The Implications of the Coalition Government's Policy during the Austerity Crisis," *Cambridge Journal of Economics* 36, no. 1 (2012): 111, http://dx.doi.org/10.1093/cje/ber033.

48. Michael J. Piore and Sean Safford, "Changing Regimes of Workplace Governance, Shifting Axes of Social Mobilization, and the Challenge to Industrial Relations Theory," *Industrial Relations: A Journal of Economy and Society* 35, no. 3 (2006): 300–302, http://dx.doi.org/10.1111/j.1468-232X.2006.00439.x.

49. Stephen F. Befort, "Labor and Employment Law at the Millennium: A Historical Review and Critical Assessment," *Boston College Law Review* 43 (2001): 380, accessed October 29, 2013, http://lawdigitalcommons.bc.edu/cgi/viewcontent.cgi?article=2201&context=bclr.

50. Baccaro and Howell, "Common Neoliberal Trajectory." Guy Standing calls this form of flexibility "subordinated" and notes that it requires workers to be more adaptable, a theme I explore in greater detail later. Liberating flexibility, on the other hand, gives workers more freedom to pursue diverse lifestyles and in this sense corresponds with employee-friendly flexibility, to be discussed later; Standing, *Beyond the New Paternalism: Basic Security as Equality* (London: Verso, 2002), 6. My analysis complicates this dichotomy, however, by showing that the broader regime of flexibility induces a subtle form of domination even for more privileged workers who enjoy liberating flexibility.

51. The four forms of flexibility discussed here are set out in Marino Regini, "The Dilemmas of Labour Market Regulation," in *Why Deregulate Labour Markets?*, ed. Gosta Esping-Andersen and Marino Regini (Oxford: Oxford University Press, 2000), 16–17.

52. Standing, *Beyond the New Paternalism*, 33.

53. Standing, "Global Feminization through Flexible Labour: A Theme Revisited," *World Development* 27, no. 3 (1999): 583, accessed October 29, 2013, http://www.guystanding.com/files/documents/Global_Feminization_Through_Flexible_Labor_-_theme_revisited.pdf.

54. Fleetwood, "Why Work-Life Balance Now?," 389.

55. Greenhouse, "A Part-Time Life, as Hours Shrink and Shift," *New York Times*, October 28, 2012.

56. Committee on Education and the Workforce, "The Schedules That Work Act (H.R. 5159)," n.d., accessed October 15, 2014, http://democrats.edworkforce.house.gov/bill/schedules-work-act; Greenhouse, "Push to Give Steadier Shifts to Part-Timers"; Jana Kasperkevic, "Elizabeth Warren to Help Propose Senate Bill to Tackle Part-Time Schedules," *Guardian*, July 23, 2014, accessed October 15, 2014, http://www.theguardian.com/money/us-money-blog/2014/jul/23/elizabeth-warren-senate-bill-part-time-schedules.

57. Fleetwood, "Why Work-Life Balance Now?," 389.

58. Alison Maitland and Peter Thomson, *Future Work: How Businesses Can Adapt and Thrive in the New World of Work* (New York: Palgrave Macmillan, 2011), 21.

59. Fleetwood, "Why Work-Life Balance Now?," 389.

60. Equal Opportunities Commission, "Enter the Timelords: Transforming Work to Meet the Future" (2007): 10, *accessed September 29, 2012*, http://www.bitc.org.uk/document.rm?id=8625.

61. Maitland and Thomson, *Future Work*, 4.

62. Ibid., 36.

63. See Ulrich Beck, *Risk Society* (London: Sage, 1992).

64. Maitland and Thomson, *Future Work*, 43, 45.

65. Garsten and Turtinen, "'Angels' and 'Chameleon,'" 181.

66. See Louise Amoore, "Risk, Reward, and Discipline at Work," *Economy and Society* 33, no. 2 (2004): 176, http://dx.doi.org/10.1080/03085140410001677111.

67. As Karl Marx famously quipped, the sphere within which labor power is bought and sold is a "very Eden of the innate rights of man. There alone rule Freedom, Property and Bentham"; Marx, *Capital: A Critique of Political Economy*, trans. Samuel Moore and Edward Aveling, ed. Frederick Engels (New York: International Publishers, 1967), 1:176.

68. See Laura E. Lyons, "'I'd Like My Life Back': Corporate Personhood and the BP Oil Disaster," *Biography: An Interdisciplinary Quarterly* 34, no. 1 (2011): 96–107, http://dx.doi.org/10.1353/bio.2011.0012.

69. Andrew Ross, *Nice Work If You Can Get It: Life and Labor in Precarious Times* (New York: New York University Press, 2009), 5.

70. Here I adapt Will Kymlicka's discussion of alienation in his *Contemporary Political Philosophy* (Oxford: Clarendon, 1990), 188–89.

71. For a similar argument, see Standing, *The Precariat: The New Dangerous Class* (London: Bloomsbury Academic, 2011), 126.

72. Tom Rath, *Strengths Finder 2.0* (New York: Gallup, 2007), 45.

73. Ibid., 46.

74. Standing, *Beyond the New Paternalism*, 50.

75. Colin Cremin, *Capitalism's New Clothes: Enterprise, Ethics, and Enjoyment in Times of Crisis* (London: Pluto, 2011), 45–46.

76. Ibid., 44.

77. Paolo Virno, "The Ambivalence of Disenchantment," in *Radical Thought in Italy: A Potential Politics*, ed. Paolo Virno and Michael Hardt (Minneapolis: University of Minnesota Press, 1996), 17.

78. Rose, *Powers of Freedom*, 161.

79. Ken Kamoche, Mary Pang, and Amy L. Y. Wong, "Career Development and Knowledge Appropriation: A Genealogical Critique," *Organization Studies* 32, no. 12 (2011): 1671, http://dx.doi.org/10.1177/0170840611421249.

80. Executive Office of the President, Council of Economic Advisers, "Work-Life Balance and the Economics of Workplace Flexibility" (2010), accessed September 4, 2012, http://www.whitehouse.gov/blog/2010/03/31/economics-workplace-flexibility.

81. Cremin, *Capitalism's New Clothes*, 34, 42.

82. Michel Foucault, *The Birth of Biopolitics: Lectures at the Collège de France, 1978–79*, ed. Michel Senellart, trans. Graham Burchell (New York: Palgrave Macmillan, 2008), 24–25.

83. Ibid., 226.

84. Miller and Rose, "Production, Identity, and Democracy," 455.

85. The term "entreployee" was first coined by Hans J. Pongratz and G. Günter Voß; see Martin Hartmann and Axel Honneth, "Paradoxes of Capitalism," *Constellations* 13, no. 1 (2006): 45, http://dx.doi.org/10.1111/j.1351-0487.2006.00439.x.

86. Maitland and Thomson, *Future Work*, 45.

87. Scott Lash and John Urry, *Economies of Signs and Space* (London: Sage, 1994), 122.

88. Piore and Safford, "Changing Regimes of Workplace Governance," 311.

89. Sharon Beder, *Selling the Work Ethic: From Puritan Pulpit to Corporate PR* (London: Zed, 2000), 108.

90. Gorz, *Critique of Economic Reason*, 59.

91. Nigel Thrift, *Knowing Capitalism* (London: Sage, 2005), 33.

92. Equal Opportunities Commission, "Enter the Timelords," 11.

93. Weeks, *Problem with Work*, 70.

94. See Lisa Adkins and Celia Lury, "The Labour of Identity: Performing Identities, Performing Economies," *Economy and Society* 4 (1999): 600, http://dx.doi.org/10.1080/03085149900000020.

95. Executive Office of the President, Council of Economic Advisers, "Work-Life Balance and the Economics of Workplace Flexibility."

96. Iris Marion Young, *Justice and the Politics of Difference* (Princeton: Princeton University Press, 1990), 57.

97. On the basis of data from ninety-seven countries (including the United Kingdom and the United States) between 1980 and 2008, the IMF argues that "policies aimed at increasing labor market flexibility *may* have an important effect in reducing unemployment" (emphasis added); Bernal-Verdugo, Furceri, and Guillaume, "Labor Market Flexibility and Unemployment," 4.

98. See Simon Deakin and Hannah Reed, "Britain—River Crossing or Cold Bath?," in Esping-Andersen and Regini, *Why Deregulate Labour Markets?*, 141.

99. Robert Perrucci and Earl Wysong, *The New Class Society: Goodbye American Dream?* (Lanham, MD: Rowman and Littlefield, 2003), xii, 48.

100. Harvey, *Spaces of Global Capitalism: Towards a Theory of Uneven Geographical Development* (London: Verso, 2006), 42.

101. Michael Hardt and Antonio Negri, *Commonwealth* (Cambridge, MA: Harvard University Press, 2009), 133.

102. Standing, "Global Feminization through Flexible Labour, 599–600.

103. Hardt and Negri, *Commonwealth*, 133–34.

104. Standing, "Global Feminization," 583.

105. Fraser, "After the Family Wage: Wage Equity and the Welfare State," *Political Theory* 22, no. 4 (1994): 611.

106. Kim England, "Home, Work, and the Shifting Geographies of Care," *Ethics, Place and Environment*, 13, no. 2 (2010): 132; see also Glenn, "Creating a Caring Society." Glenn points out that other factors driving the crisis include "increased longevity and medical advances" (84).

107. Fraser, "Feminism, Capitalism, and the Cunning of History," *New Left Review*, no. 56 (2009): 99–100; see also Joan C. Tronto, *Caring Democracy: Markets, Equality, and Justice* (New York: New York University Press, 2013), 82.

108. Fraser, "Feminism, Capitalism, and the Cunning of History," 105, 111.

109. Fraser, "After the Family Wage," 601.

110. Ibid., 605.

111. Nancy Fraser and Jo Littler, "The Fortunes of Socialist Feminism: Jo Littler Interviews Nancy Fraser," *Soundings: A Journal of Politics and Culture* 58 (2014–15): 21.

112. Tronto, *Caring Democracy*, 40.

113. Ibid., 89.

114. Jennifer Glass, Robin W. Simon, and Matthew A. Andersson, "Parenthood and Happiness: Effects of Work-Family Reconciliation Policies in 22 OECD Countries," *American Journal of Sociology* 122, no. 3 (2016): 886–929.

115. Diane Elson, "Market Socialism or Socialization of the Market," *New Left Review* 1, no. 172 (November–December 1988): 17.

116. Tronto, *Caring Democracy*, 101, 106.

117. Glass et al., "Parenthood and Happiness."

118. Glenn, "Creating a Caring Society," 88, 93.

119. Amna Silim and Alfie Stirling, "Women and Flexible Working: Improving Female Employment Outcomes in Europe," *Institute of Public Policy Research*, December 2014, accessed June 30, 2016, http://www.ippr.org/publications/women-and-flexible-working-improving-female-employment-outcomes-in-europe.

120. Chartered Institute of Personnel and Development, "Flexible Working Provision and Uptake," May 2012, accessed June 30, 2016, http://www.cipd.co.uk/hr-resources/survey-reports/flexible-working-provision-uptake.aspx, 16.

121. US Department of Labor, "Women of Working Age," n.d., accessed July 21, 2016, https://www.dol.gov/wb/stats/latest_annual_data.htm.

122. Van Parijs, *Real Freedom for All*, 222–23.

123. Beck, *Brave New World of Work*, 58. As we will see in chapter 4, the term "multi-activity society" is also used by André Gorz in *Reclaiming Work*.

124. See Weeks, *Problem with Work*, 138.

125. Tony Fitzpatrick, *Freedom and Security: An Introduction to the Basic Income Debate* (Basingstoke: Macmillan, 1999), 5.

4. Unconditional Basic Income

1. Peter S. Goodman, "Free Cash in Finland. Must Be Jobless." *New York Times*, December 17, 2016, accessed January 13, 2017, https://www.nytimes.com/2016/12/17/business/economy/universal-basic-income-finland.html; James Surowiecki, "The Case for Free Money: Why Don't We Have Universal Basic Income?" *New Yorker*, June 20, 2016, accessed January 13, 2017, http://www.newyorker.com/magazine/2016/06/20/why-dont-we-have-universal-basic-income; Gleb Tsipursky, "Free Money Is Not So Funny Anymore: Confessions of a (Former) Skeptic of Basic Income," *Salon*, August 21, 2016, accessed January 13, 2017, http://www.salon.com/2016/08/21/free-money-is-not-so-funny-anymore-confessions-of-a-former-skeptic-of-basic-income/.

2. Fitzpatrick, *Freedom and Security*, 5.

3. See Carole Pateman, "Democratizing Citizenship: Some Advantages of a Basic Income," in *Redesigning Distribution: Basic Income and Stakeholder Grants as Cornerstones for an Egalitarian Capitalism*, ed. Erik Olin Wright (London: Verso, 2006), 102.

4. Quoted in Ben Kentish, "Finland to Begin Paying Basic Income to Unemployed Citizens," *Independent*, December 23, 2016, accessed January 13, 2017, http://www.independent.co.uk/news/world/europe/finland-universal-basic-income-ubi-citizens-560-euros-monthly-job-poverty-unemployment-a7492911.html.

5. Kela, "Objectives and Implementation of the Basic Income Experiment," January 13, 2017, accessed January 13, 2017, http://www.kela.fi/web/en/basic-income-objectives-and-implementation.

6. Rutger Bregman, "Why We Should Give Free Money to Everyone," *DutchNews.nl*, April 21, 2016, accessed January 13, 2017, http://www.dutchnews.nl/features/2016/04/why-we-should-give-free-money-to-everyone/.

7. See, for example, Gina-Marie Cheeseman, "The Case for Universal Basic Income," *Triple Pundit*, April 29, 2016, accessed January 13, 2017, http://www.triplepundit.com/2016/04/ngo-givedirectly-experiments-with-basic-income-cash-transfers-in-kenya/.

8. For an excellent overview of the points of agreement between the basic income and a variety of ideologies, see Fitzpatrick, *Freedom and Security*.

9. Although Nancy Fraser suggests that in a "neoliberal regime" the basic income would "subsidize employers of low-wage, temporary labor and possibly depress wages overall," she claims that in a social democracy it could transform the relations between capital and

labor and men and women alike. This would qualify as a nonreformist reform, then, since despite "leaving intact the deep structure of capitalist property rights," it could "set in motion a trajectory of change in which more radical reforms become practicable over time"; Fraser, "Social Justice in the Age of Identity Politics: Redistribution, Recognition, and Participation," in *Redistribution or Recognition? A Political-Philosophical Exchange*, by Nancy Fraser and Axel Honneth (London: Verso, 2003), 78, 79. For a discussion of nonreformist reforms, see Gorz, *Strategy for Labor*, 7.

10. Erik Olin Wright, "Basic Income as a Socialist Project" (paper presented at the annual US-BIG Congress, New York, March 4–6, 2005), 3, accessed October 29, 2013, http://www.ssc.wisc.edu/~wright/Basic%20Income%20as%20a%20Socialist%20Project.pdf.

11. Robert Van der Veen and Philippe Van Parijs, "A Capitalist Road to Communism," *Theory and Society* 15, no. 5 (1986): 635–55, accessed October 29, 2013, http://www.ssc.wisc.edu/~wright/ERU_files/PVP-cap-road.pdf.

12. Herbert Marcuse, *One-Dimensional Man* (Boston: Beacon, 1964), xliii.

13. In asking whether the basic income is within reach, I refer to Marcuse's formulation of historical alternatives, but it is a curious coincidence that Philippe Van Parijs claims, in strikingly Marcusean language, that "the idea of a totally unconditional income rekindles the hope that not all major steps towards the emancipation of mankind are behind us: another one [the basic income] is within reach"; Van Parijs, "Competing Justifications of Basic Income," in *Arguing for Basic Income: Ethical Foundations for a Radical Reform*, ed. Philippe Van Parijs (London: Verso, 1992), 7.

14. Weeks, *Problem with Work*, 138.

15. Fitzpatrick, *Freedom and Security*, 38–39.

16. Van Parijs, "The Worldwide March to Basic Income: Thank You Switzerland!" *Basic Income Earth Network*, June 6, 2016, accessed January 25, 2017, http://basicincome.org/news/2016/06/the-worldwide-march-to-basic-income-thank-you-switzerland/.

17. Ibid., 66.

18. Gorz, *Reclaiming Work*, 83.

19. Ibid.

20. See Anthony Giddens, *The Consequences of Modernity* (Stanford: Stanford University Press, 1990), 3; and J. K. Gibson-Graham, *A Postcapitalist Politics* (Minneapolis: University of Minnesota Press, 2006), 59.

21. Van Parijs, "Basic Income: A Simple and Powerful Idea of the Twenty-First Century," *Politics and Society* 32, no. 1 (2004): 11, http://dx.doi.org/10.1177/0032329203261095.

22. Due to constraints of space, I do not analyze the US Earned Income Tax Credits or its British counterpart, the Working Tax Credit. It is worth noting that the basic income would effectively combine this form of fiscal welfare with so-called state welfare, which provides cash transfers; Fitzpatrick, *Freedom and Security*, 25. Moreover, both tax credits and the basic income function as a subsidy to employees, with the crucial distinction that the former is paid only to those in work; Van Parijs, "A Basic Income for All," in *What's Wrong with a Free Lunch?*, ed. Joshua Cohen and Joel Rogers (Boston, MA: Beacon, 2001), 18.

23. Van Parijs, "Basic Income," 11.

24. Standing, *Beyond the New Paternalism*, 130. For a classic account of the regulation of economic and political behavior by relief programs, see Piven and Cloward, *Regulating the Poor: The Functions of Public Welfare* (New York: Vintage, 1993).

25. See Fraser, "Can Society Be Commodities All the Way Down? Polyanian Reflections on the Capitalist Crisis," *Fondations Maison des Sciences de l'Homme* 18 (2012), accessed October 29, 2013, http://hal.archives-ouvertes.fr/docs/00/72/50/60/PDF/FMSH-WP-2012-18_Fraser2.pdf.

26. Fred Block, "Towards a New Understanding of Economic Modernity," in *The Economy as a Polity: The Political Constitution of Contemporary Capitalism*, ed. Christian Joerges, Bo Stråth, and Peter Wagner (London: UCL, 2005), 8.

27. Standing, *Beyond the New Paternalism*, 127, 131.

28. William Walters, *Unemployment and Government: Genealogies of the Social* (Cambridge: Cambridge University Press, 2000), 58, 57.

29. Ibid., 131, 124; Stråth and Peter Wagner, "After Full Employment: Theoretical and Political Implications," in Stråth, *After Full Employment*, 261.

30. Robert C. Lieberman, *Shifting the Color Line: Race and the American Welfare State* (Cambridge, MA.: Harvard University Press, 1998), 213.

31. Walters, *Unemployment and Government*, 58–59.

32. Rose, "The Death of the Social? Re-figuring the Territory of Government," *Economy and Society* 25, no. 3 (1996): 333, http://dx.doi.org/10.1080/03085149600000018.

33. Ibid., 334.

34. Ceren Özselçuka and Yahya M. Madra, "Enjoyment as an Economic Factor: Reading Marx with Lacan," *Subjectivity* 3, no. 3 (2010): 330, http://dx.doi.org/10.1057/sub.2010.13.

35. Glynos, "Ideological Fantasy at Work," *Journal of Political Ideologies* 13, no. 3 (2008): 283, http://dx.doi.org/10.1080/13569310802376961.

36. Standing, *Beyond the New Paternalism*, 156–57.

37. European Citizens' Initiative for an Unconditional Basic Income, "Annex," 3, accessed October 29, 2013, http://basicincome2013.eu/ubi/wp-content/uploads/2013/01/Full_Annex_ECI_unconditionnal-basic-income-2.pdf.

38. Basic Income Earth Network, "About Basic Income" (2008), accessed May 22, 2013, http://basicincome.org/bien/aboutbasicincome.html.

39. Claus Offe, "Basic Income and the Labor Contract," *Analyse and Kritik* 1 (2009): 77, accessed October 29, 2013, http://www.analyse-und-kritik.net/2009-1/AK_Offe_2009.pdf.

40. Van Parijs, "Basic Income for All," 16–18.

41. Glynos and Yannis Stavrakakis, "Lacan and Political Subjectivity: Fantasy and Enjoyment in Psychoanalysis and Political Theory," *Subjectivity* 24 (2008): 265, http://dx.doi.org/10.1057/sub.2008.23.

42. Glynos and Howarth, *Logics of Critical Explanation*, 107.

43. Glynos, "Ideological Fantasy at Work," 276, 283, 195, 191.

44. Glynos and Stavrakakis, "Lacan and Political Subjectivity," 261, 262.

45. Simon Critchley and Oliver Marchart, "Introduction," in *Laclau: A Critical Reader*, ed. Simon Critchley and Oliver Marchart (Abingdon, Oxon: Routledge, 2004), 4.

46. Pateman, "Democratizing Citizenship," 90.

47. Van Parijs, *Real Freedom for All*, 33–34.

48. Van Parijs, "Basic Income for All," 19.

49. Offe, "Basic Income and the Labor Contract," 65.

50. Pateman, "Democracy, Human Rights and a Basic Income in a Global Era," 8.

51. Fraser, "Social Justice in the Age of Identity Politics," 79.

52. Ingrid Robeyns, "Is Nancy Fraser's Critique of Theories of Distributive Justice Justified?" *Constellations* 10, no. 4 (2003): 542, http://dx.doi.org/10.1046/j.1351-0487.2003.00352.x.

53. Fraser, "Social Justice in the Age of Identity Politics," 65.

54. See Axel Honneth, "Redistribution as Recognition: A Response to Nancy Fraser," trans. Joel Golb, James Ingram, and Christiane Wilke, in Fraser and Honneth, *Redistribution or Recognition?*, 141. As I argue elsewhere, however, Honneth's theory pays insufficient attention to race and citizenship status; James A. Chamberlain, "Recognition and Social Justice: What Critical Theory Can Learn from Paid Domestic Laborers in the United States,"

New Political Science 35, no. 2 (2013): 197, http://dx.doi.org/10.1080/07393148.2013.7
90698.

55. Glynos, "Ideological Fantasy at Work," 291.

56. Ibid., 290.

57. Glynos, "Ideological Fantasy at Work," 291, 290, 291.

58. Weeks, *Problem with Work*, 99, 146.

59. Gorz, *Reclaiming Work*, 83.

60. Ute Fischer et al., "Freedom, Not Full Employment," trans. Marc Batko and Axel
Jansen, Freiheit statt Vollbeschäftigung, June 24, 2005, accessed May 28, 2013, http://www.
freiheitstattvollbeschaeftigung.de/en/theses.

61. Walters, *Unemployment and Government*, 73.

62. Lieberman, *Shifting the Color Line*, 182.

63. Joel Handler, *Social Citizenship and Workfare in the United States and Western Europe: The Paradox of Inclusion* (Cambridge: Cambridge University Press, 2004), 2.

64. Fitzpatrick, *Freedom and Security*, 4.

65. Walters, *Unemployment and Government*, 61, 63.

66. Ibid., 63.

67. Lieberman, *Shifting the Color Line*, 180–81, 206, 213; Michael White, *Against Unemployment* (London: Policy Studies Institute, 1991), 23.

68. Fitzpatrick, *Freedom and Security*, 110; White, *Against Unemployment*, 24. In the
United States, these requirements have restricted access to African Americans, for example,
owing to their higher levels and longer durations of unemployment and often precarious position within the labor market; Lieberman, *Shifting the Color Line*, 206.

69. Pateman, "Democratizing Citizenship," 111.

70. T. H. Marshall, "Citizenship and Social Class," in *Inequality and Society*, ed. Jeff
Manzer and Michael Sauder (1950; repr. New York: W. W. Norton, 2009), 149.

71. Ibid., 149–50.

72. Ibid., 149, 152, emphasis added.

73. Fraser, "A Triple Movement? Parsing the Politics of Crisis after Polanyi," *New Left
Review* 81 (May–June 2013): 127, accessed October 29, 2013, http://newleftreview.org/II/81/
nancy-fraser-a-triple-movement.

74. Fitzpatrick, *Freedom and Security*, 46.

75. Elizabeth Anderson, "Optional Freedoms," in Van Parijs et al., *What's Wrong with
a Free Lunch?*, 72.

76. Offe, "Basic Income and the Labor Contract," 63.

77. Gorz, *Critique of Economic Reason*, 207.

78. Gorz, *Reclaiming Work*, 86, 87.

79. Handler, *Social Citizenship and Workfare*, 5, 2.

80. Jamie Peck, *Workfare States* (New York: Guildford, 2001), 10.

81. Even though some proponents recognize the need to retain some means-tested benefits for people with special needs; see Fitzpatrick, *Freedom and Security*, 39.

82. Standing, *Beyond the New Paternalism*, 125, 131.

83. Handler, *Social Citizenship and Workfare*, 2–7.

84. Walters, *Unemployment and Government*, 124. In 2011 the Coalition government
replaced earlier programs such as the New Deal with its "payment for results" Work Programme, a welfare-to-work scheme delivered by "a range of private, public, and voluntary
sector organisations." According to the government, it "combines strong long-term incentives
with freedom for service providers to innovate"; Department for Work and Pensions, "The
Work Programme," (2012) accessed June 28, 2013, http://webarchive.nationalarchives.gov.

uk/+/http://www.dwp.gov.uk/docs/the-work-programme.pdf. I do not consider the details of the Work Programme itself here, since my argument centers on the broader logic of workfare, which the Work Programme also embodies.

85. Walters, *Unemployment and Government*, 127.

86. Herbert J. Gans, *The War against the Poor: The Underclass and Antipoverty Policy* (New York: Basic Books, 1995), 27–29.

87. Fraser and Gordon, "Genealogy of Dependency," 121.

88. Ruth Levitas, *The Inclusive Society? Social Exclusion and New Labour* (Basingstoke: Palgrave Macmillan, 2005), 7.

89. Rose, *Powers of Freedom*, 266.

90. William Galston, "What about Reciprocity?" in Van Parijs et al., *What's Wrong with a Free Lunch?*, 31.

91. Here I modify slightly Dominique Meda's response to the "incentive" objection, discussed by Gorz, in *Reclaiming Work*, 98.

92. Robert M. Solow, "Guess Who Likes Workfare," in *Work and Welfare*, ed. Amy Gutmann (Princeton: Princeton University Press, 1998), 5.

93. Amy Gutmann, "Introduction," in Gutmann, *Work and Welfare*, x.

94. Gorz, *Critique of Economic Reason*, 205.

95. Ibid., 207.

96. M. David Forrest, "Consensus and Crisis: Representing the Poor in the Post-Civil Rights Era," *New Political Science* 35, no. 1 (2013): 20, http://dx.doi.org/10.1080/07393148.2012.754667.

97. Rose, *Powers of Freedom*, 267.

98. Charles M. A. Clark and Catherine Kavanagh, "Basic Income, Inequality and Unemployment: Rethinking the Linkage between Work and Welfare," *Journal of Economic Issues* 30, no. 2 (1996): 401, http://www.jstor.org/stable/4452238.

99. Offe, "Basic Income and the Labor Contract," 73.

100. Fitzpatrick, *Freedom and Security*, 113.

101. Ibid., 84–85.

102. Clark and Kavanagh, "Basic Income, Inequality and Unemployment," 401.

103. Offe, "Basic Income and the Labor Contract," 73.

104. Walters, *Unemployment and Government*, 140.

105. Office of Family Assistance, "About TANF," accessed October 30, 2013, http://www.acf.hhs.gov/programs/ofa/programs/tanf/about.

106. Department for Work and Pensions and HM Treasury, "Helping People to Find and Stay in Work," August 8, 2013, accessed September 24, 2013, https://www.gov.uk/government/policies/helping-people-to-find-and-stay-in-work/supporting-pages/managing-the-work-programme.

107. Rose, "Death of the Social?," 339.

108. Walters, *Unemployment and Government*, 138.

109. Mitchell Dean, "Governing the Unemployed Self in an Active Society," *Economy and Society* 24, no. 4 (1995): 563, http://dx.doi.org/10.1080/03085149500000025.

110. Ibid.

111. Offe, "Basic Income and the Labor Contract," 73.

112. Gorz, *Reclaiming Work*, 80.

113. Van der Veen and Van Parijs, "Capitalist Road to Communism," 647.

114. Ibid., 651.

115. Van Parijs, *Real Freedom for All*, 5.

116. Ibid., 25.

117. Ibid., 23.

118. Foucault, "The Subject and Power," *Critical Inquiry* 8, no. 4 (1982): 791–92, http://dx.doi.org/10.1086/448181.

119. As Balibar puts it, equality is the "general form of the radical negation of all subjection and all mastery" or "the liberation of freedom itself" from that which would pervert it; Balibar, *Equaliberty*, 49.

120. Weber, *Protestant Ethic*, 123.

121. Ibid., 124.

5. Community beyond Work

1. Weeks, *Problem with Work*, 204, 219.

2. Hardt and Negri refer to "the common," whereas Gorz uses the more conventional "commons"; see Gorz, *The Immaterial: Knowledge, Value and Capital*, trans. Chris Turner (London: Seagull, 2010), 97. Although the concept is much less pronounced in Gorz's work, the general idea that contemporary capitalism exploits socially produced forms of common wealth is clearly present.

3. Gorz, *Immaterial*, 110, 9, 13.

4. Ibid., 52–53.

5. Ibid., 54.

6. Ibid., 9, 35.

7. Ibid., 54.

8. Ibid., 55.

9. Hardt and Negri, *Commonwealth*, 139; see also 153.

10. Hardt and Negri, *Multitude: War and Democracy in the Age of Empire* (New York: Penguin, 2004), 114.

11. Hardt and Negri, *Commonwealth*, 286, 287.

12. Gorz, *Immaterial*, 9; emphasis added.

13. Hardt and Negri, *Multitude*, 107, 114, 115. For a similar point, see Gorz, *Immaterial*, 73.

14. Gorz, *Immaterial*, 109–10.

15. Gorz, *Strategy for Labor*, 128.

16. Gorz, *Immaterial*, 113, 114.

17. Hardt and Negri, *Commonwealth*, 143, 145–48, 309, 310, 311.

18. Gorz, *Reclaiming Work*, 40.

19. Hardt and Negri, *Empire* (Cambridge, MA: Harvard University Press, 2000), 422n16.

20. Gorz, *Reclaiming Work*, 74.

21. Ibid.

22. Hardt and Negri, *Commonwealth*, 152.

23. Hardt and Negri, *Multitude*, 212.

24. Wanda Vrasti, " 'Caring' Capitalism and the Duplicity of Critique," *Theory and Event* 14, no. 4 (2011).

25. Gorz, *Critique of Economic Reason*, 13, 165.

26. See ibid., chapter 2.

27. Gorz, *Reclaiming Work*, 106, 77.

28. Ibid., 78, 65, 78.

29. Ibid., 110.

30. Gorz, *Ecologica*, trans. Chris Turner (London: Seagull, 2010), 131, 132.

31. Ibid., 132, 133.

32. Ibid., 129, 130.
33. Ibid., 130–31.
34. Ibid., 130.
35. Gorz, *Capitalism, Socialism, Ecology*, 55.
36. Gorz, *Immaterial*, 127.
37. Gorz, *Farewell to the Working Class*, 102.
38. Gorz, *Reclaiming Work*, 78.
39. Gorz, *Immaterial*, 128.
40. Hardt and Negri, *Commonwealth*, 57.
41. Hardt and Negri, *Empire*, 364.
42. Quoted in Hardt and Negri, *Commonwealth*, 59.
43. Ibid., 59, 58.
44. Ibid., 153, 152.
45. Ibid., 61.
46. Hardt and Negri, *Empire*, 102.
47. Quoted in Ibid., 103.
48. Ibid.
49. Ibid., 158.
50. Ibid., 156.
51. Ibid., 97, 344.
52. Ibid., 344.
53. Ibid., 395.
54. Ibid., 206, 210.
55. Ibid., 400.
56. Ibid., 403.
57. Ibid., emphasis added.
58. Hardt and Negri, *Commonwealth*, 310. See Gorz, *Immaterial*, 131 for a similar argument.
59. Hardt and Negri, *Empire*, 403.
60. Ibid., 407.
61. Ibid., 303.
62. Hardt and Negri, *Commonwealth*, 145, 147, 148.
63. Ibid., 309, 310.
64. Hardt and Negri, *Multitude*, 225.
65. Jean-Luc Nancy, "Un Peuple ou des Multitudes," *L'Humanité*, December 26, 2003, accessed July 8, 2016, http://www.multitudes.net/Un-peuple-ou-des-multitudes/. All translations are my own.
66. Hardt and Negri, *Multitude*, 225–26.
67. Ibid., 226.
68. Ibid., 349.
69. Hardt and Negri, *Empire*, 358.
70. Hardt and Negri, *Multitude*, 349.
71. Hardt and Negri, *Commonwealth*, viii.
72. See Hardt and Negri, *Empire*, 361, and *Multitude*, 351.
73. Hardt and Negri, *Commonwealth*, 183, 180, 181.
74. Hardt and Negri, *Empire*, 358.
75. Hardt and Negri, *Commonwealth*, 180, 181; emphasis added.
76. Ibid., 182.
77. Ibid., 182, 183.
78. Ibid., 198.

79. Ibid., 184.

80. Ibid., 196.

81. Ibid., ix, viii; Hardt and Negri, *Multitude*, xi.

82. Gorz, *Reclaiming Work*, 100.

83. Nancy, *Inoperative Community*, xxxviii.

84. Ibid., 3.

85. Ibid., xxxviii; see also Nancy, "La Comparution/The Compearance: From the Existence of 'Communism' to the Community of 'Existence,'" trans. Tracy B. Strong, *Political Theory* 20, no. 3 (1992): 372.

86. Nancy, *Inoperative Community*, 12.

87. I am grateful to Christopher Watkin for suggesting this distinction.

88. Nancy, *Inoperative Community*, 1.

89. Nancy, *Being Singular Plural*, 43.

90. Nancy, *Inoperative Community*, 1.

91. Nancy, "Thinking Better of Capital: An Interview," *Studies in Practical Philosophy* 1, no. 2 (1999): 218.

92. Nancy, *La Communauté désavouée* (Paris: Éditions Galilée, 2014), 45; my translation.

93. Nancy, *Inoperative Community*, xxxix.

94. Ibid., xxxviii.

95. Alexandre Kojève coined the term *désoeuvrement* to describe the protagonists of three novels by Raymond Queneau, whom he called *voyous désoeuvrés* (often translated as "lazy rascals"), as they find themselves without work after the end of history; see Alysia Garrison, "Kojève, Alexandre," in *Agamben Dictionary*, ed. Alex Murray and Jessica Whyte (Edinburgh: Edinburgh University Press, 2011), 114. As I will show, Nancy's use of the term, following Maurice Blanchot's, is quite different.

96. Nancy, *Inoperative Community*, 31.

97. Ibid., xxxix, xxxviii.

98. Ibid., 72.

99. Ibid., 73.

100. Ibid., 72.

101. Ibid., 73.

102. Quoted in ibid., 74.

103. Quoted in ibid., 74.

104. Ibid.

105. Ibid., 64.

106. Ibid., 41.

107. Not by chance, articulation has both a communicative dimension and a way of conveying the linkage of distinct parts, as in engineering and anatomy. When one considers the meaning of "articulation" in relation to language it conveys both separation and joining: if "articulation" means "the utterance of the distinct elements of speech," precisely what makes these elements distinct is that they precede and follow one another in a kind of linguistic chain. Similarly, in music, articulation is understood as the "*succession* of separate notes from one another" (*OED*, emphasis added). In mechanical terms, one finds a similar notion of parts that are joined together being able move independently from one another, as in an articulated vehicle or limbs of a body.

108. Nancy, *Inoperative Community*, 80.

109. Ibid., 81.

110. Nancy's critique of capital still proceeds on the basis of his ontological view of community, but rather than suggesting that capitalism involves the imposition of an essential identity, here his claim is that capital reduces everything to a universal value—exchange value—to the detriment of being-in-common. I am grateful to Christopher Watkin for highlighting this distinction.

111. Nancy, *Inoperative Community*, 75.
112. Ibid.
113. Nancy, *Being Singular Plural*, 73.
114. Ibid., 74.
115. Ignaas Devisch, *Jean-Luc Nancy and the Question of Community* (London: Bloomsbury, 2013), 177.
116. Nancy, "Thinking Better of Capital," 222.
117. I am grateful for Christopher Watkin for proposing that it is not inevitable that unworking would take on the function of work, although there is a risk that this might occur.
118. Nancy, *Inoperative Community*, 38.
119. Ibid.
120. Ibid., 37.
121. Ibid., 38.
122. Ibid., 39.
123. Ibid., xxxviii.

6. The Postwork Community

1. Marx, *Capital*, 1:714.
2. Massimo De Angelis, "Separating the Doing and the Deed: Capital and the Continuous Character of Enclosures," *Historical Materialism* 12, no. 2 (2004): 64, http://dx.doi.org/10.1163/1569206041551609.
3. Thomas Paine was among the first to propose a social dividend funded by ground rent paid to all adult members of the community, but the idea is also present in the contemporary Alaska Permanent Fund; see Simon Birnbaum and Karl Widerquist, eds., "About Basic Income," accessed October 21, 2013, http://www.basicincome.org/bien/aboutbasicincome.html#history.
4. I am grateful to Robyn Marasco for drawing out the distinction between these positions and for suggesting the terminology that I adopt here.
5. Hayek, *Constitution of Liberty*, 81.
6. Richard D. Woolf, "Critics of Capitalism Must Include Its Definition," *Truthout*, May 26, 2015, accessed January 19, 2017, http://www.truth-out.org/news/item/30678-critics-of-capitalism-must-include-its-definition.
7. Gorz, *Critique of Economic Reason*, 119.
8. Ibid., 119–20.
9. Ibid., 35.
10. Gibson-Graham, *Postcapitalist Politics*, 92.
11. Ibid., 59.
12. Ibid., 86.
13. Ibid., 88.
14. Christopher Watkin, "A Different Alterity: Jean-Luc Nancy's 'Singular Plural,'" *Paragraph* 30, no. 2 (2007): 61.
15. Todd May, *Reconsidering Difference: Nancy, Derrida, Levinas, and Deleuze* (University Park: Pennsylvania State University Press, 1997), 41.
16. Ibid., 23, 40.
17. Geoffrey Pleyers, "'Nuit debout': Citizens Are Back in Squares in Paris," *Open Democracy*, April 8, 2016, accessed January 18, 2017, https://www.opendemocracy.net/geoffrey-pleyers/nuit-debout-citizens-are-back-in-squares-in-paris; Aurélien Soucheyre, "Nuit debout: Réécrire la Constitution, par tous et pour tous," *l'Humanité*, April 14, 2016, accessed January 18, 2017, http://www.humanite.fr/nuit-debout-reecrire-la-constitution-par-tous-et-pour-tous-604695; Stathis Kouvelakis and Frédéric Lordon, "Overturning a World," *Jacobin*,

May 4, 2016, accessed January 18, 2017, https://www.jacobinmag.com/2016/05/nuit-debout-france-el-khomri-labor-law/; and "Nuit debout: Frédéric Lordon; 'Pour en finir avec l'empire du capital,'" *Le Nouvel Observateur*, April 16, 2016, accessed January 18, 2017, http://temp sreel.nouvelobs.com/politique/20160415.OBS8653/nuit-debout-frederic-lordon-pour-en-finir-avec-l-empire-du-capital.html.

18. "Senator Bernie Sanders on Democratic Socialism in the United States," November 19, 2015, accessed January 18, 2017, https://berniesanders.com/democratic-socialism-in-the-united-states/.

19. My translation; quoted in Soucheyre, "Nuit debout."

20. I am grateful to Robyn Marasco for raising this concern.

21. Wright, "How to Be an Anticapitalist Today," *Jacobin*, December 2, 2015, accessed January 18, 2017, https://www.jacobinmag.com/2015/12/erik-olin-wright-real-utopias-anti capitalism-democracy/.

BIBLIOGRAPHY

Adkins, Lisa, and Celia Lury. "The Labour of Identity: Performing Identities, Performing Economies." *Economy and Society* 4 (1999): 598–614. http://dx.doi.org/10.1080/03085149900000020.

Advisory, Conciliation and Arbitration Service. "Acas Consultation on: Draft Code of Practice on the Extended Right to Request Flexible Working." February 2013. Accessed October 27, 2013. http://www.acas.org.uk/media/pdf/2/r/Consultation_draft_COP_FW.pdf.

Agamben, Giorgio. "What Is a Destituent Power?" Translated by Stephanie Wakefield. *Environment and Planning D: Society and Space* 32 (2014): 65–74.

Amoore, Louise. "Risk, Reward, and Discipline at Work." *Economy and Society* 33, no. 2 (2004): 174–96. http://dx.doi.org/10.1080/03085140410001677111.

Anderson, Elizabeth. "Optional Freedoms." In *What's Wrong with a Free Lunch?*, edited by Joshua Cohen and Joel Rogers, 70–74. Boston, MA: Beacon, 2001.

Appelbaum, Lauren. "Sanders: Full Employment Needed for All." *RespectAbility Report*, July 8, 2015. Accessed January 20, 2017. http://therespectabilityreport.org/2015/07/08/sanders-full-employment-needed-for-all/.

Arendt, Hannah. *The Human Condition*. Chicago: University of Chicago Press, 1958.

Baccaro, Lucio, and Chris Howell. "A Common Neoliberal Trajectory: The Transformation of Industrial Relations in Advanced Capitalism." *Politics and Society* 39, no. 4 (2001): 521–63. http://dx.doi.org/10.1177/0032329211420082.

Balibar, Étienne. *Equaliberty: Political Essays.* Translated by James Ingram. Durham: Duke University Press, 2014.

Basic Income Earth Network. "About Basic Income." 2008. Accessed May 22, 2013. http://basicincome.org/bien/aboutbasicincome.html.

Bauman, Zygmunt. *Work, Consumerism, and the New Poor.* Maidenhead, UK: Open University Press, 2005.

Beck, Ulrich. *The Brave New World of Work.* Cambridge: Polity, 2000.

———. *Risk Society.* London: Sage, 1992.

Beckett, Clare. *Thatcher.* London: Haus, 2006.

Beder, Sharon. *Selling the Work Ethic: From Puritan Pulpit to Corporate PR.* London: Zed, 2000.

Befort, Stephen F. "Labor and Employment Law at the Millennium: A Historical Review and Critical Assessment." *Boston College Law Review* 43 (2001): 351–460. Accessed October 29, 2013. http://lawdigitalcommons.bc.edu/cgi/viewcontent.cgi?article=2201&context=bclr.

Berlin, Isaiah. "Two Concepts of Liberty." In *Liberty: Isaiah Berlin,* edited by Henry Hardy. Oxford: Oxford University Press, 2002.

Bernal-Verdugo, Lorenzo E., Davide Furceri, and Dominique Guillaume. "Labor Market Flexibility and Unemployment: New Empirical Evidence of Static and Dynamic Effects." International Monetary Fund Working Paper 12/64. March 2012. Accessed April 24, 2012. http://www.imf.org/external/pubs/ft/wp/2012/wp1264.pdf.

Bertram, Chris, Corey Robin, and Alex Gourevitch, "Let It Bleed: Libertarianism and the Workplace." *Crooked Timber,* July 1, 2012. Accessed September 24, 2014. http://crookedtimber.org/2012/07/01/let-it-bleed-libertarianism-and-the-workplace/.

Birnbaum, Simon, and Karl Widerquist, eds. "History of Basic Income." 2008. Accessed June 10, 2013. http://www.basicincome.org/bien/aboutbasicincome.html#history.

Block, Fred. "Towards a New Understanding of Economic Modernity." In *The Economy as Polity: The Political Constitution of Contemporary Capitalism,* edited by Christian Joerges, Bo Stråth and Peter Wagner, 3–16. London: UCL, 2005.

Bowring, Finn. "André Gorz: Autonomy and Equity in the Post-Industrial Age." *Sociological Review* 53, no. 1 (2005): 134–47.

———. "Misreading Gorz." *New Left Review,* no. 217 (1996): 102–22.

Bregman, Rutger. "Why We Should Give Free Money to Everyone." *DutchNews.nl.* April 21, 2016. Accessed January 13, 2017. http://www.dutchnews.nl/features/2016/04/why-we-should-give-free-money-to-everyone/.

Cabinet Office and Prime Minister's Office. "PM's Speech on the Fightback after the Riots." August 15, 2011. Accessed February 15, 2013. http://www.number10.gov.uk/news/pms-speech-on-the-fightback-after-the-riots/.

Chamberlain, James A. "Recognition and Social Justice: What Critical Theory Can Learn from Paid Domestic Laborers in the United States." *New Political Science* 35, no. 2 (2013): 182–202. http://dx.doi.org/10.1080/07393148.2013.790698.

Chartered Institute of Personnel and Development. "Flexible Working Provision and Uptake." May 2012. Accessed June 30, 2016. http://www.cipd.co.uk/hr-resources/survey-reports/flexible-working-provision-uptake.aspx.

Cheeseman, Gina-Marie. "The Case for Universal Basic Income." *Triple Pundit,* April 29, 2016. Accessed January 13, 2017. http://www.triplepundit.com/2016/04/ngo-givedirectly-experiments-with-basic-income-cash-transfers-in-kenya/.

Clark, Charles M. A., and Catherine Kavanagh. "Basic Income, Inequality and Unemployment: Rethinking the Linkage between Work and Welfare." *Journal of Economic Issues* 30, no. 2 (1996): 399–406. http://www.jstor.org/stable/4452238.

Cohen, Joshua, and Joel Rogers. *What's Wrong with a Free Lunch?* Boston, MA: Beacon, 2001.

Committee on Education and the Workforce. "The Schedules That Work Act (H.R. 5159)." N.d. Accessed October 15, 2014. http://democrats.edworkforce.house.gov/bill/schedules-work-act.

Countouris, Nicola, and Mark Freedland. "Injunctions, *Cyanamid*, and the Corrosion of the Right to Strike in the UK." UCL Labour Rights Institute On-Line Working Papers. *LRI WP 1/2010*: 1–20. Accessed October 27, 2013. http://www.ucl.ac.uk/laws/lri/papers/Injunctions_Cyanamid_the-corrosion-of-the-right-to-strike-in-the-UK.pdf.

Cremin, Colin. *Capitalism's New Clothes: Enterprise, Ethics, and Enjoyment in Times of Crisis.* London: Pluto, 2011.

Critchley, Simon, and Oliver Marchart. "Introduction." In *Laclau: A Critical Reader*, edited by Simon Critchley and Oliver Marchart, 1–13. Abingdon, Oxon: Routledge, 2004.

De Angelis, Massimo. "Separating the Doing and the Deed: Capital and the Continuous Character of Enclosures." *Historical Materialism* 12, no. 2 (2004): 57–87. http://dx.doi.org/10.1163/1569206041551609.

Deakin, Simon, and Hannah Reed. "Britain—River Crossing or Cold Bath?" In *Why Deregulate Labour Markets?*, edited by Gosta Esping-Andersen and Marino Regini, 115–47. Oxford: Oxford University Press, 2000.

Dean, Mitchell. "Governing the Unemployed Self in an Active Society." *Economy and Society* 24, no. 4 (1995): 559–83. http://dx.doi.org/10.1080/03085149500000025.

Deveaux, Monique. *Gender and Justice in Multicultural Liberal States.* Oxford: Oxford University Press, 2006.

Devisch, Ignaas. *Jean-Luc Nancy and the Question of Community.* London: Bloomsbury, 2013.

Department for Work and Pensions. "The Work Programme." December 2012. Accessed June 28, 2013. http://webarchive.nationalarchives.gov.uk/+/http://www.dwp.gov.uk/docs/the-work-programme.pdf.

Department for Work and Pensions and HM Treasury. "Helping People to Find and Stay in Work." August 8, 2013. Accessed September 24, 2013. https://www.gov.uk/government/policies/helping-people-to-find-and-stay-in-work/supporting-pages/managing-the-work-programme.

"Donald Trump's News Conference: Full Transcript and Video." *New York Times*, January 11, 2017. Accessed January 20, 2017. https://www.nytimes.com/2017/01/11/us/politics/trump-press-conference-transcript.html.

Elson, Diane. "Market Socialism or Socialization of the Market." *New Left Review* 1, no. 172 (November–December 1988): 17.

England, Kim. "Home, Work, and the Shifting Geographies of Care." *Ethics, Place and Environment* 13, no. 2 (2010): 131–50.

Equal Opportunities Commission. "Enter the Timelords: Transforming Work to Meet the Future." 2007. Accessed September 29, 2012. www.bitc.org.uk/document.rm?id=8625.

European Citizens' Initiative for an Unconditional Basic Income. "Annex." Accessed October 29, 2013. http://basicincome2013.eu/ubi/wp-content/uploads/2013/01/Full_Annex_ECI_unconditionnal-basic-income-2.pdf.

Executive Office of the President, Council of Economic Advisers. "Work-Life Balance and the Economics of Workplace Flexibility." 2010. Accessed September 4, 2012. http://www.whitehouse.gov/blog/2010/03/31/economics-workplace-flexibility.

Explanatory Note to the Unfair Dismissal and Statement of Reasons for Dismissal (Variation of Qualifying Period) Order 2012 No. 989. Accessed November 5, 2012. http://www.legislation.gov.uk/uksi/2012/989/note/made.

Farber, Henry F., and Bruce Western. "Ronald Reagan and the Politics of Declining Union Organization." *British Journal of Industrial Relations* 40, no. 3 (2002): 385–401. http://dx.doi.org/10.1111/1467-8543.00240.

Fiorito, Jack. "The State of Unions in the United States." *Journal of Labor Research* 28, no. 1 (2007): 43–68. Accessed October 29, 2013, http://connection.ebscohost.com/c/articles/23815043/state-unions-united-states.

Fischer, Ute, Stefan Heckel, Axel Jansen, Sascha Liebermann, and Thomas Loer. "Freedom, Not Full Employment." Translated by Marc Batko and Axel Jansen. Freiheit statt Vollbeschäftigung, June 24, 2005. Accessed May 28, 2013. http://www.freiheit stattvollbeschaeftigung.de/en/theses.

Fitzpatrick, Tony. *Freedom and Security: An Introduction to the Basic Income Debate.* Basingstoke: Macmillan, 1999.

Fleetwood, Steve. "Why Work-Life Balance Now?" *International Journal of Human Resource Management* 18, no. 3 (2007): 387–400. http://dx.doi.org/10.1080/095 85190601167441.

Forrest, M. David. "Consensus and Crisis: Representing the Poor in the Post-Civil Rights Era." *New Political Science* 35, no. 1 (2013): 19–43. http://dx.doi.org/10.10 80/07393148.2012.754667.

Foucault, Michel. *The Birth of Biopolitics: Lectures at the Collège de France, 1978–79.* Edited by Michel Senellart. Translated by Graham Burchell. New York: Palgrave Macmillan, 2008.

——. "The Subject and Power." *Critical Inquiry* 8, no. 4 (1982): 777–975. http://dx.doi.org/10.1086/448181.

Frank, Thomas. *One Market under God.* New York: Anchor, 2000.

Fraser, Nancy. "After the Family Wage: Wage Equity and the Welfare State." *Political Theory* 22, no. 4 (1994): 591–618.

——. "Can Society Be Commodities All the Way Down? Polanyian Reflections on the Capitalist Crisis." *Fondations Maison des Sciences de l'Homme* 18 (2012): 1–13. Accessed October 29, 2013. http://hal.archives-ouvertes.fr/docs/00/72/50/60/PDF/FMSH-WP-2012-18_Fraser2.pdf.

——. "Feminism, Capitalism, and the Cunning of History." *New Left Review*, no. 56 (2009): 97–117.

——. *Scales of Justice: Reimagining Political Space in a Globalizing World.* New York: Columbia University Press, 2009.

——. "Social Justice in the Age of Identity Politics: Redistribution, Recognition, and Participation." In *Redistribution or Recognition? A Political-Philosophical Exchange*, by Nancy Fraser and Axel Honneth, 7–109. London: Verso, 2003.

——. "A Triple Movement? Parsing the Politics of Crisis after Polanyi." *New Left Review* 81 (May–June 2013): 119–32. Accessed October 29, 2013. http://newleftreview.org/II/81/nancy-fraser-a-triple-movement.

Fraser, Nancy, and Linda Gordon. "A Genealogy of 'Dependency': Tracing a Keyword of the US Welfare State." In *Justice Interruptus: Critical Reflections on the "Post-socialist" Condition*, by Nancy Fraser, 121–49. New York: Routledge, 1997.

Fraser, Nancy, and Axel Honneth. *Redistribution or Recognition? A Political-Philosophical Exchange.* London: Verso, 2003.

Fraser, Nancy, and Jo Littler. "The Fortunes of Socialist Feminism: Jo Littler Interviews Nancy Fraser." *Soundings: A Journal of Politics and Culture* 58 (2014–15): 21–33.

Fredman, Sandra. "The New Rights: Labour Law and Ideology in the Thatcher Years." *Oxford Journal of Legal Studies* 12, no. 1 (1992): 24–44. http://dx.doi.org/10.1093/ojls/12.1.24.

Freud, Sigmund. *Civilization and Its Discontents.* Translated by James Strachey. New York: W. W. Norton, 2010.

Galston, William. "What about Reciprocity?" In *What's Wrong with a Free Lunch?*, edited by Joshua Cohen and Joel Rogers, 29–33. Boston, MA: Beacon, 2001.

Gans, Herbert J. *The War against the Poor: The Underclass and Antipoverty Policy.* New York: Basic Books, 1995.

Garrison, Alysia. "Kojève, Alexandre." In *Agamben Dictionary*, edited by Alex Murray and Jessica Whyte. Edinburgh: Edinburgh University Press, 2011.

Garsten, Christina, and Jan Turtinen. "'Angels' and 'Chameleon': The Cultural Construction of the Flexible Temporary Agency Worker in Sweden and Britain." In *After Full Employment: European Discourses on Work and Flexibility*, edited by Bo Stråth, 161–96. Brussels: P. I. E. Peter Lang, 2000.

Gibson-Graham, J. K. *A Postcapitalist Politics.* Minneapolis: University of Minnesota Press, 2006.

Giddens, Anthony. *The Consequences of Modernity.* Stanford: Stanford University Press, 1990.

Glass, Jennifer, Robin W. Simon, and Matthew A. Andersson. "Parenthood and Happiness: Effects of Work-Family Reconciliation Policies in 22 OECD Countries." *American Journal of Sociology*, 122, no. 3 (2016): 886–929.

Glenn, Evelyn Nakano. "Creating a Caring Society." *Contemporary Sociology* 29, no. 1 (2000): 84–94.

Glynos, Jason. "The Grip of Ideology: A Lacanian Approach to the Theory of Ideology." *Journal of Political Ideologies* 6, no. 2 (2001): 191–214. http://dx.doi.org/10.1080/13569310120053858.

——. "Ideological Fantasy at Work." *Journal of Political Ideologies* 13, no. 3 (2008): 275–96. http://dx.doi.org/10.1080/13569310802376961.

Glynos, Jason, and David Howarth. *Logics of Critical Explanation in Social and Political Theory.* London: Routledge, 2007.

Glynos, Jason, and Yannis Stavrakakis. "Lacan and Political Subjectivity: Fantasy and Enjoyment in Psychoanalysis and Political Theory." *Subjectivity* 24 (2008): 256–74. http://dx.doi.org/10.1057/sub.2008.23.

Goodman, Peter S. "Free Cash in Finland. Must Be Jobless." *New York Times*, December 17, 2016. Accessed January 13, 2017. https://www.nytimes.com/2016/12/17/business/economy/universal-basic-income-finland.html.

Gorz, André. *Capitalism, Socialism, Ecology.* Translated by Martin Chalmers. London: Verso, 2012.

——. *Critique of Economic Reason.* Translated by Gillian Handyside and Chris Turner. London: Verso, 1989.

——. *Ecologica.* Translated by Chris Turner. London: Seagull, 2010.

——. *Farewell to the Working Class: An Essay on Post-Industrial Socialism.* Translated by Michael Sonenscher. London: Pluto, 1982.

——. *The Immaterial: Knowledge, Value and Capital.* Translated by Chris Turner. London: Seagull, 2010.

——. *Paths to Paradise: On the Liberation from Work.* Translated by Malcolm Imrie. London: Pluto, 1985.

——. *Reclaiming Work: Beyond the Wage-Based Society.* Translated by Chris Turner. Cambridge: Polity, 1999.

——. *Strategy for Labor: A Radical Proposal.* Translated by Martin A. Nicolaus and Victoria Ortiz. Boston, MA: Beacon, 1968.

Greenhouse, Steven. "A Part-Time Life, as Hours Shrink and Shift." *New York Times,* October 28, 2012.

——. "A Push to Give Steadier Shifts to Part-Timers." *New York Times,* July 15, 2014. Accessed October 14, 2014. http://www.nytimes.com/2014/07/16/business/a-push-to-give-steadier-shifts-to-part-timers.html.

——. "Wisconsin's Legacy for Unions." *New York Times,* February 22, 2014. Accessed October 14, 2014. http://www.nytimes.com/2014/02/23/business/wisconsins-legacy-for-unions.html?_r=0.

Grimshaw, Damian, and Jill Rubery. "The End of the UK's Liberal Collectivist Social Model? The Implications of the Coalition Government's Policy during the Austerity Crisis." *Cambridge Journal of Economics* 36, no. 1 (2012): 105–26. http://dx.doi.org/10.1093/cje/ber033.

Gutmann, Amy. "Introduction." In *Work and Welfare,* edited by Amy Gutmann, vii–xv. Princeton: Princeton University Press, 1998.

Handler, Joel. *Social Citizenship and Workfare in the United States and Western Europe: The Paradox of Inclusion.* Cambridge: Cambridge University Press, 2004.

Hardt, Michael, and Antonio Negri. *Commonwealth.* Cambridge, MA: Harvard University Press, 2009.

——. *Empire.* Cambridge, MA: Harvard University Press, 2000.

——. *Multitude: War and Democracy in the Age of Empire.* New York: Penguin, 2004.

Hartmann, Martin, and Axel Honneth. "Paradoxes of Capitalism." *Constellations* 13, no. 1 (2006): 42–58. http://dx.doi.org/10.1111/j.1351-0487.2006.00439.x.

Harvey, David. *A Brief History of Neoliberalism.* Oxford: Oxford University Press, 2005.

——. *Spaces of Global Capitalism: Towards a Theory of Uneven Geographical Development.* London: Verso, 2006.

Hastings, Max. "Years of Liberal Dogma Have Spawned a Generation of Amoral, Uneducated, Welfare Dependent, Brutalised Youngsters." *Daily Mail,* August 12, 2011. Accessed February 15, 2013. http://www.dailymail.co.uk/debate/article-2024284/UK-riots-2011-Liberal-dogma-spawned-generation-brutalised-youths.html.

Hayek, Friedrich A. *The Constitution of Liberty.* Chicago: University of Chicago Press, 1960.

Honneth, Axel. "Redistribution as Recognition: A Response to Nancy Fraser." Translated by Joel Golb, James Ingram, and Christiane Wilke. In *Redistribution or Recognition? A Political-Philosophical Exchange*, by Nancy Fraser and Axel Honneth, 110–97. London: Verso, 2003.

Howell, Chris. "The Changing Relationship between Labor and the State in Contemporary Capitalism." *Law, Culture and the Humanities* 12 (2012): 1–11. http://dx.doi.org/10.1177/1743872112448362.

——. "From New Labour to No Labour?" *New Political Science* 22, no. 2 (2010): 201–29.

Kamoche, Ken, Mary Pang, and Amy L. Y. Wong. "Career Development and Knowledge Appropriation: A Genealogical Critique." *Organization Studies* 32, no. 12 (2011): 1665–79. http://dx.doi.org/10.1177/0170840611421249.

Kasperkevic, Jana. "Elizabeth Warren to Help Propose Senate Bill to Tackle Part-Time Schedules." *Guardian*, July 23, 2014. Accessed October 15, 2014. http://www.theguardian.com/money/us-money-blog/2014/jul/23/elizabeth-warren-senate-bill-part-time-schedules.

Kela. "Objectives and Implementation of the Basic Income Experiment." January 13, 2017. Accessed January 13, 2017. http://www.kela.fi/web/en/basic-income-objectives-and-implementation.

Kentish, Ben. "Finland to Begin Paying Basic Income to Unemployed Citizens." *Independent*, December 23, 2016. Accessed January 13, 2017. http://www.independent.co.uk/news/world/europe/finland-universal-basic-income-ubi-citizens-560-euros-monthly-job-poverty-unemployment-a7492911.html.

Kouvelakis, Stathis, and Frédéric Lordon. "Overturning a World." *Jacobin*, May 4, 2016. Accessed January 18, 2017. https://www.jacobinmag.com/2016/05/nuit-debout-france-el-khomri-labor-law/.

Kymlicka, Will. *Contemporary Political Philosophy*. Oxford: Clarendon, 1990.

Lash, Scott, and John Urry. *Economies of Signs and Space*. London: Sage, 1994.

Levitas, Ruth. *The Inclusive Society? Social Exclusion and New Labour*. Basingstoke: Palgrave Macmillan, 2005.

Lieberman, Robert C. *Shifting the Color Line: Race and the American Welfare State*. Cambridge, MA.: Harvard University Press, 1998.

Lyons, Laura E. " 'I'd Like My Life Back': Corporate Personhood and the BP Oil Disaster." *Biography: An Interdisciplinary Quarterly* 34, no. 1 (2011): 96–107. http://dx.doi.org/10.1353/bio.2011.0012.

Maitland, Alison, and Peter Thomson. *Future Work: How Businesses Can Adapt and Thrive in the New World of Work*. New York: Palgrave Macmillan, 2011.

Marcuse, Herbert. *Eros and Civilization: A Philosophical Inquiry into Freud*. Boston, MA: Beacon, 1974.

——. *One-Dimensional Man*. Boston, MA: Beacon, 1964.

Marshall, T. H. "Citizenship and Social Class." In *Inequality and Society*, edited by Jeff Manzer and Michael Sauder, 148–54. New York: W. W. Norton, 2009. Originally published in 1950.

Marx, Karl. *Capital: A Critique of Political Economy*, Vol. 1. Translated by Samuel Moore and Edward Aveling. Edited by Frederick Engels. New York: International Publishers, 1967.

——. *Grundrisse: Foundations on the Critique of Political Economy.* Translated by Martin Nicolaus. New York: Vintage, 1973.

May, Todd. *Reconsidering Difference: Nancy, Derrida, Levinas, and Deleuze.* University Park: Pennsylvania State University Press, 1997.

Mezzadra, Sandro, and Brett Neilson. *Border as Method, or, the Multiplication of Labor.* Durham: Duke University Press, 2013.

Mill, John Stuart. *On Liberty.* Indianapolis: Hackett, 1978.

Miller, Peter, and Nikolas Rose. "Production, Identity, and Democracy." *Theory and Society* 24, no. 3 (1995): 427–67. http://dx.doi.org/10.1007/BF00993353.

Mulholland, Hélène. "Senior Lib Dem and Unions Condemn Proposal to Scrap Unfair Dismissal." *Guardian*, October 26, 2011. Accessed October 27, 2013. http://www.theguardian.com/politics/2011/oct/26/unions-condemn-report-unfair-dismissal.

Nancy, Jean-Luc. *Being Singular Plural.* Translated by Robert D. Richardson and Anne E. O'Bryne. Stanford: Stanford University Press, 2000.

——. *La communauté désavouée.* Paris: Éditions Galilée, 2014.

——. "Communism, the Word." In *The Idea of Communism*, edited by Costas Douzinas and Slavoj Žižek. London: Verso, 2010.

——. "La Comparution/The Compearance: From the Existence of 'Communism' to the Community of 'Existence.'" Translated by Tracy B. Strong. *Political Theory* 20, no. 3 (1992): 371–98.

——. *The Inoperative Community.* Edited by Peter Connor. Translated by Peter Connor, Lisa Garbus, Michael Holland, and Simona Sawhney. Minneapolis: University of Minnesota Press, 1991.

——. "Un Peuple ou des Multitudes." *l'Humanité*, December 26, 2003. Accessed July 8, 2016. http://www.multitudes.net/Un-peuple-ou-des-multitudes/.

——. "Thinking Better of Capital: An Interview." *Studies in Practical Philosophy* 1, no. 2 (1999): 214–32.

NLRB v. Mackay Radio and Telegraph Co., 304 U.S. 333 (1938).

"Nuit debout: Frédéric Lordon; 'Pour en finir avec l'empire du capital.'" *Le Nouvel Observateur*, April 16, 2016. Accessed January 18, 2017. http://tempsreel.nouvelobs.com/politique/20160415.OBS8653/nuit-debout-frederic-lordon-pour-en-finir-avec-l-empire-du-capital.html.

Offe, Claus. "Basic Income and the Labor Contract." *Analyse and Kritik* 1 (2009): 49–79. Accessed October 29, 2013. http://www.analyse-und-kritik.net/2009-1/AK_Offe_2009.pdf.

Office of Family Assistance. "About TANF." Accessed October 30, 2013. http://www.acf.hhs.gov/programs/ofa/programs/tanf/about.

Office of Scott Walker. "Reforms and Results." Accessed September 17, 2012. walker.wi.gov/Documents/Act_10_Success_Recap.pdf.

Özselçuka, Ceren, and Yahya M. Madra. "Enjoyment as an Economic Factor: Reading Marx with Lacan." *Subjectivity* 3, no. 3 (2010): 323–47. http://dx.doi.org/10.1057/sub.2010.13.

Pasulka, Nicole. "Right-to-Work Laws, Explained." *Mother Jones*, March 16, 2012.

Pateman, Carole. "Democracy, Human Rights and a Basic Income in a Global Era." Paper presented at the Basic Income Earth Network Congress, Dublin, June 20–21,

2008. Accessed May 24, 2013. http://www.basicincome.org/bien/pdf/dublin08/ple
nary1speaker2pataeman.doc.

——. "Democratizing Citizenship: Some Advantages of a Basic Income." In *Redesigning Distribution: Basic Income and Stakeholder Grants as Cornerstones for an Egalitarian Capitalism,* edited by Erik Olin Wright, 101–19. London: Verso: 2006.

——. *The Sexual Contract.* Stanford: Stanford University Press, 1988.

Peck, Jamie. *Workfare States.* New York: Guildford, 2001.

Peck, Jamie, and Adam Tickell. "Neoliberalizing Space." *Antipode* 34, no. 3 (2002):
380–404. http://dx.doi.org/10.1111/1467-8330.00247.

Perrucci, Robert, and Earl Wysong. *The New Class Society: Goodbye American Dream?*
Lanham, MD: Rowman and Littlefield, 2003.

Piore, Michael J., and Sean Safford. "Changing Regimes of Workplace Governance,
Shifting Axes of Social Mobilization, and the Challenge to Industrial Relations Theory." *Industrial Relations: A Journal of Economy and Society* 35, no. 3 (2006):
299–325. http://dx.doi.org/10.1111/j.1468-232X.2006.00439.x.

Piven, Frances Fox, and Richard A. Cloward. *The Breaking of the American Social
Compact.* New York: New Press, 1997.

——. *Regulating the Poor: The Functions of Public Welfare.* New York: Vintage, 1993.

Plato. *The Trial and Death of Socrates.* Translated by G. M. A. Grube. Indianapolis:
Hackett, 2000.

Pleyers, Geoffrey. " 'Nuit debout': Citizens Are Back in Squares in Paris." *Open Democracy,* April 8, 2016. Accessed January 18, 2017. https://www.opendemocracy.net/
geoffrey-pleyers/nuit-debout-citizens-are-back-in-squares-in-paris.

Rath, Tom. *Strengths Finder 2.0.* New York: Gallup, 2007.

Rawls, John. *A Theory of Justice.* Cambridge, MA: Harvard University Press, 1999.

Regini, Marino. "The Dilemmas of Labour Market Regulation." In *Why Deregulate
Labour Markets?,* edited by Gosta Esping-Andersen and Marino Regini, 11–29. Oxford: Oxford University Press, 2000.

Robeyns, Ingrid. "Is Nancy Fraser's Critique of Theories of Distributive Justice Justified?"
Constellations 10, no. 4 (2003): 538–54. http://dx.doi.org/10.1046/j.1351-0487.
2003.00352.x.

Roediger, David. *The Wages of Whiteness: Race and the Making of the American Working Class.* London: Verso, 2007.

Rogers, Daniel T. *The Work Ethic in Industrial America, 1850–1920.* Chicago: University of Chicago Press, 1979.

Rose, Nikolas. "The Death of the Social? Re-figuring the Territory of Government."
Economy and Society 25, no. 3 (1996): 327–56. http://dx.doi.org/10.1080/03085
149600000018.

——. *Powers of Freedom: Reframing Political Thought.* Cambridge: Cambridge University Press, 1999.

Ross, Andrew. *Nice Work If You Can Get It: Life and Labor in Precarious Times.* New
York: New York University Press, 2009.

Sartre, Jean-Paul. "Existentialism Is a Humanism." 1946. Translated by Philip Mairet.
Accessed October 8, 2013. http://www.marxists.org/reference/archive/sartre/works/
exist/sartre.htm.

"Senator Bernie Sanders on Democratic Socialism in the United States." November 19, 2015. Accessed January 18, 2017. https://berniesanders.com/democratic-socialism-in-the-united-states/.

Shklar, Judith. *American Citizenship: The Quest for Inclusion.* Cambridge, MA: Harvard University Press, 1991.

Silim, Amna, and Alfie Stirling. "Women and Flexible Working: Improving Female Employment Outcomes in Europe." *Institute of Public Policy Research*, December 2014. Accessed June 30, 2016. http://www.ippr.org/publications/women-and-flexible-working- improving-female-employment-outcomes-in-europe.

Solow, Robert M. "Guess Who Likes Workfare." In *Work and Welfare*, edited by Amy Gutmann, 3–22. Princeton: Princeton University Press, 1998.

Soucheyre, Aurélien. "Nuit debout: Réécrire la Constitution, par tous et pour tous." *l'Humanité*, April 14, 2016. Accessed January 18, 2017. http://www.humanite.fr/nuit-debout-reecrire-la-constitution-par-tous-et-pour-tous-604695.

Standing, Guy. *Beyond the New Paternalism: Basic Security as Equality.* London: Verso, 2002.

——. "Global Feminization through Flexible Labour: A Theme Revisited." *World Development* 27, no. 3 (1999): 583–602. Accessed October 29, 2013. http://www.guystanding.com/files/documents/Global_Feminization_Through_Flexible_Labor_-_theme_revisited.pdf.

——. *Global Labour Flexibility: Seeking Distributive Justice.* Basingstoke: Macmillan, 1999.

——. *The Precariat: The New Dangerous Class.* London: Bloomsbury Academic, 2011.

State of Wisconsin. 2011–12 Legislature. January 2011 Special Session. *Senate Bill 11.* Accessed September 17, 2012. docs.legis.wisconsin.gov/document/proposaltext/2011/JR1/SB11.pdf.

Stråth, Bo, ed. *After Full Employment: European Discourses on Work and Flexibility.* Brussels: P. I. E. Peter Lang, 2000.

Stråth, Bo, and Peter Wagner. "After Full Employment: Theoretical and Political Implications." In *After Full Employment: European Discourses on Work and Flexibility*, edited by Bo Stråth, 261–78. Brussels: P. I. E. Peter Lang, 2000.

Surowiecki, James. "The Case for Free Money: Why Don't We Have Universal Basic Income?" *New Yorker*, June 20, 2016. Accessed January 13, 2017. http://www.newyorker.com/magazine/2016/06/20/why-dont-we-have-universal-basic-income.

Thrift, Nigel. *Knowing Capitalism.* London: Sage, 2005.

"Transcript: Vice President Biden's Convention Speech." *National Public Radio*, September 6, 2012. Accessed March 12, 2013, http://www.npr.org/2012/09/06/160713378/transcript-vice-president-bidens-convention-speech.

Tronto, Joan C. *Caring Democracy: Markets, Equality, and Justice.* New York: New York University Press, 2013.

Tsipursky, Gleb. "Free Money Is Not So Funny Anymore: Confessions of a (Former) Skeptic of Basic Income." *Salon*, August 21, 2016. Accessed January 13, 2017. http://www.salon.com/2016/08/21/free-money-is-not-so-funny-anymore-confessions-of-a-former-skeptic-of-basic-income/.

US Congress. "Summary: H.R. 5159—Schedules That Work Act." N.d. Accessed June 24, 2016. https://www.congress.gov/bill/113th-congress/house-bill/5159.

——. "Summary: S. 1772–14th Congress (2015–16). N.d. Accessed June 2, 2016. https://www.congress.gov/bill/114th-congress/senate-bill/1772.

——. "S. 1772: Schedules that Work Act." Accessed June 24, 2016. https://www.con gress.gov/bill/114th-congress/senate-bill/1772/text.

US Department of Labor. "State Right-to-Work Laws and Constitutional Amendments in Effect as of January 1, 2009, with Year of Passage." December 2008. Accessed November 12, 2012. http://www.dol.gov/whd/state/righttowork.htm#.UKFCBIXOZV4.

——. "Women of Working Age." N.d. Accessed July 21, 2016. https://www.dol.gov/wb/stats/latest_annual_data.htm.

Van der Veen, Robert, and Philippe Van Parijs. "A Capitalist Road to Communism." *Theory and Society* 15, no. 5 (1986): 635–55. Accessed October 29, 2013. http://www.ssc.wisc.edu/~wright/ERU_files/PVP-cap-road.pdf.

Van Parijs, Philippe. "Basic Income: A Simple and Powerful Idea of the Twenty-First Century." *Politics and Society* 32, no. 1 (2004): 7–39. http://dx.doi.org/10.1177/0032329203261095.

——. "A Basic Income for All." In *What's Wrong with a Free Lunch?*, edited by Joshua Cohen and Joel Rogers, 3–26. Boston, MA: Beacon, 2001.

——. "Competing Justifications of Basic Income." In *Arguing for Basic Income: Ethical Foundations for a Radical Reform*, edited by Philippe Van Parijs, 3–29. London: Verso, 1992.

——. *Real Freedom for All: What (If Anything) Can Justify Capitalism?* Oxford: Oxford University Press, 1995.

——. "The Worldwide March to Basic Income: Thank You Switzerland!" *Basic Income Earth Network*. June 6, 2016. Accessed January 25, 2017. http://basicincome.org/news/2016/06/the-worldwide-march-to-basic-income-thank-you-switzerland/.

Virno, Paolo. "The Ambivalence of Disenchantment." In *Radical Thought in Italy: A Potential Politics*, edited by Paolo Virno and Michael Hardt, 13–33. Minneapolis: University of Minnesota Press, 1996.

Vrasti, Wanda. " 'Caring' Capitalism and the Duplicity of Critique." *Theory and Event* 14, no. 4 (2011).

Wagner, Peter. "The Exit from Organised Modernity: 'Flexibility' in Social Thought and in Historical Perspective." In *After Full Employment: European Discourses on Work and Flexibility*, edited by Bo Stråth, 35–63. Brussels: P. I. E. Peter Lang, 2000.

Walters, William. *Unemployment and Government: Genealogies of the Social*. Cambridge: Cambridge University Press, 2000.

Watkin, Christopher. "A Different Alterity: Jean-Luc Nancy's 'Singular Plural.' " *Paragraph* 30, no. 2 (2007): 50–64.

Weber, Max. *The Protestant Ethic and the Spirit of Capitalism*. Translated by Talcott Parsons. New York: Routledge, 2002.

Weeks, Kathi. *The Problem with Work: Feminism, Marxism, Antiwork Politics, and Postwork Imaginaries*. Durham: Duke University Press, 2011.

White, Michael. *Against Unemployment*. London: Policy Studies Institute, 1991.

Whiteside, Noel. "Britain and France in Comparison." In *After Full Employment: European Discourses on Work and Flexibility*, edited by Bo Stråth, 107–33. Brussels: P. I. E. Peter Lang, 2000.

Willman, Paul, and Alex Bryson. "Union Organization in Great Britain." *Journal of Labor Research* 28, no. 1 (2007): 93–115. http://web.ebscohost.com/ehost/detail? vid=3&sid=87414c4a-e116-4482-92ac-d14a909772d3%40sessionmgr10&hid=25 &bdata=JnNpdGU9ZWhvc3QtbGl2ZQ%3d%3d#db=bth&AN=23815053.

Woods, Ashley, and David Sands. " 'Right to Work' Michigan: Gov. Rick Snyder Says New Legislation Gives Union Workers 'Freedom.' " *Huffington Post*, December 6, 2012. Accessed December 18, 2012. http://www.huffingtonpost.com/2012/12/06/ right-to-work-michigan-snyder-unions_n_2250601.html.

Woolf, Richard D. "Critics of Capitalism Must Include Its Definition." *Truthout*, May 26, 2015. Accessed January 19, 2017. http://www.truth-out.org/news/item/ 30678-critics-of-capitalism-must-include-its-definition.

Wright, Erik Olin. "Basic Income as a Socialist Project." Paper presented at the annual US-BIG Congress, New York, March 4–6, 2005. Accessed October 29, 2013. http:// www.ssc.wisc.edu/~wright/Basic%20Income%20as%20a%20Socialist%20Project.pdf.

———. "How to Be an Anticapitalist Today." *Jacobin*, December 2, 2015. Accessed January 18, 2017. https://www.jacobinmag.com/2015/12/erik-olin-wright-real-utopias-anticapitalism-democracy/.

———. "Introduction." In *Redesigning Distribution: Basic Income and Stakeholder Grants as Cornerstones for an Egalitarian Capitalism*, edited by Erik Olin Wright, ix–xii. London: Verso: 2006.

Young, Iris Marion. *Justice and the Politics of Difference*. Princeton: Princeton University Press, 1990.

INDEX

9 781501 714863